DAVID OGG who died in 1965 was one of the greatest seventeenth century scholars of his time. Born in Glasgow he attended the University there before winning a scholarship to Lincoln College, Oxford, where he became a pupil of Sir Charles Firth, then Regius Professor. During the war of 1914-18 he served at sea as an officer in the R.N.V.R. and subsequently assisted Sir Julian Corbett, the great historian of the Tudor Navy, in his official History of Naval Operations. Elected Fellow and Tutor in Modern History at New College, Oxford, he taught there for thirty years, subsequently being elected an Emeritus and finally an Honorary Fellow. After his retirement from official teaching duties at Oxford he held a number of Visiting Professorships in America.

During his Oxford career he produced a number of books amongst which the best known are *Europe in the seventeenth century* (1925), *England in the reign of Charles II* (2 vols) (1934, revised edition 1956) and *England in the reign of James II and William III* (1955).

D1375191

DAVID OGG

EUROPE OF THE
ANCIEN RÉGIME
1715-1783

FONTANA/COLLINS

First published in the Fontana Library 1965
Eighth Impression July 1977

© David Ogg 1965

Made and printed in Great Britain by
William Collins Sons & Co Ltd Glasgow

Preface

It is a pleasure to record publicly my debt of gratitude to those who have helped, by their suggestions and corrections, in the preparation of this book. Dr. L. A. K. Staveley revised the section on Science, Dr. H. K. Andrews that on Music, Professor J. S. Bromley gave valuable assistance in the chapters dealing with economic matters, and Professor A. Goodwin enabled me to benefit by his unrivalled knowledge of the eighteenth century. My son, Mr. A. J. Ogg, F.R.C.S., cleared up some points for me in matters of Public Health. Mr. Richard Ollard, in his revisal of the whole book, removed many blemishes. To all of these I gratefully record my obligations. But the mistakes are entirely my responsibility.

DAVID OGG

July 1964

CONTENTS

CONTENTS

MAPS

PART ONE

INSTITUTIONS

ECONOMIC LIFE

DIPLOMACY

THE GREAT WARS

Chapter 1

SOME ASPECTS OF THE ANCIEN REGIME

The term *Ancien Régime* has been applied to that period of French civilisation which, commencing after the conclusion of civil and religious strife in the seventeenth century, ended suddenly and violently in 1789. More loosely, the term has been applied to other nations where the old order of things was displaced gradually; and it may be claimed that, especially in France, only the forces of inertia were holding together a system which, for more than a century, many intelligent men had come to regard as anachronistic and unjust. Accordingly, what unity this book may possess is derived from the fact that it is bounded by two chapters, each complementary to the other, of which the first describes some relics of a decayed medievalism, still surviving long after their original justification had disappeared, while the last outlines a penetrating analysis of human society intended, not only to remedy the defects of existing institutions, but to prepare the way for a better and happier way of life. The antithesis between these two things became more acute in the course of the eighteenth century, culminating in the French Revolution. Illustrations of the pre-revolutionary structure of society in western Europe have been selected mainly from England and France, the two nations which played the largest part in European affairs, and for which the contemporary historical material is most abundant.

I POPULATION AND PUBLIC HEALTH

At the outset there is one certain fact—the great increase of population in eighteenth-century Europe. Since the middle years of the seventeenth century the subject of population had become of increasing interest, and demographers had provided estimates (largely conjectural), based mainly on taxation statistics and registers of births and deaths. There already existed some original material for these estimates. Commencing in the sixteenth century, weekly Bills of Mortality were published for the London parishes; after 1720 similar information for Berlin was conveyed in the *Acta Medicorum Berolinensium.* There were also notable writers on the subject, including Sir William Petty and Gregory King in England; and the investigations of the astronomer Edmund Halley, by inaugurating the science of life statistics, helped to guide the earliest life insurance ventures. It is of interest that the average number of persons in a family was estimated at between 4 and 5. Several states, including Spain, attempted to take a national census; in 1753, however, the British House of Commons rejected a proposal for this purpose, on the ground that the information would be of value to the enemy. We may be sure only of a general increase of population, accentuated in the years after 1750, and most marked in Great Britain and Belgium; indeed, it has been estimated that the total population of Europe advanced from about 100 millions in 1650 to about 187 millions in 1800, a rate of advance probably unparalleled in any previous period. Contemporaries, uninformed about these facts, were divided on the question whether an increase was desirable. Montesquieu expressed fears of under-population[1] and, in the middle years of the century, the Physiocrats[2] insisted on abundance of population as an essential of prosperity. But, as early as 1761, a Scottish economist Robert Wallace, in his *Various Prospects of Mankind, Nature and Providence,* expressed fears that, but for wars and vices, mankind would double itself in every third part of a century. The pessimistic views of Malthus were thus anticipated by nearly forty years.

[1] Montesquieu, *Lettres Persanes* (1721), no. CXXII.
[2] below, p. 96.

Some estimates of population are as follows.[1] Between 1700 and 1800 the population of Great Britain increased from 8 millions to nearly 15 millions; France from 23 millions to about 28 millions; Spain from 7 to 10 millions; the Italian states from 9 to 13 millions; Belgium from 1½ millions to 3 millions; Sweden from 1.6 millions to 2.3 millions; Prussia from 1.7 millions to 3.1 millions; the Dutch Netherlands from 1.1 millions to 1.7 millions. The population of Russia at the end of the period was estimated at 31 millions. Density of population was greatest in Belgium and Lombardy; least in Spain, Sweden and Norway. Of the larger cities London had an estimated populace of about half a million, Paris about half that number, Vienna a quarter of a million and Berlin 120,000. It must be added that these figures are approximate and, to some extent, conjectural.

We can be more certain about the mortality rates, especially in the cities. In London the rate per thousand was 52 during the "gin period" (1728-57), as contrasted with 29 in the first decade and 19 in the last decade of the nineteenth century. A similar decline in the mortality rates can be found in all the large towns. Expressed in another way, it may be said that, in the earlier half of the eighteenth century, the number of deaths in the greater cities often exceeded the number of births, and the population was maintained by immigration from the countryside. All this helps to provide evidence that the average expectation of life, calculated from birth, was much less than it is to-day; in France it was 25-27 years. Necker, who succeeded Turgot as finance minister, estimated that a quarter of the inhabitants of France died before the age of 3; a quarter before the age of 25, and another quarter before 50. In the course of 50 years, therefore, about three fourths of the population died off; moreover a worker, particularly a farm worker, who survived to the age

[1] These statistics are selected from W. Bowden, M. Karpovich and A. F. Usher, *An Economic History of Europe since 1750*, (American Book Company, 1937).

of 50 was likely to be worn out. This was the age at which benefits were to commence in a scheme of contributory old age pensions passed by the English House of Commons[1] in 1772, but the Bill appears to have been rejected by the Lords.

In such circumstances there was no need for the welfare state since death was usually the substitute for the old age pension. What were the main factors accounting for the high mortality rate? In England, until about 1757, gin drinking among the poor took a heavy toll; but increased duties on spirits and better regulation of their sale brought the scourge within bounds. Smallpox was probably the most serious of the "killers", though it was mitigated to some extent by inoculation with human virus; not till Jenner used virus from the cow (vaccination) was a great diminution effected. Typhus, from lice, and malaria, from mosquitoes, were among the diseases left by armies on the march, causing many thousands of deaths among the German peasantry in the Seven Years War. The almost complete absence of sanitation as we know it and abundance of horse manure and flies in the streets were responsible for the enteric diseases, notably typhoid and infantile diarrhœa, the latter of which carried off so many children. Malnutrition was another source of disease, evident in tuberculosis and rickets; moreover, as there was little opportunity for segregating the sick, infection spread rapidly. There was also plague, which continued to be endemic in the eastern Mediterranean; it appeared in Marseilles in 1720, in Sicily in 1743, in Poland and Russia in 1770, but otherwise western Europe was spared this menace. There were however certain negative factors. These included the comparative infrequency of large-scale starvation; leprosy had almost entirely disappeared, and syphilis was no longer the scourge that it had been in the sixteenth century.

Increase of population suggests improved conditions of health throughout Europe; what were the causes of this im-

[1] W. Cobbett, *Parliamentary History of England*, XVII, Dec. 11, 1772.

provement? They were many and it is difficult to estimate their comparative importance. In England, with the decline of the apprenticeship system, the birth rate rose because craftsmen married earlier and, on well managed estates, cottages were built for the workers. There was also an increase in the number of city hospitals, accompanied by a slow improvement in medical science and teaching—students had now to "walk the wards", and study disease not only in books, but in the human body. The great Dutch physician Boerhaave created a famous school at Leyden, which was emulated by that in Edinburgh, with the result that waves of well-trained doctors joined in the Scottish invasion of the south. Later in the century, thanks to the pioneer work of John Hunter, surgery, while still a craft, became also a science. This medical advance was helped by the use of drugs new to Europe—quinine ("Jesuits' Bark") for malaria and opium for its pain-killing qualities, an invaluable drug when there were no anæsthetics.

Less directly, there were other measures helping to raise the standard of public health. In the larger cities water supplies were either introduced or improved; scavenging services were made more efficient, and street lighting reduced the number of homicides. Especially in the later years of the century many classes had a better and more ample dietary, with bread and meat of improved quality. Coffee, tea, cocoa and chocolate provided salutary alternatives to wine, beer and spirits. Town dwellers began to appreciate the country and the sea. Mountains (popularised by Rousseau) attracted many tourists—indeed the word "tourist" was then coming into use—and guide books were published for them. Londoners, following the example of George III, frequented Weymouth, and Parisians went to Dieppe in order to see the ocean and even to bathe in it. When it is added that more soap was being used in this period it may be claimed that the advantages of fresh air and bodily cleanliness are comparatively modern discoveries.

Within the last century human longevity in Europe has been greatly extended mainly by sanitation and advances in science, an advance in which the plumber has ably assisted the physician. Improvement has been most marked in the decline of infantile mortality; and, in our estimates of life expectancy, we must always distinguish between that at birth and that at an age, such as early adolescence, when the perils of infancy have been surmounted. This improvement has affected mainly what are called the lower classes who, in the past, were often weakened by excessive labour, or insufficient food or inadequate breathing space, conditions which did not affect so seriously what we call the upper classes, whose longevity was little different from that experienced by their counterparts of to-day. In an enquiry into the life span of this small class, selected from various European nations, it was found that of twelve representative statesmen the average length of life was 77 years; for the same number of higher ecclesiastics the figure was 81. Ten Deists and Sceptics, with an average of 66 years, showed a less satisfactory performance, in spite of the fact that this group included Voltaire, who lived to be 84. A batch of twenty scholars and thinkers provided an average of 70 years; twelve artists and musicians gave the slightly better figure of 72. We may conclude from these details that religious orthodoxy, or rather the routine performance of ecclesiastical functions, may have favoured longevity, while scepticism appears to have diminished it. More important, we have to recognise that a long life span was the lot of a small minority which, having survived the perils of infancy, was assured of adequate food and fresh air.

With the general increase of population, sharply accentuated after 1750, this privileged minority constituted an ever-diminishing proportion of the populace, a fact of momentous consequences. The underdogs were multiplying with almost explosive force. For the economist this means that, particularly in England, there was available a large supply of cheap labour, without which the Industrial Revolution would scarcely have been possible. To some sociologists, however, it appears that herein we have a cause, direct or indirect, of wars such as those of the Revolutionary and Napoleonic eras, the assumption being that wars, like infanticide, provide a biological corrective to excess population. This theory is attractive to the many who seek a " scientific " explanation of historical events. But, even if the assumption can be substantiated, it remains true that, in comparison with malnutrition and disease, war is low on the scale of biological " killers "; in the pre-atomic age it was a poor genocide. Moreover, wars continued to be waged for old-fashioned reasons—greed, lust for power or revenge, desire to impose one's way of thinking on other men. We are on surer ground if we say that this pressure of population, when an expanding outer fringe of the unprivileged was weighing more heavily on the core of monopoly and exemption at the centre, was bound to lead to social change or even revolution. In France, this was sudden and violent; in England, the readjustment was gradual, extending from about 1782 to 1848. It is now necessary to consider some of the characteristics of this central core of the privileged, the continued existence of which was threatened by innumerable critics, and by the increasing impact of an unenfranchised majority.

II THE FIEFS

These characteristics were mostly survivals, usually distorted or corrupted, from a remote past. One example was derived from military service. Throughout the middle ages defence was a paramount necessity, not only against the foreign invader, but against the native rebel. Hence the importance of fealty and its converse, treason; hence also the institution of the *feudum* or fief, by which the crown conferred land on a vassal, subject to a contract (*foedus*) by which the vassal undertook to perform service, usually military service, in return for the land. There was a rough equation between the holders of fiefs, who provided protection and those, not in possession of fiefs, who supplied labour. In the course of centuries the equation came to be seriously disturbed, mainly because the crown had to use mercenaries for its wars; but the principle implied by the existence of the fief was still held to be valid even as late as the eighteenth century. The unprivileged continued to supply their labour and, in many cases, were obliged to perform military or naval service; the holders of military fiefs, on the other hand, no longer provided service in a feudal host. They had long ceased to perform the conditions on which they held their lands, but they nevertheless retained these lands as if they were their private property; moreover, payment of a tax to the crown on the sale or transfer of a fief served to confirm the territorial rights of the feudatories. In England a change had been effected by the Act usually described as that for abolishing the feudal tenures (1660), a measure which, while extinguishing tenure by knight service (which had long fallen into desuetude), left the knightly tenants in full possession of their lands. A similar process occurred in other countries and it was felt, not unreasonably, that such enfranchised tenants should pay compensation to the crown in respect of obligations no longer fulfilled. In Prussia Frederick William in 1717 imposed a tax on those who thus benefited by the abolition of knight service.

This evolution, affecting the majority of what we call the landed classes, might not have been so important were it not for the fact that the possession of a fief brought with it a number of rights, including jurisdiction and the right to impose personal services. In many cases also it included at least a claim to exemption from national taxation, since the feudatory was still supposed to pay by the military service which he had long ceased to perform. For compensation of these things, one has sometimes to apply an inverted logic. The feudal sword had long been rusting in the scabbard, but the spade still kept its polish from constant use. In England manorial lords maintained rights over their copyhold tenants until early in the twentieth century, but the profits therefrom were negligible, in comparison with those from wool, or corn or minerals; in France, on the other hand, where the landed classes were less actively engaged in agriculture or industry, this jurisdictional right, or *Directe,* was a valuable source of income, and was often levied by a lord who, though he had parted company with the land, still retained these medieval prerogatives over its occupants. By sub-infeudation as well as by sale and transfer these rights had become extremely complicated, but they were protected by the law as if they were private property, and in the eighteenth century they were coming to be more harshly enforced, usually by bailiffs. Similar conditions prevailed on the vast estates of northern Germany, where the lord exercised *Gerichtherrschaft,* or right of jurisdiction, as distinguished from *Grundherrschaft,* or right of ownership of the soil and its products. In France the same distinction was implied by the contrast of *Domaine Directe* and *Domaine Utile.*

These manorial rights varied so greatly from place to place and were often so bizarre in their interpretation that, in France, they provided material for a comparatively new learned profession, that of *feudiste,* or expert in the lore of fiefs. The *feudistes* developed a certain connoisseurship in a subject that had more exceptions than principles, more absurdity than reason. Several enlightened men advocated the abolition of fiefs; these men included the Marquis d'Argenson and the Physiocrats; they were supported by the *philosophes.* In 1776 an employee of Turgot named Boncerf, in his *Les Inconvenients des Droits Féodaux* maintained that, by the lavish grant of such fiefs, the crown had been greatly impoverished and had to be compensated by more national taxation, from which so many feudatories claimed exemption. The fiefs should be abolished by the state, with adequate compensation to the seigneurs. In this way all the *cens*,[1] *corvées*,[2] *banalités*[3] and innumerable other exactions would be removed. These moderate proposals roused the ire of the Paris *Parlement* which ordered the books to be burnt and declared, in an edict, that once tenants were relieved of their feudal services, they would not hesitate to go farther. If Boncerf's proposals were adopted, what would become of private property, "*ce bien si sacré?*". It may be added, by way of contrast, that in the Austrian dominions feudal rights were gradually mitigated, and were almost entirely abolished by Joseph II.

III GILDS AND CORPORATIONS

The complexities of the fief were paralleled by another set of feudal survivals—the gilds and corporations for the exercise of a craft, or mystery. These existed throughout eighteenth-century Europe in varying degrees of vigour; they were weakening in England, but they remained strong in France and in many parts of Germany. Basically, the gild was a corporation and friendly society that included masters, journeymen and apprentices. The apprentice, who had to complete a period of " servitude " (lasting from four to seven years) within the household of the master, might hope to become a journeyman, but it was more difficult to become a master, unless he happened to be the son or son-in-law of a master. This exclusiveness, and also the high fees prevented many journeymen from becoming completely " free " of their craft. The gilds did not extend to wholesale trade, nor to banking nor exchange; their province was limited to trades and handicrafts as practised in a corporate town. They provided some protection against exploitation, and enforced standards of craftsmanship in their

---

[1] A form of quit rent. [2] Labour services. [3] An obligation such as to have one's corn ground at the lord's mill or one's grapes pressed at his wine press.

industries; otherwise there might have been shoddy workmanship and " sweated " labour.

In France the most common type of organisation was the *métier juré,* or sworn body of craftsmen, headed by the *jurandes,* or patriarchates of masters. They were controlled partly by the crown, partly by the municipality; they were forbidden to form coalitions for raising prices; regulation of hours of labour and supervision of materials and workmanship were among their prerogatives. As a corporation the *métier juré* had a seal; it might also possess property, and it had a place in public processions. To some of them police duties were entrusted; for example, the *épiciers* (spice merchants) had the function of inspecting weights and measures, and the goldsmiths had to keep registers of their purchases. On occasion, groups of *métiers* made contributions to the state, is in 1759 when the *Six Corps* or major gilds of Paris paid a large sum to the Treasury for war expenses, and in 1762 when they borrowed enough money to build and equip a ship of 72 guns. Moreover, they helped in the raising of taxes, because they were assessed in groups, and the *jurandes* had the duty of apportioning the total among the members.

Creation of new *métiers* was a source of revenue for the crown. Any pretext, such as the marriage or coronation of the King, would suffice for setting up new monopolies, thus weakening the position of those already endowed with such privileges. The threat implied by this procedure might be bought off by a monetary payment to the crown, as happened with the Parisian gilds in 1757; but ten years later, in spite of this arrangement, new *métiers* were created throughout the kingdom. This was the last of such new creations. Another royal device for obtaining money from the corporations was the elevation of gild membership to an office, which could be put up for sale. The office conferred additional prestige on the holder, and was thought to give added security because of (nominal) limitation of numbers; otherwise the difference was one of degree rather than of kind. But this process created more vested interests, the consequences of which were seen in 1776 when Turgot, engaged in abolishing many of the gilds of Paris, was obliged to exempt those gildsmen who were holders of offices, for their abolition would have involved repayment by the state of the purchase price. Herein was an increasingly serious limitation of the prerogative exercised by Louis XV and Louis XVI. It was this entrenchment of the privileged classes in their monopolies that made reform difficult or even impossible, a factor accounting for a certain fragility or brittleness in the social structure of France throughout the period before the Revolution. Like the fiefs on the land, the immunities in the towns had come to be equated with private property, endowed with all the sanctity which then attached to private property.

The corporations were by no means limited to economic activities, for they included the church, the universities and the learned professions. The church, the earliest example of a corporate organisation, had trained statesmen, administrators and educators; indeed, the whole fabric of medieval civilisation in western Europe was shaped in an ecclesiastical mould. By contrast, in Russia and Poland, where the secular clergy were weak or uneducated, the level of civilisation was appreciably lower. In Europe, especially in France and Spain, the church was endowed with vast wealth, derived from lands, tithe, town property and gifts, so unevenly distributed that there was a glaring contrast between the rich emoluments of the higher clergy and the poverty of the parish priests. In England, where this contrast existed, though to a less extent, the church had been assigned a public and responsible position in the constitution, and could make no secret attempts to influence national policy; moreover, the Anglican bishops, though monopolist and often intolerant, did not have the power and seldom had the wish to persecute. It was otherwise on the continent. In France and Germany there were many instances of clerical injustice and oppression. French bishops could make use of *lettres de cachet* in order to commit to prison persons who had made their confession to a Jansenist priest.[1] In Germany many archbishops and bishops ruled their extensive lands as secular princes, responsible to themselves alone; they had the legal right to expel heretics, a right exercised in the winter of 1731-2 by the Archbishop of Salzburg who, with the help of imperial troops, drove thousands of Protestants out of his dominions. As well as the higher clergy there was the Inquisition, still powerful in Spain and in some of the Italian states, an organisation intent, as in Spain, on the maintenance of racial and religious uniformity; or elsewhere, as in Naples and the Papal States, on the extirpation of human abnormality in conduct or belief. In different degrees, throughout the continent of Europe, the church, as represented by the higher clergy and the Inquisition, provided not only the strongest bulwark against change, but one of the clearest threats, whether actual or potential, to independence of thought.

Of the other learned professions the most important historically was that large class which we loosely describe as lawyers. In England (as contrasted with Scotland and the continental states) the almost unbroken continuity of the common law (as distinct from statute law) with that of medieval times helped to confer on it a prestige which no other institution possessed, and to bestow on its practitioners a social position higher than that of any other secular pursuit. The Lord Chancellor was a member, and often an influential member, of British Cabinets; in the House of Lords the Law Lords provided the technical knowledge enabling the Upper House to act as a supreme judicial tribunal. Education for the Bar was provided at the Inns of Court, ancient and influential corporations situated in the heart of the city of London, where young men, mostly of good family, received a training qualifying them not only for service in the courts but, in many cases, for service in the House of Commons. In this way there was formed a close association between Bar and Legislature, such

[1] below, p. 259.

25

as existed nowhere else, an association so close that the British constitution has been defined as a lawyer-made constitution. In three respects English common law was unique. It embodied a certain national or even patriotic element in the opposition maintained by its advocates to "foreign" systems, such as the civil and canon law; many of its principles could be adduced in favour of liberty of the subject, a fact evidenced in the American Revolution and in several famous judgements by eighteenth-century judges and, thirdly, notwithstanding many medieval survivals and injustices, it was a uniform system, from Berwick-on-Tweed to Land's End. In spite of its abuses (not remedied until the early decades of the nineteenth century) English jurisprudence provided an element of continuity such as no other nation possessed.

When we turn to the law and its practitioners in France we are presented with an interesting contrast. There was no national jurisprudence, the main distinction being that between the *Pays de Droit Ecrit,* provinces in the south and south-west, where Roman Law principles still survived, and the *Pays de Droit Coutumier,* in the north, north-east and centre, where over 300 different sets of customary laws prevailed. The administration of justice was in the hands of 31 sovereign courts, headed by 15 *Parlements,* of which that of Paris was the most important, if only because its jurisdiction extended to such a large area of northern and central France. The system has been compared to one of concentric circles, having the *Parlement de Paris* at the centre, the *Grande Chambre* of which included about 50 dukes and peers of France who sat there as hereditary advisers of the crown. In this way there was a faint but deceptive resemblance between the Paris *Parlement* and the British House of Lords.

But this bald summary does less than justice to the complexity of French judicial administration. While, in England, a great deal of this was performed by unpaid justices of the peace, in France there were thousands of functionaries, exalted and humble, most of whom had bought the offices which qualified them to practise in innumerable courts. As judicial functions were often attached to administrative bodies, a storehouse of government salt might serve as a granary and a tribunal.[1] Moreover, as most of the frontier provinces had been incorporated comparatively late in French history, there were many differences of rule and procedure arising from this source. The higher functionaries, such as the first presidents of the *Parlements,* owed their tenure to royal commissions, and so could neither buy nor sell nor bequeath their offices, but any of these things could be done by their inferiors. Here indeed was a great caste—the *noblesse de robe*—which, in its power and pretensions, became a serious rival of the old nobility of the sword. The young aspirant to judicial honours might inherit his office, or it might be bought for him by a parent—as Montesquieu did for his son—the only qualification for the magistracy being that the candidate should be " sufficient and capable ". That condition was satisfied by the writing of a short commentary on a passage selected from Justinian; and, as the same passage was usually selected, it was not difficult for the young member of a " robe " family to satisfy his examiners.

The system had its defenders and critics. Of the defenders the most noteworthy was Montesquieu, who valued venality and heredity in the judicial system because, in his view, these qualities gave cohesion to one of the " intermediate corps " which served to maintain a balance between absolutism on the one hand and mob rule on the other. Venality of office was defended by others on the ground that it provided an incentive whereby the man who had made money could purchase an office for himself and his family; moreover, this property qualification was thought by some to ensure continuity and dependability. But the critics of the system were more numerous. Fénelon and Saint Simon, as representatives of the old nobility, had no sympathy with the claims of an upstart

[1] F. D. Ford, *Robe and Sword: the Regrouping of the French Aristocracy after Louis XIV* (1953), ch. III.

noblesse de robe; the Marquis d'Argenson held that venality of office was a corruption impeding the establishment of a better order of things. Voltaire objected to a system that made the administration of justice a family trade, and he regarded the presidents and counsellors of the *Parlements* with dislike and contempt.

Voltaire's attitude is accounted for by the fact that, in his day, the *Parlements* and the *noblesse de robe* generally were the most formidable representatives of reaction, the most securely entrenched of vested interests, the exponents of an intolerance more extreme than that of any of the religious orders. It should be recalled that some of the most notorious cases of religious persecution in the century were the work not of the clergy but of local magistrates.[1] Even the Paris *Parlement* was not free from this taint in spite of the fact that, since the seventeenth century, it had acquired a certain reputation for its espousal of popular or semi-popular causes, such as Jansenism and Gallicanism; moreover, during the abeyance of the States General (1614-1789) it had at times tried to emulate the exploits of its English counterpart. A comparison between these two national institutions provides an interesting study in historical evolution. Both took shape at the beginning of the fourteenth century under the direction of powerful kings; and at first they had much in common, for they began as supreme royal councils and supreme judicial tribunals. But whereas the English Parliament was " afforced " by the attendance of knights of the shire and burgesses from the boroughs the Paris *Parlement* never assumed a representative character On the contrary, it added to its functions that of a close corporation of lawyers, limiting its composition to member of the " robe " families and insisting on preservation of the privileges for which most of its members had paid. It main tained an organised resistance against every attempt to extend the basis of taxation—the most badly-needed reform in eight eenth-century France—and although, in 1771, it was abolishe

[1] below, p. 342.

by the reforming Chancellor Maupeou,[1] it was soon restored, with the other *Parlements,* to await final extinction at the Revolution. The British Parliament was certainly no democratic institution, nor was the House of Commons a representative body in our sense of the term; but, within its walls, could be heard free debate on every matter of national import. This is one reason why the revolution proceeded so much more slowly and gently in England than in France.

IV PROPERTY IN ENGLAND

Hitherto this chapter has been concerned with rights or monopolies associated, however indirectly, with property, as exemplified by fiefs, gilds and corporations. It is now proposed to consider briefly some of the privileges which, without any intermediary, flowed directly from the possession of property, particularly landed property. Of these privileges England, not France, provided the clearest examples. In England the freeholders, in effect, constituted the nation, for they sat in Parliament, they elected members of the House of Commons, they served on Grand Juries and from their number were selected the justices of the peace. Full rights of citizenship were enjoyed only by the Anglican freeholder; the others were only on the fringe. The distinction was more moral than economic, for it was held that property, especially a landed estate, provided a rampart against intimidation from above and corruption from beneath. The poor man, it was thought, would easily succumb to bribes and threats; he had none of that backbone of independence to be found only in those more amply endowed. Thus, in 1734, during a debate on one of the many Place Bills introduced into the Commons, Walpole, defending the presence of office holders in the House, alleged that their private property alone provided a guarantee against corruption. Generally, by the conferment of offices, sinecures and

[1] below, p. 267.

pensions, the crown could be assured of adequate support in both Houses. Later in the century it was contended by Archdeacon Paley that, if such props had been available to ministers in the colonial legislatures, the breakaway of the American colonies might never have occurred.

But eulogy of property was not dependent on the sophistries of parliamentary debate. All the thinkers of the period, including Locke, Hume and Blackstone, insisted on protection of private property as the basis not only of justice but of civilisation itself; without the leisured class brought into existence by this institution, there would be no art, or letters or science. By contrast, it may be added, where there are no property rights, there can be no theft—a proof that civilisation, as we know it, has not even begun. From this admittedly narrow point of view, England was considered the most highly civilised state in eighteenth-century Europe, because property was protected there by a penal code more brutal than any to be found elsewhere; indeed, by the end of the century, there were more than 200 felonies on the statute book, the great majority of them connected with violation of property rights. Men were executed for stealing five shillings; a girl was hanged for stealing a handkerchief. These savage punishments had been authorised not by a tyrant, but by a legislature composed almost entirely of property owners. In practice, the code was frequently mitigated by the compassion of juries or the discretion of judges.

Nor was this subjection to a merciless code the only disability suffered by the property-less in England, for they might be forced into military or naval service from which owners of property were exempt. In 1758, when the Commons were debating amendments to a Habeas Corpus Bill a member, defending the enforcement of service on the poor, argued that every man is bound to defend the state either by his property or his person. " Property or Person "—that was the alternative. If, continued the speaker, men of property were forced into naval or military service, they would lose the opportunity of electing members of parliament, sent to Westminster in order to safeguard private property.¹ The argument is unanswerable.

It is of some significance that these rights were enforced most vigorously in England, where owners of property had the backing of a legislature. This may have been in the mind of Adam Smith when, in his discussion of negro slavery, he distinguished between the law on the one hand and its enforcement on the other. In a colony where the government is arbitrary, he maintained,² the laws, such as they may be, for the protection of a slave are likely to be enforced; whereas, in a state governed by a legislature, when a magistrate protects a slave against brutality, he may be accused of interfering with rights of property. Wherever there are representative institutions—and these in the eighteenth century consisted almost exclusively of property owners—a magistrate cannot do this with impunity; whereas, in an autocracy, so great are his powers, that he can interfere even with these sacred rights.

All the abuses of the *Ancien Régime,* it has been said, were articles of private property. This was most clearly revealed in the London prisons, notably the debtors' prisons, such as the Fleet and the Marshalsea. In 1729 the Commons addressed themselves to consideration of these establishments, and heard reports of barbarities committed therein by wardens and gaolers, as well as of fraudulent conversion of legacies left by charitable persons for the aid of prisoners. But the Commons soon found themselves thwarted by an insuperable obstacle—the custodians of the prisons had bought or inherited their offices, which were their freeholds. Moreover, in order to make doubly sure, the wardens of debtors' prisons were in the habit of secretly conveying away their freeholds to relatives and accomplices so that, in the event of a law suit, they

¹ W. Cobbett, *Parliamentary History,* xv, Feb. 21, 1758.
² Adam Smith, *Wealth of Nations,* bk. iv, ch. 7, pt. 2.

appeared to be without assets on which damages could be levied.[1] The result was that reform of the prisons had to be indefinitely postponed; Parliament could do many things, but it could not invade a man's freehold. Here was one of the more sinister characteristics of the *Ancien Régime*—this authorised trading on the misery of human beings, whether prisoners or negro slaves, as a right derived from the possession of property.

It is a truism that, in the history of jurisprudence, rights of property always come before rights of the person. This was abundantly evidenced even as late as the eighteenth century. The land was more important than the man who tilled it; the perpetuity of a family estate counted for more than the well-being of the heir, as witness the popularity of the entail (with a family settlement) in England, the *substitution* in France, the *mayorazgo* in Spain and the *fideikommisz* in Germany and Austria. This was more subtle than the distinction between the haves and the have-nots for, actually, many merchants and tradesmen were better off than those who derived their status from land. In England the acquisition of that status was easy, because there was a continuous flow of capital, accumulated in the towns, into landed estates purchased in the country; the peerage was never a closed caste, for its doors were open to those who, having made a fortune in trade or office, acquired a seat in the country and founded a noble family. Money thus made possible not so much a change of status as the acquisition of status, for only the freeholders in England had full civic rights. This had two good effects. It provided capital for agriculture and it mitigated the rigidity of caste. Hence a contrast with conditions on the continent, where all the members of a noble family were accounted noble, and trade was regarded with contempt.

The landed classes of western Europe were influenced by two main motives—the perpetuity and aggrandisement of their estates. The first was secured by the marriage settlement or

[1] W. Cobbett, *op. cit.*, VIII, Feb. 26, 1729.

entail which regulated the succession, usually for two generations, in such a way that the " owner " was little more than a life tenant; the second object was obtained by a well-planned marriage. In these days of parental authority matrimonial alliances were usually arranged by the parents, who often sacrificed the natural inclination of their children to this desire for aggrandisement, whether in money or lands; to such an extent indeed that, even in wedding announcements, the bride was sometimes rated according to her reputed wealth.[1] From this point of view the landed classes in England constituted a close preserve, open only to men who had inherited or bought an estate. But there was a small loophole through which a woman of a certain type could enter. Until 1753, so chaotic was the administration of the English marriage laws, that an adventuress could gate-crash into the sacred precincts by means of a secret marriage with a young, irresponsible heir. For this purpose a metropolitan Gretna Green was provided by the numerous public houses in the Fleet district, where a " clergyman " was always within call, ready to unite (for a fee) a designing woman with a young heir who had been well primed for the sacred ceremony. These secret weddings, though highly irregular, were usually considered valid. But this was not the end of the matter. Often the ill-assorted pair would separate, and the heir would (bigamously) marry a woman of his own class, keeping secret the fact of his first marriage. On his death, the original wife, armed with her marriage certificate, might appear on the scene, to the utter undoing of the second " wife ", who had to face the fact that (unknowingly) she had been living in adultery, and that her children were bastards. It was a case of this kind that brought the marriage laws to the attention of the House of Lords.

In consequence, Lord Chancellor Hardwicke drew up his Clandestine Marriage Bill, which was passed by the Upper House and sent down to the Commons, where it was first

---

[1] e.g., *The Gentleman's Magazine*, October 1731. "—Barratt Esq. to Miss Baker, a £20,000 fortune ".

debated in May 1753. There was considerable opposition,[1] and it was contended that, as the Bill had been initiated in the Upper House, the peers obviously designed to monopolise all the rich heiresses for themselves. One of the opposition, contending that wealth should circulate freely, even suggested that a gentleman's or farmer's daughter was a good match for the son of a lord, because she brought in fresh blood. This was possibly the first public occasion in England when the sanctity of private property was impugned; a measure which we now recognise as a good one was attacked on the ground that it closed a back door into the sacred preserves of ownership. The Bill passed the Commons, and is now the basis of the English law of marriage. Briefly, by the requirement of publication of banns, marriages were made public and secret weddings were declared illegal. So the hostelries in the Fleet district had to close down the matrimonial side of their business, which was thereupon transferred to distant Gretna Green (where the Scottish law of marriage prevailed); and near-by Carlisle developed a minor industry in the provision of wedding breakfasts.[2] But there still remained an undercurrent of opposition to Hardwicke's Act. As late as 1781 the demand for its repeal provided good political propaganda, skilfully directed by C. J. Fox, who alleged that the Act was intended to separate the "high" from the "vulgar" by preventing their marriage.[3] This, he declared, was contrary to the constitution. In this way, opposition to a salutary measure was deflected to an attack on those class distinctions which the institution of private property did so much to preserve.

In one other respect private property in England can be regarded as distinctive, even unique. For long, the law had insisted on a clear distinction between realty and personalty; the first, consisting of lands and tenements that could neither be concealed nor removed, served two purposes, for it pro-

---

[1] W. Cobbett, *op. cit.*, xv, May 7, 1753.
[2] Ibid, xxii, May 27, 1781.
[3] ibid, xxii, pp. 396 ff.

vided the owner with status and also with responsibility, since
the lands could be forfeited on conviction for treason. In this
way an element of allegiance and continuity—so essential in
the evolution of early society—was preserved. By contrast, no
such guarantee was provided by personalty or moveables, since
these could be concealed or taken away; consequently, the law
conferred special privileges on holders of realty that were
denied to those whose wealth consisted merely of money or
chattels. Moreover, it was of some social importance that only
the landed classes could make provision for their posterity;
realty, which must always descend to an heir and could never
ascend to an ancestor, was the bond uniting generations of
feudal and post-feudal society, ensuring both fidelity to the
reigning dynasty and continuity of the family throughout the
political and economic ups and downs of human life.

But, in eighteenth-century England, this disparity between
the two types of property was greatly diminished because, by
then, public finance had been modernised, and there existed
institutions, such as the Bank of England, for the provision of
credit. In William III's reign sums of unprecedented magnitude had to be raised for the war against Louis XIV; these
were obtained by the new device of appealing for loans to the
public (as distinct from the professional financiers). The
interest on these loans was secured on the yield from the
taxes, and by a system of consolidation, it was arranged that a
deficiency in one source of revenue would be made up from
other sources; moreover, as some of these loans were for as
long a term as 99 years, the investor could provide not only for
himself and his relatives but also for his descendants. Provision for one's posterity, hitherto the monopoly of the
landed classes, was now available for the moneyed man as
well as for executors and trustees. Confidence was created by
the regularity with which the interest was paid, to such an
extent indeed that it was stated in the Commons in 1737 that
at least a quarter of the British funds belonged to foreigners.[1]

[1] ibid, x, 134.

" Faith in Parliament " declared Walpole in that year " is pledged to prevent reduction of interest without consent of proprietors ".[1] This integrity of the government was sharply contrasted with that in several continental countries, particularly France, where the *rentiers* had often to accept reduced interest or even a repudiation of their holdings. Moreover, the stability of a state can be roughly gauged by the rate of interest which it has to pay to its creditors; in eighteenth-century England there was a steady reduction in the interest rate on government funds, and in 1749, after the conclusion of a long war, Henry Pelham could proudly boast in the Commons that " the Three Per Cents stand at Par ".[2] Here was the most concise and convincing exposition of England's financial stability. All this was of momentous social and political consequence. The National Debt, which had provided a rampart against Jacobitism was afterwards to provide a rampart against Jacobinism; so many Englishmen had invested in the government that they were unlikely to welcome its overthrow. Herein is one of the reasons why England was spared violent revolution.

V EVOLUTION OF PERSONALITY

As love and marriage were closely related to broad acres and gilt-edged securities, so human personality was joined to substantial things, namely, the four bodily humours : blood, phlegm, black bile and yellow bile. This theory, derived from Hippocrates and the doctrine of the four elements, was a commonplace of medical practice, with amendments derived from such writers as Bodin and Montesquieu, who insisted on the influence of climate. The four humours, which could be described as built-in constituents of the human body, might become " corrupt ", and " corrupt " bile would produce melancholia unless adequately purged. So too with other ailments. Climate served almost as a thermostat, producing a fairly con-

[1] ibid, X, 183-4.　　　　[2] ibid, XIV, Nov. 16, 1749.

stant type of character according to latitude—brave and active in the north, in the opinion of some writers, sluggish and torpid in the opinion of others. Hot climates engendered an indolence conducive to slavery; the Orient favoured fertility of imagination and so on. In other words what we now term personality was determined by internal secretions as regulated by temperature and climate. Human character was therefore referred not to what we call psychology, but to a balance of chemical reactions; here indeed was a primitive and unscientific biochemistry. Because of the variety of meanings attributed to it, the word " humour " provides a key to some of the more remote recesses of modern civilisation. In eighteenth-century France to say that a man had no humour (*humeur*) meant that he had no " corners " and was easy to get on with; even in modern France the word more often means bad humour than good. In England, on the other hand, the word acquired an additional meaning—a sense of balance or proportion, keenly sensitive to the ridiculous, as seen in the phrase " sense of humour ", a personal quality possessed by those who are usually easy to get on with. This phrase like " sense of honour " was unknown in England until the nineteenth century.

It is debatable whether human character has been deepened and enriched in the course of centuries, but it is indisputable that our vocabularies for describing shades of character have been greatly enlarged. It is even possible that, among the more recondite effects of the revolutionary and romantic movements, there emerged something new—the idea of human individuality in its own right—as contrasted with the older conception which submerged personality in the family, or the corporation or the landed estate. As Funck Brentano[1] said of the *Ancien Régime* : " individuals did not exist then ", or, more accurately, the individual had not yet been detached from his milieu; he was not yet considered a personality, dis-

[1] F. Funck Brentano, *The Old Régime in France*, English trans. 1929, p. 34.

tinctive and unique. This change did not come overnight, nor can we assign any date to its occurrence. The new concept found expression in different forms, many of them bizarre. There appeared on the scene devotees of solitude, some of whom fled to the mountains, where they could indulge in an introspection unattainable within the conventions of civilisation. Now, introspection is essentially personal and individual; many were experiencing a need for it, a fact which may help to explain why mountains and solitary places, including graveyards, hitherto regarded with horror, exercised an increasing fascination for sensitive minds This changed attitude to nature, culminating in the Romantic Revival, may be connected with the gradual emergence of the individual from the herd.

The change can be illustrated from a number of sources, including religion and language. In religion, Methodism was revolutionary in so far as it brought the individual right into the foreground, making him the object of divine affection—

Jesu, lover of my soul.

Here was a clue to the success of the movement, for the poorer elements of society had never before been assured of such a personal, intimate solicitude on their behalf. In no other phase of religion was this personal element so strong as in Methodism, nor did any other creed penetrate so deeply into the humblest ranks of society, including even such pariahs as the coal miners who, in this period, were outside the pale. All this provided a barrier against violence and revolution, a barrier which did not exist in France.

It is in language, however, that one finds clearest evidence of this gradual emergence of individuality and personality. Language often provides the most sensitive register of deep-seated changes in civilisation, though it is rarely used by the historian. Now, it was not until the eighteenth century that the European vernaculars became fully developed; grammars and dictionaries were published, and in 1694 the French Academy produced the first edition of its Dictionary. This was a momentous event, because hitherto Latin or a latinised form of the vernacular had been the vehicle of learned discussion; but now the national languages had to meet the demands of rapidly developing civilisations, and new ideas had to be expressed in new words. In this respect it is interesting to compare the French Dictionary of 1694 with that of 1777. In the latter there were, as we might expect, many new words as well as old words to which a new meaning was attached. Among the entirely new words were "*patriote*" and "*patriotisme*". The fact that these were late arrivals in French vocabulary may help us to understand why Voltaire congratulated Frederick the Great on his victories over the French.

Among other new words in the 1777 edition were "*optimisme*", probably derived from the views of Leibniz and the ideas of human perfectibility then in vogue among some of the *philosophes*; also the word "*personnalité*", which was defined as the character or quality of a person. There was a similar evolution in the English language, changes of emphasis or implication rather than of meaning, some of them so minute as to escape detection. Thus, the words *human* and *humane* were interchangeable in the early eighteenth century; whereas, to-day, we use the former to denote a species and the latter to denote a personal quality or virtue of that species. This is why Locke's *Essay Concerning Humane Understanding* is commonly misquoted as *Essay Concerning Human Understanding*; like his contemporaries, Locke was using the word *humane* in an objective, not in a subjective sense. Almost invariably, in this development of words to meet new needs, the advance is from the concrete to the abstract. Of this, a clear example is our word *tolerant,* an old word which, by the nineteenth century, had been amplified to include tolerance of other people's opinions; whereas, formerly, it was limited to tolerance of something physical, such as poison, or hard work or exposure. Already, by their analysis of the connection between sense impressions and the processes of human thought, such thinkers as Locke, Hume and Condillac had laid the foundations of what we call psychology, but it was not until the post-revolutionary, post-romantic period that the demand was fully met for new words or amplified old words intended to convey those shades of differentiation in human character and personality with which we are so familiar to-day. Here indeed is a worth-while subject of intelligent research—the elucidation of linguistic developments which indicate subtle changes in human civilisation.

Of this the most abundant examples will be found in the many words ending in -ism, nearly all of them of nineteenth-century origin. It might even be claimed that, particularly in our Anglo-Saxon societies, with their comparative tolerance, their innumerable cults, their absence of authoritarian dogma and their subtle shadings of opinion, the -ism has become a linguistic necessity, useful at times for disguising our meaning, or even for saying something when we are not sure what we really do mean. In some branches of literature, as in art, there is great scope for the diffuse and the chiaroscuro, but the legitimate use of the -ism exceeds its abuse. Practically unknown in the *Ancien Régime*, it has become the literary hall mark of our age. A few examples will make clear the nature of this extension of our vocabularies. Take such groups of words as piety and pietism, clerical and clericalism, obscurity and obscurantism, peace and pacifism, opportunity and opportunism, feminine and feminism—the list might be indefinitely extended—it will be found that, while the first word of each group is old and concrete, the second is new and abstract, relating to a quality of character, or a cult or a type of opinion. Our literary currency would be much the poorer in the absence of such new mintings. This is the main difference between the language of the *Ancien Régime* and that of to-day; it illustrates a change of mentality not unlike that evidenced in the development of the individual from childhood to maturity for, while the child can appreciate only what is visible and in the foreground, the adult can think in terms of the subjective and the unseen.

VI TWO EXPONENTS OF THE ANCIEN REGIME: BIELFELD AND PALEY

Of literature advocating change or reform there is no end; dissent is more vocal than conformity. This is specially true of eighteenth-century France, when new vistas for humanity appeared to be opening up, and enthusiasts rushed into print, anxious to remove one more stumbling block from the pathway to the millenium. On the other hand, it is rare to find an author who, notwithstanding certain reservations, is satisfied with the conditions around him, and goes to the trouble of giving reasons for his satisfaction. It may be claimed that such writers, regrettably few, are more representative of ordinary, inarticulate opinion than the reformers and propagandists. In the period with which this book is concerned there appear to be no Frenchmen in this category—the French are usually critical of their environment—but there were two writers, a Prussian and an Englishman who, on the whole, acquiesced in existing conditions. These were the Baron de Bielfeld and Archdeacon Paley.

J. F. Bielfeld (1716-70) was born in Hamburg and served under Frederick the Great as Inspector General of Prussian universities. The two volumes of his *Institutions Politiques* were published at The Hague in 1760. " We are lucky to be living in this century " he wrote " when kings are seeking every means of making their subjects happy ". Nothing of barbarity remains, he added, in contrast with such an age as that of Machiavelli; " one is revolted by his maxims ". In the first volume, devoted mainly to social and economic matters, the author showed that he was no reactionary, but a man of progressive and enlightened ideas, for he condemned torture (except when used to investigate conspiracies); he advocated the abolition of feudal fiefs and customary laws; he pleaded for the exercise of humanity in war. Deploring the prejudice which excluded the nobility from trade, he advocated the establishment of national banks, the making of good roads and encouragement of agriculture, in which respects he claimed that England was superior to France. National prosperity, in his view, was associated not with hoarding of bullion, but with its free circulation. Especially in large, wealthy states there was a place for luxury—" commerce and art would languish without luxury". The influence of the Enlightenment is seen in Bielfeld's opinion that the clergy should be excluded from secular matters, and that civil marriage should be instituted. One of the duties of the sovereign is to " polish " the nation, which can best be done by setting up academies, as in France. Our author had little patience with " cranks ", such as enthusiasts for the state of nature and advocates of perpetual peace. These views do little more than reflect the enlightened elements in the domestic policy pursued by Frederick the Great.

Otherwise, Bielfeld insists on the preservation of a static state, where everyone is kept in his place and the police are endowed with large powers. This immobile organisation is held together by religion, which habituates the subject to obedience; the ruler and the upper classes need not believe in religious tenets, but they must not communicate their scepticism to the lower classes. The nobility are rightfully exempt from taxation because they serve the state in war, at court and in embassies; also, with their large establishments, they consume more taxed commodities than do common men. Burgesses should not be allowed to acquire land, for their place is in the towns. As the sovereign is the source of all laws, his edicts ought to be embodied in a code, on which the subject should be forbidden to make comments, for such comments open the door to disaffection. Children of the poor should be taught only useful or mechanical occupations, because the arts and refinements of civilisation are the monopoly of the upper classes. The police must control the Press in order to prevent the spread of immorality and unrest; they should enforce measures for preventing gluts and famines, and they ought to maintain a general supervision over the exercise of trades and crafts. A well-regulated, compact state is much easier to govern than a loose, unorganised body of men.

In his second volume Bielfeld considers matters of foreign policy. He distinguished between three kinds of European state: those able to wage war on their own account, as England and France; those in need of alliances and subsidies, as Austria, Russia, Prussia and Spain, and those unable to maintain troops in peace time, such as Portugal, Sardinia, Sweden, Denmark and the Netherlands. It is, he declares,[1] a fundamental maxim that each state should use every legitimate means for the conservation or increase of its actual and relative power (obviously much would depend on the interpretation of the word "legitimate"). This maxim, our author states, is dictated by "Natural Law", and a government acting on any other principle is guilty of "criminal negligence". Here is an anticipation of the views of Hegel, Treitschke and Hitler, as relevant for the twentieth century as for the eighteenth. A sovereign, according to Bielfeld, can carry out this duty by one of two methods—by a "war" system or a "politic" system. If he rules over a large state with warlike subjects, he should adopt the first method, and should organise his state in a military way. Otherwise, he must adopt more pacific methods, for which a good deal of ability is required. Thus, he can make shrewd purchases of territory; he can arrange marriages likely to bring in profitable successions; family alliances, "pacts of confraternity" and a "clientage" system among one's neighbours are all means to the same end. The weakness or decadence of neighbouring states will often facilitate the pursuit of such a policy. Compactness of territory should be aimed at, as a distant province is difficult to defend. A prince can break off a treaty if its fulfilment would prejudice the state. These maxims are set forth in a book which begins with a denunciation of Machiavelli.

It may be objected that Bielfeld is of more Prussian than

[1] Bielfeld, *Institutions Politiques*, II, p. 85.

European significance, but nevertheless no other writer has made such a frank avowal of the principles which actuated, in greater or less degree, the policies of the more powerful nations in the *Ancien Régime*. As well as this, there is an element of menace in Bielfeld's book. Wars of aggression are as old as history, but now they are justified on the most exalted moral grounds.

William Paley (1743-1805), a descendant of Yorkshire yeoman families, was educated at a north-country school and at Christ's College, Cambridge, of which society he afterwards became a fellow and tutor. In 1782 he was appointed Archdeacon of Carlisle, having already held several country livings. In 1785 he published his *Principles of Morals and Political Philosophy*. Based on his college lectures (which were well attended), this proved to be the most famous text book of the century, fifteen editions being published in the lifetime of the author. Paley, a genial, sociable man, having no claim to originality, abounded in shrewd commonsense; the popularity of his book may be attributed to the fact that it represented the views of the average, not too intelligent Englishmen of the period, particularly those who distrusted innovation or reform. Hence its value for the student of history. Frequently a vein of sophistry can be detected in his arguments.

As with Bielfeld, his approval of the existing régime was not unreserved; on the contrary he suggested a number of reforms, some of which would be acceptable to-day. Anticipating Bentham, he maintained that the chief object of the lawgiver should be to increase human happiness. When engaged in a " just " or " defensive " war, the ruler should aim not simply at increase of territory, but at the promotion of happiness in the country which he acquires. In home affairs he thought that there were too many offices at the disposal of the crown, most of them of too great value; in the church, too many preferments were given to " illiterate and frivolous " sons of the nobility. In his discussion of taxation he broke fresh ground, for he advocated a reduction of taxes on married couples and on all who, by agricultural improvements or encouragement of industry, were adding to the national wealth. Unaware perhaps of the great increase of population going on around him, he emphasised the importance of expanding the number of productive workers.

Otherwise, Paley found more to commend than condemn. He justified the non-residence of clergy on the unconvincing ground that, as the total revenue of the church may be regarded as a common fund for the support of the national church, it does not matter from which portion a non-resident clergyman is paid. Hence, he continues, the pecuniary value of a preferment need bear no relation to the amount of labour which it involves. On the same analogy the right of a freeholder to vote can be purchased, but the voter must not accept a bribe for his vote; so too, the sale of advowsons is justified, provided that the patron does not accept a bribe. These distinctions are somewhat subtle. Regarding subscription to the Thirty-Nine Articles Paley had no sympathy with those who, in his own day, were demanding some relaxation; for, according to him, the law did not intend acceptance of controversial opinions, but simply exclusion from office of three undesirable classes of men—Papists, Anabaptists and Puritans, all of them hostile to the episcopal institution. He defended the existing system whereby the church courts exercised jurisdiction over the interpretation of Wills and the administration of personalty on the ground that, before Henry VIII's Statute of Wills, all matters of probate were within the jurisdiction of the church. So too with divorce, which was then under the control of the ecclesiastical courts.

On the subject of the British constitution Paley was informative. Adhering to the early Whig view that the crown was one of three Estates, he maintained that the king would not use the veto capriciously, because of the restraint implied by the passing of the annual army vote. The old favouritism, he contended, had disappeared, as " proved " by the fact that the crown often conferred office on persons who had previously been in opposition. The House of Lords, he continues, serves three purposes—it enables the king to reward merit; it secures the stability of monarchy, and it helps to stem the progress of popular fury. " Large bodies of men are subject to sudden phrenzies ". The Lords can be trusted to reject Bills that are founded on the folly or violence of the lower orders of the community. As for the House of Commons, about one half of its members obtain their seats by the choice of freeholders, the other half by purchase, or by the nomination of great landlords. " If the properest persons be elected, what matters it by whom they are elected?". Whatever the defects of the existing system, it secures a great weight of property in the Commons by ensuring that many seats are accessible only to men of large fortunes; moreover, it is a good thing that so many of the Commons are nominated by the nobility, as this promotes community of interest. " An independent parliament is inconsistent with the existence of monarchy "—perhaps the most candid admission ever made about the eighteenth-century legislature.

On the subject of the administration of justice Paley expressed opinions which, even in his day, were beginning to be challenged. In regard to crimes, he adhered to the popular view that the facility with which a theft can be committed, e.g. stealing clothes from bleaching grounds, is an aggravation of the offence, and justifies a more severe penalty. In general, he favoured the opinion that there should be many felonies on the statute book, with discretionary powers for mitigating the penalty. " The penal laws were never meant to be carried into indiscriminate execution ". But in practice they often were. The legislature, our author notes, trusts that the crown will relax the severity of the punishments. It was just this uncertainty about infliction of the penalty that reformers afterwards strove to remove. Had Paley lived into the reign of George IV he might have heard complaints that many petitions to the crown for mercy were held up for months because George, absenting himself from his royal duties, was "convalescing" at Brighton.

Paley attributed the frequency of executions in England to three causes—much liberty, great cities and the infrequency of punishments, short of death, that would serve as an adequate deterrent. Transportation he considered unsuitable because, in his view, it was a "slight" punishment for those who have neither property, nor friends nor reputation. So the Archdeacon appears to have preferred the gibbet, an emblem, according to him, not of English ferocity but of English freedom. Here his reasoning, which is not easy to follow, appears to be based on a contrast between England and foreign countries. In the latter, there is more personal surveillance and an absence of the principle of proof before conviction, whereas British insistence on the liberty of the subject, and the existence of public courts for the trial of all offenders, serve to reinforce the argument for exemplary punishment of all who have been found guilty. In other words, English liberty was something good but, like most good things, it had to be paid for; it was paid for by the poor—on the gallows. Considering the high proportion of sophistry in Paley's reasoning, it is not difficult to understand how his audiences and readers—many of them destined to be country magistrates—were reconciled to the infliction of savage punishments on the lower classes. But, in fairness to the Archdeacon, it must be added that imprisonment was not then a common form of punishment, as hanging or transportation were the usual alternatives.

Regarding the causes of crime Paley thought that aversion to work was responsible for half the vices of "low life". To the vices of high life he was more indulgent, as witness his argument that luxury can be defended, provided it is limited to persons of high rank. So Paley, like many of his contemporaries, amended one of the beatitudes to read: "blessed are the exalted and the rich, for their virtue shall be of more account than that of the poor".

Chapter II

CONTINENTAL EMPIRES.
MONARCHIES. REPUBLICS

The break up of western European civilisation by the Protestant Reformation had brought into existence the national monarchies of modern times, wholly or partially free from clerical control; but many of them retained the Divine Right sanction by which the church had hallowed the rule of medieval kings. To this the sixteenth century added the support of Roman Law; and so, by the eighteenth century, kingship had the allegiance of lawyer and priest. No institution could have stronger support. Moreover experience confirmed what theory had advocated. Until the emergence of the American federation in 1783 the republics, such as Switzerland and Venice, were too small to be of account, and had to seek safety in neutrality; the Swedish democratic experiment was ended in 1772 by the restoration of absolute monarchy, just in time to avoid partition such as had dismembered the weak, elective monarchy of Poland only a few months before. In a century when clergy, nobility and the professions were unsparingly criticised, absolute monarchy, sometimes little different from personal despotism, was rarely challenged, and was even regarded as the only medium through which radical reform could be effected.

I CONTINENTAL EMPIRES

As a consequence mainly of the Reformation and the Thirty Years War the powers of the Holy Roman Emperor, who traced his prerogative to Charlemagne, had been greatly diminished, but he still retained some personal prestige as the pre-eminent secular ruler of western Christendom. That prestige, medieval and semi-ecclesiastical in character, was contrasted with the material bases, money and large armies, on which power now rested; in comparison the imperial armies and finances were ludicrously small. The office of emperor was still nominally elective, choice being made by nine electors, who included the archbishops of Mainz, Cologne and Trier, five great German princes and the king of Bohemia; but, since the fifteenth century, choice had been limited to the Habsburg family. A break in this tradition occurred in 1742-5, during the Austrian Succession War, when the office was exercised by Charles VII, of the Wittelsbach family—the chief German rivals of the Habsburgs. He was succeeded by Francis Stephen of Lorraine, husband of Maria Theresa, and on his death was followed by emperors of the House of Habsburg-Lorraine until the extinction of the empire in 1806. By the eighteenth century the old imperialist claims in Italy had been very nearly abandoned; in Germany they were resented, notably by Frederick of Prussia, as the intrusion of a non-German family.

The constitution of the empire still further emphasised its ineffectiveness. The Imperial Diet, which met at Ratisbon, consisted of three Estates—princely electors, nobles and towns —all of them represented by deputies, many of them lawyers, and the concurrence of all three Estates was necessary for the promulgation of a law. This was difficult, especially when a question of religion was involved because, on such occasions, by the *jus eundi in partes,* each Estate divided into Catholic and Protestant sections. Legal jurisdiction was vested in the Imperial Court sitting at Wetzlar, a tribunal notorious for the fact that it was thousands of cases in arrear. Crowning this unwieldy edifice was the Aulic Council in Vienna, a supreme body which occasionally exercised a control not unlike that formerly wielded by the British government over the native princes of India, for it acted on petitions from subjects aggrieved by the conduct of their rulers. It was to the Aulic Council that landowners in Brandenburg appealed against the imposition by Frederick William of a tax on the conversion into freehold of lands formerly held by knight service.[1] Another case was that of the celebrated jurist and patriot J. J. Moser who had drawn up a protest on behalf of the Württemberg Estates against the arbitrary conduct of the Duke. For this, the Duke consigned him to prison but, on his appeal, the Aulic Council ordered his release. These examples suggest a certain paternal element in the imperial prerogative, but it was not often exercised.

As the Habsburgs derived little more than prestige from their office they were dependent for revenue on their hereditary lands in Austria, the Milanese and Belgium, and their two kingdoms of Hungary and Bohemia. These provinces and kingdoms still preserved their local Estates, which were summoned irregularly or not at all. In the course of the eighteenth century their place was taken by an elaborate civil service, having its headquarters in Vienna.[2] Differences of race, religion and language made impossible the creation of a unified state from such scattered dominions; a spirit of separatism from within and the threat of conquest from without served to make the Habsburg empire one of the most unstable of all European polities. Only the Pragmatic Sanction[3] of 1713 united it into some kind of unity, and that proved to be little more than a paper guarantee.

The Muscovite Empire was limited by conditions imposed by geography and climate. These conditions were incidental to the existence of a great land mass, stretching across eastern Europe and northern Asia, much of it uncleared forest, or swamp, or desert, a vast area in which climate is influenced as much by longitude as by latitude. As one travels eastwards to the Urals the winter temperature, on the same latitude, steadily diminishes. Moscow is on the same parallel as Edinburgh; in January, the Crimea, on the 45th parallel, has the

[1] above, p. 20.   [2] below, p. 207.   [3] below, p. 125.

same mean temperature as Stockholm, which is 60 degrees north, whereas in summer it has the average temperature of Madeira (34th parallel).[1] In north-eastern Siberia Verkhoyansk in winter is the coldest town in the world. These extremes, typical of a continental climate, have influenced Russian economy, as they may have influenced Russian character. There were however some mitigating factors. The rivers, though frozen during variable parts of the year, provide transport in summer and winter; except in the tundra of the Arctic circle, snow prevents freezing of the soil and promotes the cultivation of cereals, of which rye is the most important. Also, the Russian Empire is very rich in minerals; indeed, it is doubtful whether they have yet been fully exploited.

These facts alone may be sufficient to explain why Siberia has for so long been regarded as a penal settlement; whereas the frontier brought hope to the pioneer in the west, it usually brought despair to the Russian in the east. Otherwise, there were some analogies between the evolution of the British Empire in North America and that of the Muscovite Empire in Asia. In both there were forest lands to be cleared and uncharted deserts to be crossed; there were similar extremes of temperature; nomadic tribes resented any intrusion into their way of life and, while the British colonist had, for long, to face the hostility of the French, in Siberia the settlers had to reckon with Tartar tribes, many of them under the protection of the Porte. The conquest and settlement of these vast areas provide one of the great epics of modern history. Even before the eighteenth century some pioneer work had been done by the land-owning monasteries of north-east Russia, and by the merchant princes of Novgorod; the Pacific had been reached by explorers and, by 1741, the discovery of the Behring Straits led to the establishment of a seal-trapping industry which spread to Alaska and even as far south as the coast of California. Contact with China was maintained through

[1] For this see P. Milioukov, C. Seignobos and L. Eisenmann, *Histoire de Russie*, I, pp. 45 ff.

Irkutsk, near the Mongolian frontier, a strategic point for the caravans bringing in tea, silks and oriental goods. But these communications provided no more than the tentacles of empire and, at the beginning of the century, there were probably not more than 300,000 Russians in Siberia.

The Russian Empire may be said to date from 1721 when Peter the Great proclaimed himself Emperor (*Imperator*). In this way was inaugurated the Third Rome and the Second Jerusalem, having for its emblem the double-headed eagle of Byzantium, an auspicious event coinciding with the signing of the treaty of Nystadt,[1] whereby Russia acquired Ingria, Estonia and Livonia at the expense of Sweden. These conquests gave to Russia a Baltic coast line from Viborg to Riga. Except for Ingria, the new possessions were not colonised by Russians, as they were already administered mainly by an aristocracy of German origin, but, economically, they were of great importance as they supplied so much of the canvas, timber, flax, tar and hemp, all of them in demand by the west, especially by England. These products accounted for about two-thirds of Russian exports in the eighteenth century. Southern Finland was added in 1743 after a short war with Sweden. In consequence Arkhangel, ice-bound during a great part of the year, fell into decay and Russia became not only the greatest of the Baltic powers but a force to be reckoned with by western diplomacy. In the east the most notable achievement of Peter's reign was the establishment of a great iron and copper industry in the Urals,[2] to which serfs were " ascribed " as unfree workers. Farther east, penetration consisted of little more than the setting up of a number of frontiers, according to occupation. At first Siberia was valued for its furs, so the earliest pioneers were the trappers, followed by the miners and seal hunters. Labour was provided by numerous escaped serfs, by serfs sentenced to hard labour by their masters, by communities of dissidents, such as the Old Believers, who objected to Peter's westernising policy, and by

[1] below, p. 132.   [2] below, p. 116.

the agents of trading companies. The Cossacks, who were subsidised by an annual grant of cloth and munitions from Moscow, acted as frontiersmen and as a police force, usually, but not always, faithful to the Tsars.

Russian imperialism was extended in the reign of Catherine II (1762-96). This began in 1772 with the first Partition of Poland, when she acquired an area having its western boundary on the Dwina, stretching south nearly to Kiev and the Dnieper, an area formerly part of the Grand Duchy of Lithuania; almost contemporary with this was the acquisition from Turkey of the steppe lands on the north shore of the Black Sea. These were among the conquests of the Russo-Turkish War, which was ended by the treaty of Kutchuk Kainardji in 1774; added to them was the right of mercantile navigation on the Black Sea and passage into the Mediterranean through the Straits. Azov had already been gained by the treaty of Belgrade in 1739; the Crimea was freed from Turkish sovereignty in 1783, and in 1794 Odessa was founded. In the wheat-bearing lands between the Black Sea and Caspian, where fresh acquisitions were made, was the New Russia, a symbol of conquest and expansion; still more, by the treaty of Kutchuk Kainardji Catherine was designated Protectress of the Christians in the Balkan lands, an office which prompted her to begin a process of undermining Ottoman power in the Balkans, in the hope of creating a new Byzantium on the shores of the Bosphorus. But the Turk proved too resilient for the achievement of such an ambition. Nevertheless, Catherine's dominion extended into three continents and, though the Asiatic and American portions were very thinly peopled, the Russian empire could claim to be one of the largest since the days of Ancient Rome.

The Turkish empire in Europe during a great part of this period consisted mainly of the Balkan Peninsula (including Greece) as far as the Danube; the north coast of the Black Sea (until 1774); the principalities of Moldavia and Wallachia. In Asia it extended to Asia Minor, Armenia, Kurdistan, Irak,

Mesopotamia and Syria; the African possessions were Egypt, Tripoli and Algiers; Turkish suzerainty was also exercised over Cyprus, Crete, the Aegean Islands and Wallachia. In some of these areas imperial control was nominal, consisting mainly in the exaction of tribute. So far as the European possessions were concerned, the climax of Ottoman power was reached at the treaty of Belgrade (1739), in terms of which Austria gave up most of the conquests that had been acquired at the treaty of Passarowitz (1718), including Belgrade, Serbia, Bosnia and Wallachia; thenceforward, the Danube and the Save were the north-western boundaries of Turkey in Europe. But a long period of peace, followed by the Russo-Turkish war of 1768-74, proved disastrous to the Porte and, as already related, of advantage to Russia.

The Ottoman Turks, who were probably descended from a nomadic Siberian tribe, included Near-East and Asiatic elements in their ancestry. Having no culture of their own they borrowed extensively—their Mohammedan faith from the Arabs, their arts from Persia and Byzantium. Habituated by generations of plunder, they had no manufactures, save those of brass ware, carpets and perfumery; nor (except among the upper classes) did they have any pride in household possessions. The Turk was either a soldier, a farmer or a government official. As a soldier, he was stolid rather than brave, but was capable of subjection to discipline; as a farmer, he was hard working; as a government official he despised the wretched salary allotted him by his government, preferring more indirect means of making a livelihood. The city of Constantinople was not a capital in the modern sense, but little more than a meeting place of east and west. Imbued with fatalism, the Turk had little or no intellectual curiosity, believing that everything worth knowing had already been expounded in the Koran; moreover, his pride in Turkish achievements—always heroic and at the expense of races whom he regarded as his inferiors—was naïve, often a mixture of historical fact and myth as with most nomadic peoples and lacking the sophistication of Western European history. It can therefore be understood that, so far as use of original sources is concerned, we cannot have an account of the civilisation of Turkey in Europe comparable in either fullness or authenticity with that of the western states.

In the Turkish polity there was no distinction between secular and spiritual; the sultan, as descendant of the ancient Caliphate, was both pope and emperor. Nor was there any distinction between law and theology, both of them having their repositories in the *ulemas* who, under the direction of the Grand Mufti, were a body of experts in law and theology, from whom civil servants, judges and teachers were recruited. Nominally absolute, the sultan had to conform to the decisions of the *ulemas* as otherwise he might be the victim of a *jehad* or holy war, in which he could be deposed and murdered by his subjects. He might also be at the mercy of his Grand Vizier, who acted as his representative and performed many of the functions of head of the state. Spread of the Islamic faith by conquest was the supreme duty enjoined on the executive; but fortunately, in the eighteenth century, the sultans, including Ahmed III (1703-30) and Mahmud I (1730-54) were men of peace and even of culture; indeed, it was because of his devotion to these things that Ahmed was deposed. The army was made up of *sipahis*, the holders of military fiefs, and janissaries—sons of Christian subjects forced into military service at an early age. In this period the janissaries were little better than an armed mob. The navy, modelled on the Venetian galleys, was manned by slaves and criminals; its powerlessness against a modern fleet was demonstrated at Tchesmé in 1770, when the Russian ships annihilated the Turkish galleys.[1]

The Balkan provinces were administered not by Turks but by Greeks, mostly from the Phanariot or Lighthouse district of Constantinople; their rule was usually both irresponsible and oppressive. Trade and commerce were mainly in the hands of Greeks, Armenians and Levantines. Since the sixteenth century the French, in virtue of a series of Capitulations, had enjoyed special trading privileges in Constantinople, but they had to face the rivalry of the English. Generally, as has been well said, the Turks did not settle in Europe; they merely camped out. But the Turkish imperial system, though obtuse and corrupt on modern standards, was not without its redeeming features. Christian subjects were taxed, but not persecuted. Slavery existed, but manumission was frequent, since the sultan himself was always the son of a female slave, who was usually freed after she had served her purpose. All the sultan's servants, however exalted their office, were technically his slaves. So far as toleration was concerned, eighteenth-century Turkey compared favourably with western Europe.

II MONARCHIES

Of the European monarchies in this period Spain, Prussia, Sweden and Denmark call for brief reference; England and France are treated with somewhat greater fullness. Poland, the crown of which was elective, was sometimes regarded as a republic, but is here treated as a monarchy. The United Dutch Provinces, which began as a federation of states, were obliged at times to submit to the rule of a hereditary stadholder, endowed with almost monarchic powers, but are here classed as a republic. It should be added that the word republic (*respublica*), as used in this period, did not always have its modern connotation, for it might mean no more than " state ".

Spain benefited by its transfer, in terms of the treaties of Utrecht, from Habsburg to Bourbon rule, though its first Bourbon ruler, Philip V, suffered from prolonged periods of melancholia, and his second wife Elizabeth Farnese dragged the nation into foreign entanglements and war. Nominally, the Spanish monarchy was a divinely-instituted autocracy, tempered by the control which the *cortès* of the various states were supposed to exercise. But the *cortès* of Aragon ceased to meet and, though the *cortès* of Navarre and Castile were still summoned, their importance was negligible, for they met only in order to swear allegiance to the new sovereign or to give formal support to important royal edicts. Philip V, who did much to centralise the administration mainly by reducing the number of councils which had impeded the work of his predecessors, ruled with the help of one supreme council—the Council of Castile—a body which exercised judicial, executive and legislative functions. For the details of administration Philip introduced secretaries on the French model; *intendants* were permanently established by his successor Ferdinand VI, all of them responsible to the Council of Castile. Although the Basque provinces retained something of their old autonomy, including their civil legislation, and although Catalonia, with its distinctive dialect and commercial enterprise, remained a somewhat discordant element in the nation nevertheless, under her Bourbon rulers, Spain achieved a degree of unity and a standard of administrative efficiency such as were unknown in the past.

Under the rule of Frederick William and his son Frederick the Great the kingdom of Prussia was unique because of royal concentration on one object—the creation of administrative and fiscal efficiency in order to provide sufficient money for the maintenance of an army which, in proportion to the population, was by far the largest in Europe. In this object these two rulers succeeded, but at the cost of creating an artificial, top-heavy state that did not survive the test of time. Frederick William did much to eliminate local particularism, including that of the Estates, his object being to centralise government in king and privy council, assisted by a hierarchy of boards and departments which extended their tentacles to the humblest local officials. Departments that had previously worked separately or in isolation were conjoined in 1723 into a General

Directory of War, Finance and Royal Domains. Subordinate to this supreme body were councils whose duties were subdivided on a geographical basis, not unlike that prevailing among the French secretaries of state. The provincial nobility were conscripted into the system and from them were appointed the *Landräte* or Sub Prefects, who were paid civil servants, having jurisdiction over local areas (*Kreise*). They were assisted by commissaries who controlled the towns within their jurisdiction. Direction of the judicial system, of religion and education was delegated to a supreme council, and the shaping of foreign policy was entrusted to a Cabinet. With Teutonic thoroughness everything was regulated and provided for; nor was there any room for initiative in this vast pyramidal structure. As nowhere else, state service became the most honourable human activity and it is not surprising that, in the twentieth century, Nazi doctrinaires eulogised the administration of Frederick William as the supreme model.

The system was continued and developed by his son Frederick the Great. New councils, for Silesia, commerce and the army were set up in order to assist the General Directory, which remained the core of the system; and even greater use was made of the Fiscals, who were little distinguishable from spies on the civil servants. In consequence, the Prussian civil service became the hardest worked, the poorest paid and the most carefully scrutinised of all the civil services of Europe. In contrast with his father, however, Frederick introduced into the administration a larger proportion of the nobility; and, as this class already had a monopoly of army commands, the prestige and social apartness of the upper classes in Prussia was greatly intensified. Moreover, with years, Frederick became more meticulous and distrustful; he conducted many visits of inspection, embarrassing his subordinates by innumerable memoranda and instructions, not all of them capable of application, with the result that evasion and concealment were often resorted to.

The Scandinavian polities were more rudimentary. Population was sparse and widely scattered; towns of considerable size were few; and, although there were eminent men in technology,[1] science and literature,[2] a reading public was only in process of formation. Still more, these nations did not have the rich medieval heritage so characteristic of western Europe. There remained traces of the old epic achievement in the ideals demanded of their kings, though this had been modified by a very different ideal—that of the godly prince, so favoured by the Lutheran reformers. What impeded the development of the northern states was the great number and power of the nobility. The twin kingdoms of Denmark-Norway were more fortunate in this respect than Sweden, because in 1660, by an absolutist *coup d'état,* the powers of the Danish nobility had been greatly reduced; consequently, though they continued to maintain their peasants in a state of serfdom, they ceased to be a political menace. It was otherwise in Sweden. The nobility in 1718 numbered over 1,000 families, out of a population of one and a half millions, and it has to be recalled that all the members of a noble family were accounted noble. In the Swedish Diet the nobility, who greatly preponderated in numbers and influence, provided the centre of political life;[3] but, as many of them were very poor and willing to accept bribes, it was not difficult for a foreign power such as France to exert great influence. Sweden experienced two violent changes of constitution—in 1720, when much of the prerogative was vested in the Diet and in 1772 when, by a reverse process, the powers of the crown were restored. The intervening period is described by some historians as "the period of anarchy", by others as "the period of liberty". Of these verdicts the former is probably the more true.

In the later part of the sixteenth century the area covered by Poland and Lithuania was second only to that occupied by Russia; but eventually, in consequence of the partitions, prac-

---

[1] below, p. 116.   [2] below, pp. 189-90.
[3] *The European Nobility in the Eighteenth Century,* ed. A. Goodwin (1953), ch. viii, "Sweden" by M. Roberts.

tically all the ancient duchy of Lithuania was acquired by Russia. By the beginning of the eighteenth century, of a Polish-Lithuanian population of about 11 millions, the Poles accounted for one half, the other half consisting of Russians, Germans, Lithuanians and Jews. About half the inhabitants were Catholics, a third were of the Orthodox Russian faith, the remainder were Jews and Protestants. The great majority of the peasants were serfs, dominated by more than 20,000 of the lesser nobility who, in consequence of the weakness of the crown, were free to increase the labour dues and *corvées* at will. Trade was monopolised by the Jews, who constituted a large part of the population of the towns. In this period the Polish crown became little more than the prize in a gamble played by the greater powers. After the death of John Sobieski in 1697 Augustus II, Elector of Saxony, was chosen by the Polish Diet; he ruled until his death in 1733, except for an interval between 1704 and 1709 when Stanislas Lesczinski, afterwards father-in-law of Louis XV, was held on the throne as a puppet of Charles XII of Sweden. A disputed succession on the death of Augustus II in 1733 provided a pretext and a name for the Polish Succession War,[1] which was really a revival of the old Franco-Austrian hostility; the result, so far as Poland was concerned, was the election of Augustus's son Augustus III, who reigned, largely as the nominee of Russia, until his death in 1763. His successor was Stanislas Poniatowski, the lover and confidant of Catherine the Great, whose rule lasted until his deposition in 1795.

The so-called nobility of Poland—the *szlachta*—consisted of a large, indeterminate body, including magnates and small landowners, all intensely jealous of their rights, and devoted to an abstraction which they called "liberty". They were represented in the General Diet by deputies, elected at local Dietines, whose hands were tied by rigid instructions. Towns and clergy were outside this scheme of representation, but archbishops and bishops sat in the Senate, which was a part of the

[1] below, pp. 134-6.

Diet. The Diet elected the king who, on the theory that his office was contractual, promulgated in the *Pacta Conventa* the limitations which he himself imposed on his rule. These limitations which, at first, were not unlike the terms of the English coronation oath, became more stringent in the course of the century, apparently as a concession to the liberty-loving *szlachta*. The election had to be unanimous. Moreover, by the *liberum veto* any member of the Diet could hold up business indefinitely; accordingly, insistence from outside on the maintenance of this personal right provided a guarantee of anarchy. This was the main object of Russian policy in Poland; it was made easier by increasing antagonism between the Catholic majority on the one hand and the minority of Greek Orthodox and Protestant—the Dissidents—on the other. These religious troubles became acute in the years immediately before the first Partition (1772) and led to the formation of informal groups intent on securing their rights by union. Such was the Confederation of Radom, formed by the Dissidents in 1767 with the support of Russia, and the Confederation of Bar, formed in the following year by the Catholics, in alliance with France and the party of independence. All this was a tacit admission that the Polish Diet was unable to regulate its own affairs, so partition was the inevitable consequence.

In the monarchies hitherto considered there existed Estates, of medieval origin, consisting normally of three bodies—clergy, nobility and burgesses—usually summoned at the discretion of the crown. The medieval origin of this system may be deduced from the fact that Estate means a status derived from a particular kind of tenure, so three types of tenant provided the chambers of an assembly of Estates. In theory at least such a body might impose serious restrictions on the royal prerogative, and in Sweden they did so in the years between 1720 and 1772; but elsewhere they proved ineffective. One reason for this is that the three components had come to be unevenly matched. In spite of the alleged rise to power of the middle classes the burgesses, mostly merchants, shop keepers and townsmen, were considered greatly inferior to the clergy and nobility; and so, in the event of serious disagreement, the two upper Estates would usually combine against the third. Moreover, the crown might conciliate a troublesome burgess by giving him an office, or threatening to deprive him of one which he held. There was no mixing of Estates; indeed in Scotland, where the old system survived until 1707, this was forbidden by law. Before that date, while the English House of Commons was claiming cognizance of every aspect of national life, the Scottish third Estate was limited to such matters as weights and measures and the regulation of industry, with the result that the political evolution of Scotland was greatly retarded. This may well be true also of other nations where this medieval system survived.

Two monarchies have now to be considered in neither of which were there Estates. In France the States General were in abeyance between 1614 and 1789; in England the term was still used, and some thought of King, Lords and Commons as the three Estates. Moreover, the great majority of the English House of Commons consisted technically of burgesses representing towns; and they were so denominated, in contrast with the knights of the shire. But, in reality, the old system had disappeared—not by formal abolition, but by the *mixing* of Estates. A great middle class had come into existence in the sixteenth century, but its members exercised power, not as representatives of that class, but as newly created peers, or as landowners who, having made money in the towns, bought estates in the country and completely severed their relations with the towns where they had made their wealth. These men and the sons of peers, many of them of recent creation, turned to parliament as a means of enhancing their status, with the result that, in the later part of the sixteenth century, the character of the House of Commons began to be completely transformed. That House already contained a territorial nucleus in the 80 English knights of the shire; they were joined by sons of peers and members of the new, landed gentry who, though they had no difficulty in obtaining the suffrage of the boroughs, were not really burgesses at all. The result was that, by the eighteenth century, the English House of Commons, the greatest legislative body in the world, was predominantly an assembly of landowners, with an admixture of merchants, lawyers, soldiers and men-of-letters, many of them alien to the "middle classes"; as well as this, a considerable proportion of the Commons was, by means of the clientage system, nominated by members of the House of Lords. The Commons could hold their own with the Lords not because their composition was so dissimilar but because it was so similar. In effect therefore the medieval system, which had allotted a definite place to nobility, higher clergy, knights of the shire and burgesses had been swept away.

In its place was substituted an indivisible trinity of king, lords and commons, each of them regarded as a check on the other two. None of them was regarded as independent; indeed, an independent king would be considered a despot. The Revolution of 1689 had preserved for the crown a great part of its old prerogative, including the rights of declaring war, making peace, appointing and dismissing ministers; but since that date there had developed certain conventions of the constitution, a process accentuated in the reigns of Anne and the first two Georges. Among these conventions was the institution of a cabinet, not yet recognised by law; and the principle of responsibility of ministers, based on the maxim that the king can do no wrong, a maxim enunciated in neither statute nor official instrument. Both these conventions were above party distinctions, and their practical effect was to vest a large proportion of the prerogative in a cabinet responsible to parliament. With his German literalness and instinctive belief in force, George III could hardly have been expected to understand these things. Of what use was a king if he did not govern? Such may well have been his reasoning. In a narrow academic sense the Revolution had left him with powers little different from those of his Stuart ancestors; why should he not exercise them? The precedent was a bad one. Accordingly, in the long ministry of Lord North (1770-82) this conscientious but obtuse monarch acted, not as a constitutional ruler, but as a king, prime minister and cabinet rolled into one, ignoring alike the repeated requests of North to accept his resignation, and the popular demand for the recall of Chatham as head of the administration, insisting at all times on the enforced submission of the colonists and the use of Indian guerrillas against them. If we ignore the spirit and the unwritten conventions of the constitution as they had evolved at that time, and if we regard George as heir to the prerogative which the Stuarts had abused, then some kind of case can be made for his conduct during the war of the American Revolution which, not inappropriately, was known to many contemporaries as " the King's War ". Such a case has recently been made by a new school of historians, based on the royal " correctness " in his interpretation of the constitution, and the " selfishness " of both his opponents and the colonists. But formal correctness is no substitute for commonsense; and as for selfishness, it is the easiest of all objections to urge against an opponent. In any case, it is indisputable that this revival of Stuart absolutism had disastrous results. If this melancholy incident be excepted, it may be said that the British constitution of the eighteenth century was that of a hereditary monarch ruling with the advice of ministers responsible to parliament.

In contrast with the status assigned to British monarchs after the Revolution of 1688, the Bourbon kings enjoyed a personal prestige second only to that of the Holy Roman Emperor, with whom they shared a certain sacerdotal element; moreover, the example set by Louis XIV, together with the teaching of Bossuet and the unswerving loyalty of the French people in triumph and disaster, all supported the view that, in theory at least, there were no limits to the powers of the French monarch. On several occasions Louis XV declared that supreme executive and legislative power resided in him alone. But neither he nor his unfortunate grandson was of the stuff from which despots are made. They exercised a *puissance reglée* in contrast to a *puissance absolue*; both of them had some regard for public opinion, indeed Louis XV confessed that although he appointed his ministers, the public dismissed them. In his edicts Louis XVI often showed a solicitude, however genuine, for the welfare of his subjects, and at no time could his conduct be considered irresponsible. If " constitutional" means rule with the advice of ministers, then the French monarchy of this period was constitutional, though the ministers were responsible to the king alone. A number of supreme councils advised him on matters of state. These were *Conseils de Gouvernement,* empowered to issue executive decrees which were beyond the control of the *Parlements*; from these supreme bodies Louis XIV had excluded the nobility, and they conducted their deliberations in the presence of the sovereign. Foreign policy and other important matters were the province of the *Conseil d'Etat d'en Haut,* the members of which were chosen by the king; they were closely associated with the *Conseil des Dépêches*, which was responsible for internal affairs, and acted as a final court of appeal from the *Parlements*. Finance was the province of the *Conseil Royal des Finances.* A *Conseil Royal du Commerce* was established in 1730, but it was overshadowed by the financial council. There were other councils, some of them overlapping; but the effective work of supervision was exercised by the Chancellor, head of the judicial system, and by the Controller General of the Finances, who maintained regular communication with the *intendants,*[1] thereby keeping in touch with conditions in the provinces. There were also four secretaries of state, one for war, one for foreign affairs, one for the navy and colonies, and one, that of *maison du roi,* for the supervision of Paris and the royal palaces and for the affairs of the clergy and Huguenots. These six officials controlled the administration from the

[1] below, p. 250.

centre; their functions, numerous, arduous and complicated, provided the schools in which great administrators were trained. As well as this, there were ministers, some of them loosely designated first ministers, such as Dubois, Fleury, Turgot and Maurepas who exercised considerable influence, but of these only Dubois and Turgot held a ministerial office.

The only serious obstacle encountered by the executive was that of the *Parlements,* particularly that of the *Parlement* of Paris. As most of the royal edicts were registered by this body, it was natural that its members, many of them high officials and great dignitaries, should claim some share in legislation. To many contemporaries there appeared to be an analogy with the English Parliament, and in the anonymous *Judicium Francorum* (1732) it was claimed that, in the abeyance of the States General, the *Parlement* of Paris was the parliament of the nation. But how unfounded was this claim can be seen by reference to its procedure when there was conflict with the crown. On refusal to register an edict, the king might issue *lettres de jussion*; if that failed, he could hold a *lit de justice* in which he appeared in person in *Parlement* and ordered registration. Or he might resort to another tribunal—the *Grand Conseil*—which, though concerned mainly with appeals in disputes among the religious orders might, in an emergency, be brought in for the ratification of royal decrees. The king could commit individual *parlementaires* to prison, or he could exile the whole body to Pontoise, with a threat of exile to a more distant place such as Blois—a severe penalty to home-loving Parisians.

On its side *Parlement* had its devices for holding up unacceptable legislation. It might record its protest; or, as in 1717, it appended to its registration of the Bull *Unigenitus* the rubric: " registered, but not accepted ". More effective was strike action, by which the *Parlement* refused to perform its judicial functions. To this, the royal counter move was to bring in " blackleg " labour, but litigants might well hesitate to entrust their causes to such substitutes, and so the judicial administration of the country might be held up. Here was an example of the ill consequences following the confusing of judicial and legislative functions, so characteristic of the French constitution; attempts to combine them necessarily failed. It was a disaster for France that, after the reforms of Maupeou[1] in 1771, the *Parlements* were restored in 1774; for, in spite of their espousal of popular causes, they provided the strongest bulwark against reform. The one national institution that might have co-operated with the crown in the work of legislation had itself become a close corporation of lawyers, a vested interest, opposed not only to the taxation of the privileged, but to every change that threatened to affect their interests.

In a letter[2] to Louis XVI Turgot declared:

> Your nation has no constitution. It is a society composed of different orders, imperfectly united, and of a people whose members have very few social links among themselves, with the result that each one is concerned exclusively with his own interests.

At first sight this might seem applicable to any society. But Turgot may have had in mind that process in eighteenth-century French society which hardened and even ossified the strata into which a small minority of the nation was divided. The classes that could, in any sense, be regarded as privileged probably numbered not more than half a million in a population of well over 20 millions. Of the unprivileged majority about a quarter lived in prosperity, one half was in a precarious position and a quarter lived in misery. It may be said that similar conditions prevailed in western Europe and even worse conditions east of the Elbe; why should France have suffered a revolution that spared other lands? Historians will always be divided on this question. It may be that, in contrast with England, where there was a more free intermingling of classes, France was not cushioned against violent shock; or

[1] below, p. 267.
[2] Quoted in P. Sagnac, *La Formation de la Société Française Moderne*, (1946), II, p. 249.

that, unlike the central European states, she did not have an efficient administration able to maintain order in a crisis; or that, in comparison with the Latin and Slavonic communities, she had a population sufficiently prosperous and educated to resent the surviving injustices of an outworn medievalism. Or it may be that the history of France demonstrated the existence of a volcanic element in her people.

III REPUBLICS

The republics in this period included the city states of Genoa and Venice, the Swiss Confederation, the United Provinces of the Netherlands. To these were added in 1783 the United States of America.

Genoa and Venice retained only relics of their former greatness. Divided into factions by her noble families, rent by internal conspiracies and foreign intervention Genoa, like Sardinia, had to maintain a policy of oscillation between France, Spain and Austria as formerly she had had to contest with Venice for supremacy in the Levant. In 1528 her great admiral Andrea Doria had added one more to the many Genoese constitutions by placing the republic under a Doge, who held office for only two years and was assisted by two Consuls and a Censor. Since 1481 she had been in possession of Corsica, but a succession of revolts in the island led by Paoli and Theodore of Neuhof (the so-called king of Corsica) obliged Genoa to sell her rights in Corsica to France (1768). Still a maritime state of some importance, and commercially active by her Bank of St. George she was obliged, like Venice, to yield some of her trade to Leghorn, Ancona and Trieste. In contrast, Venice had a constitution noted for its stability, or rather reputation for stability. Its structure was compared to that of a pyramid—a great council of merchant nobles at the base; then a Senate and a Council of Ten, the whole surmounted by a Doge, who held office for life. The extensive territories on the mainland were governed by *provedittori* for districts and *podestàs* for towns. But the system was inelastic and aroused discontent, particularly in Dalmatia; moreover, the republic had already been deprived of many of her overseas possessions. By the treaty of Passarowitz (1718) these were limited to Istria, Corfu, the Ionian Islands and Dalmatia. Only by a strict policy of neutrality was Venice preserved.

Until 1798 Switzerland consisted of 13 cantons united in a federal republic, the independence of which dated from the treaty of Westphalia. Each canton preserved its autonomy in internal affairs under a federal government which, in the eighteenth century, met alternately at Zürich, Berne or Lucerne; not until 1848 did Berne become the capital. Some of the cities, notably Zürich and Berne, governed large areas outside the walls. Lucerne and Fribourg were among the Catholic cantons; the Protestant cantons included Zürich, Berne and Basel. In government Berne, Lucerne and Fribourg were considered aristocratic, while the others were considered " democratic ", or a mixture of the two types. In language the cantons were divided according as French, German or Italian was spoken; there was also a native patois called Welche. Geneva was then a separate state, allied to the cantons, but not a part of the confederation until 1801. Considering the size of its population—about a million—Switzerland was noted for the number of its famous men, including Rousseau, Necker, Euler and the Bernouilli family. Of these Rousseau and Necker were Genevans.

In this period the Swiss Confederation was one of the most prosperous of states, a prosperity based on small, mixed farms, cultivated by independent farmers who produced grain and cheese for local markets. The fact that such large areas of the countryside were ruled by cities had the effect of excluding both the seigneur and serfdom; it was in virtue of this absence of a nobility that Switzerland could claim to be the most " democratic " state in Europe. Although primarily agricultural, some of the cantons were partly industrialised. There were cotton and silk industries; the iron mines of the Jura were worked, and there were foundries in Berne and Schaffhausen. The chief national industry was the making of clocks, watches and mechanical toys. Each canton had its own coinage. Considerable revenue was derived from the hiring out of about 70,000 mercenaries, mainly to France and Spain, and from the provision of transport through the St. Gothard to and from Italy. Banking was another national enterprise, conducted with great success in Geneva, and Swiss bankers established themselves elsewhere, notably in France. Like the Dutch, the Swiss were free from the intolerance which impeded the development of other states; it is therefore not surprising that they strove hard to maintain their neutrality. The Swiss Confederation embodied not the conception of democracy as we know it, but of republicanism as exemplified in the ancient city states of Greece. Hence the opinion, expounded by such idealists as Rousseau, that peace and liberty were attainable only in such small political units.

The United Dutch Provinces had come into existence at the successful conclusion of a heroic struggle against Philip II of Spain, and the terms of the Union of Utrecht (1579) provided the Magna Carta of a new and energetic republic. The Union was a federation of seven provinces, each autonomous, even to the extent of maintaining its own navy; each sending delegates, controlled by strict instructions, to the meetings of the States General at The Hague. As the decisions of the States General had to be by unanimous vote, the wonder is that the system worked; commonsense and a spirit of realism probably provide the explanation. The seven provinces were unevenly matched for, while Holland, Zeeland and Frisia were maritime, Utrecht, Over Yssel, Groningen and Gueldres were continental and mainly agricultural. More important, Holland was by far the most wealthy and enterprising, its contributions to the central exchequer being more than that of all the other provinces put together. Calvinism flourished in Zeeland and among the sailors and peasantry, but there still survived a strong Catholic element, amounting possibly to more than a third of the population, and the Protestantism of the wealthy burghers of Amsterdam was often little more than nominal. In the background was the Orange family, its monarchical and centralising ambitions providing an alternative to the republicanism and separatism of the Union of Utrecht. Only the fact of foreign invasion, as in 1672 and 1747, forced this academic republicanism into the background and brought forward a prince of Orange, entrusted with absolute power, as the saviour of the state. The status of the princes of Orange was derived from the fact that, at different times, they might be stadholders of some or even all of the provinces, and this antithesis between the separatism of the states and the centralising ambitions of the House of Orange ran like a thread through the fabric of Dutch history.

There was no "democracy" as we understand it in the Dutch polity of the eighteenth century; what at first had looked like a democracy turned out to be a narrow oligarchy.[1] Rigid class distinction became characteristic of this "republic". Power was in the hands of the upper middle class, mainly the rich, patrician burghers of Holland; these men dominated the town councils; they served on the directorates of the great trading companies; they controlled elections of representatives to the States General. By the eighteenth century, when they were designated Regents, many of them had inter-married with the territorial nobility and had become a closed caste, wearing a distinctive dress, and hostile not only to the "mob" but to the lower bourgeoisie. At the other end of the scale were the peasants, artisans and fishermen who, like their prototypes in Sweden, naturally turned to the monarchy, or the institution having the potentialities of monarchy, as the source of salvation against the monopoly of burgher Regents and oligarchs. The Dutch had this unique advantage that, while they were not normally burdened by the ambitions and expense of a monarch, they could, in moments of

[1] For this see G. J. Renier, *The Dutch Nation*, (1944), bk. 1, ch. 4.

crisis, invoke the aid of an Orange stadholder and confer on him, if only for the occasion, the powers of an absolute ruler. This anomalous state of affairs was not ended until 1815, when a hereditary monarchy was created for the Orange family.

The republic of the United States has this in common with the old Dutch republic that it began with the repudiation of a monarch who, it was alleged, had violated the fundamental contract between king and people. But the American example had much wider significance, for it involved not only the rejection of George III and hostilities against his troops, but also a social revolution which, so far as the American colonies were concerned, swept away many of the characteristic institutions of the *Ancien Régime*. This had begun long before the outbreak of war. Hereditary titles and privileges had been abolished in all the states; the suffrage had been extended to include a large majority of the adult white population, and a beginning had been made in the abolition of primogeniture and entails. The criminal code, less savage than that of England, was still further mitigated, and in no state were there more than 20 capital offences, as contrasted with 200 in the home country. In most states the penalties or disqualifications imposed on particular religious beliefs had been abrogated, and the foundations were laid not only of religious freedom for the individual, but of a secular state, entirely detached from any religious communion.[1] Of this revolution the French Revolution may be regarded as an almost inevitable sequel.

The spirit of the American Revolution permeates the wording of the Declaration of Independence of 1776. Here were brought together—in what amounted to a declaration of war—those ideals of human rights which hitherto had been safely enclosed within the covers of books or the walls of academic class rooms. These ideals included the natural equality of

[1] For this see J. Franklin Jamison, *The American Revolution Considered as a Social Movement*, (1926). Republished as a Beacon paperback in 1956.

men, their right to life, liberty and the pursuit of happiness,
the doctrine that all government is derived from the consent of
the governed and that, when the government violates the ends
for which it is instituted, it is the right of the people to alter
or abolish it. These words read almost like an extended para-
phrase of the text of Rousseau's *Du Contrat Social*: " man is
born free and everywhere he is in chains ". The American
constitution, as defined in the Philadelphia Congress of 1787,
was an amalgam in which was embedded much of the aspiration and idealism of the past. The idea of a written constitution may have been derived from Puritan experiment in the
seventeenth century; from Coke may have originated the view
that, as common law includes natural law and natural right, it
can therefore overrule Acts of Parliament, a principle exemplified in the American Supreme Court; from Locke and
Montesquieu came the doctrine of division of powers; from
the academic jurists was derived devotion to the nebulous
deity known as Natural Right, while from Rousseau was
created some kind of cosmos out of another nebula—the
General Will.

Would this work? A series of amendments to the constitution and a civil war have made it possible.

Chapter III

OVERSEAS SETTLEMENT AND TRADE

I NAVIGATION. SHIPPING. SETTLEMENT

In the eighteenth century the continents of Europe and Asia were linked together by little more than trade. Events in the Orient at least ensured that this was conducted in peace; for after the death of Aurungzebe in 1707, the Mogul dynasty in India entered upon a period of decline, and at the same time Turkey, fully occupied on her Russian and Asiatic frontiers, ceased to be a menace to western Europe. The result was that China, then ruled by the Manchus, stood out as the great power in Asia. While the Manchus were consolidating their influence in Tibet and Formosa, the Bourbons and Hanoverians were contesting for supremacy in the west, and in this way there was preserved some kind of cosmic balance of power. China did not invite or welcome trading relations with Europe; on the contrary, she merely tolerated them, insisting on the segregation of "barbarian" merchants in specified areas, and proclaiming that the celestial empire had no need for the products of the foreigner. So these two great aggregates of power, each of them inscrutable to the other, remained at a safe and respectful distance.

In these conditions of comparative stability in east-west relations and the development of settlements in the two Americas, exploration was limited to filling in the gaps, which were widest in the Pacific. Among the areas investigated were eastern Siberia and the Behring Straits. China was of special interest to the Jesuit missionaries, one of whom, J. B. Du

Halde, published an account of its geography and history in 1735. Ten years later La Condamine, a French explorer, after spending several years in South America, published a record of his travels; in 1772 an account of Arabia was produced by the Dane Carsten Niebuhr. The Scot James Bruce, in the years 1768-72, penetrated into Abyssinia in his search for the sources of the Nile; later in the century another Scot, Alexander Mackenzie, traversed the whole breadth of Canada, reaching the Pacific on June 22nd, 1793. In 1768, 1772 and 1776 Captain Cook completed, at the orders of the Admiralty, three world voyages of importance, in one of which he tried to find a north-west passage. He did however discover New Caledonia and he gave his name to the strait dividing the two islands of New Zealand. After 1763 more attention was paid to the Pacific, particularly the South Seas; and, before the end of the century, Tahiti, Samoa and the New Hebrides were added to the charts.

These explorations, though less important than many of an earlier age, had some scientific interest, and several of them were government-sponsored. They were facilitated by improvements of two navigational instruments—the sextant and the chronometer. Working independently in the years 1730-1 the Englishman John Hadley and the American Thomas Godfrey devised a modern form of sextant for taking altitudes and so determining the latitude. Longitude continued to be calculated by lunar distances until, in 1759, John Harrison perfected his chronometer, for which he received a grant from the British government. Navigation thus became more accurate, but it was still subject to the dangers and limitations of sailing-ship days. Among these dangers were infrequency and inadequacy of lighthouses (reflectors were not installed until after 1770), the ravages of piracy on all the oceans and of " wrecking " on many coasts. If a sailor survived these he might well succumb to typhus in the badly ventilated accommodation between decks, or to scurvy, because of the absence of fresh meat and green vegetables. The menace of scurvy may be deduced from the account[1] of Anson's voyage round the world in 1740-4. Of the 961 men who left England with him in his three ships, 626 had died, mainly from scurvy, by the time the fleet reached Juan Fernandez. As well as this, the ships themselves were subject to severe limitations. Especially in tropical seas the wooden hulls were attacked by fungi; and, even in northern waters, might become foul after six months at sea; moreover, the use of timber imposed a serious limit on the size of the hull, because there is a maximum length beyond which the wood will buckle. Consequently, ships were small on our standards; indeed, a ship of 700 tons (or about a quarter of the tonnage of a modern cross-channel steamer) was considered large—too large for many of the Channel ports. With smaller ships and longer voyages the cost of ocean transport must have been heavier than it is to-day; but, even thus, it was much cheaper than transport by land.

Expansion of overseas trade brought with it a greater degree of specialisation in all activities connected with shipping. In the early years of the century the father of James Watt was a builder, a merchant, a mathematical instrument maker and a shipowner. The word "merchant" was then a very elastic term, but such a variety of activities became more rare as the century progressed, though it was not until the early part of the nineteenth century that shipowning became a whole-time occupation. An intermediate stage in this process was the ownership of vessels by small partnerships and the employment of ship's "husbands" (usually ex-masters), who stayed ashore in order to make arrangements for re-fitting and ships' stores. One more degree of specialisation was introduced when ships' brokers acted as intermediaries between "husbands" and merchants. At the same time marine insurance became well established among the maritime nations. In England this had developed late in the preceding century from the

[1] In Everyman's Library edition, p. 151.

meetings of brokers and underwriters at Lloyds Coffee House, and the city of London acquired a reputation for the fidelity with which it conducted marine insurance, a reputation attested by the fact that French owners insured their ships with English insurers even in war time. Amsterdam was the centre of marine insurance on the continent, followed by Venice and Genoa. Another new development was that of the bill brokers and dealers in bullion, as practised by the Goldsmids and Mocattas in England, and on the continent, by the Rothschilds; these are example of capitalists, most of them Jews who, by their financing of overseas trade, were playing the part of merchant bankers.

From the insurance point of view the East India trades were the most hazardous and offered least incentive to individual enterprise; accordingly, all the maritime nations, including Spain and Prussia, had privileged companies for their eastern trade. These companies varied greatly in their importance, ranging from the comparatively small organisations maintained by Spain, Sweden, Denmark and Prussia to the great East India companies of England, France and Holland. The French company suffered badly from defeats inflicted on its troops in the Seven Years War; for a time its activities were suspended altogether, and it ceased to play an active part in the French economy. It was otherwise with the English and Dutch companies, both of them founded in the early years of the seventeenth century. The first of these, unable to break the Dutch monopoly in the Spice Islands, had turned to India as a second-best alternative; and, by the middle years of the eighteenth century, was in control of Bengal, Bombay, Madras and a great part of southern India. The company, which maintained its own troops, was drawn away from trade to political and military activity, a policy dictated by French rivalry, and by the necessity of conciliating or subjugating the native princes. Not until after the Regulating Act of 1774 and the publicity of the long trial of Warren Hastings (1788-95) was a more disinterested British rule made possible in

India. The Dutch company, from its headquarters in Batavia, was also obliged by force of arms to defend its dominion in Java and Ceylon, and this enforced assumption of territorial power seriously interfered with its trade. This is the main reason why the Dutch company suffered a decline.

In other trades there was less need for this corporate organisation, and many of the old Regulated companies either declined or disappeared, though the Hudson's Bay Company still survives. The Levant and the West African trades were thrown open to private enterprise, but the Levant Company and the Royal African Company still maintained a precarious existence in the eighteenth century until they were finally dissolved. Trade with Russia and the Baltic was open to all.

Of the overseas empires the Spanish and Portuguese may claim historical precedence. By the treaty of Tordesillas (1494) there had been formulated a division of future acquisitions on the general principle that everything 370 leagues westward of a line of longitude passing through the Cape Verde islands and the Azores should belong to Spain, while all to the east of this line should go to Portugal. This was not strictly adhered to but, by the eighteenth century, Spain was in possession of Mexico, central America and the whole of South America with the exception of Brazil on the east and the Guianas in the north. The Philippines provided a distant outpost, having trading connections with Spain and the west coast of Mexico. By implication, the treaty of Tordesillas conferred on Spain nominal but practically limitless claims to lands on the north American continent, claims enforced in a broad belt of territory stretching from Florida to the modern California. In the eighteenth century there was a re-organisation of this empire, when new viceroyalties were carved out of the old viceroyalty of Peru, and captains-general were established at Puerto Rico, Havana, Guatemala, Caracas, Santiago and Manila. Entry into this closed empire was limited nominally to Spaniards; indeed, until 1778, this privilege was confined to Castilians, and trade could be conducted only through the port of Cadiz, where there were many foreign agents acting for Spanish merchants. After about 1778 there was an improvement in Spanish colonial administration, and intendants were introduced for the management of local affairs; generally, the policy of the home government was to protect the native Indians, though there was often a wide gap between royal edicts and the conduct of the settlers. A host of missionaries, many of them Jesuits, combined the work of conversion with exploitation of natural resources.

Inevitably, the attempt to seal off such vast empires broke down, mainly because the demands of the Spanish colonists for slaves and manufactured goods could not be met by the home country. These demands were supplied mainly by smugglers, especially from Jamaica; there was also a small amount of legitimate trade in terms of the *Asiento*, which was conferred on England by the treaty of Utrecht, and was exercised for some years by the South Seas Company. The *Asiento* authorised the annual delivery of 4,800 slaves and the visit, once a year, of a trading ship to the isthmus of Panama. But the Spaniards needed far more than 4,800 slaves annually, a need met by enterprising English, New England and French slavers. As the necessities of the colonists became more insistent and the penetration of foreigners more audacious, there occurred frequent clashes between the *guarda costas* and the English freebooters, leading eventually to war between the two nations. The first great breach in the Spanish empire occurred in the Seven Years War, when England captured Cuba and Florida. Cuba was restored by the peace treaty, but thereafter the rigid control of the past was relaxed. At home there was a similar relaxation. With the ending of the Cadiz monopoly in 1778, thirteen Spanish ports, including Barcelona, were admitted to the colonial trade. This change coincided with the development of Spanish industry and capitalism, the two economic forces which obliged the Spaniards themselves to abandon the attempt to maintain a closed empire.

Among the many imports from the Spanish Empire were the precious metals, mainly silver, with tobacco, dye stuffs, mahogany and hides. Other imports, such as cocoa, vanilla and chocolate were of social rather than economic importance. Chocolate, from Mexico, was a mixture of cocoa, maize and pepper; its popularity was due to the belief, in many quarters, that it was less noxious than coffee. Extensive use of these commodities tended to undermine the old monopoly of spices.

During the period of her annexation to Spain (1581-1640) Portugal had lost a great part of her eastern empire to the Dutch, though she still retained outposts in the Far East and in India. Brazil was of great importance in the Portuguese economy because, among other things, it supplied gold, sugar and cotton and, later in the century, diamonds and coffee. The Amazon provided easy access to the interior, where there were many mining ventures, some of them conducted by Englishmen, a freedom of enterprise which served to contrast the two South American empires. But the great imports of gold did not prove an unmixed blessing for Portugal, because much of it (with port wine) was transmitted to England in return for textiles which, in the opinion of at least one Portuguese statesman (Pombal) should have been manufactured at home; moreover, Portugal was deficient in shipping, and so most of her Atlantic trade was conducted in English and Dutch ships. As a result there was no development of industry or capitalism such as was occurring even in Spain, and so Portugal remained one of the most backward nations in Europe. In the words of the historian Jacques Pirenne she was little more than an annexe to Brazil.

The true heirs of the great Portuguese explorers were the Dutch. In the west they possessed Dutch Guiana (Surinam) in the north of South America, also the two islands of Curaçao and St. Eustatius in the Caribbean. In the east they had stations in Ceylon, in Bengal and on the Coromandel and Malabar coasts; they had a monopoly of trade with Japan through the port of Nagasaki, and they had a small settlement

at the Cape. Java, with its capital Batavia, was their main
stronghold in the east, where labour was supplied by Chinese
immigrants, who were reduced to a semi-servile status, against
which they made at least one unsuccessful rebellion. Under
the efficient management of their East India Company, the
Dutch had made a great success of their island empire in the
east, importing vast quantities of spice, coffee, silks and porcelain, much of which was re-exported. Their East India
Company conducted its business on a strictly capitalist and
monopolist basis. But, mainly because of increased competition from English and French, as well as the greater cost of
military defence, there was a decline in profits during the
eighteenth century, and more Dutch capital was invested in
European states.

In its extent the French Empire was second only to the
Spanish, but in many parts it was thinly peopled. On the
North American continent it included Canada and Louisiana;
in South America French Guiana; in the Caribbean, it consisted mainly of the Antilles, which included St. Domingue,
Guadeloupe and Martinique; in Africa, Senegal; in the Indian
Ocean Madagascar and Mauritius; in India, Pondicherry,
Chandernagore and Masulipatam. From these sources, notably
from the Antilles, France derived great wealth in the eighteenth century, as attested by the many new and imposing
buildings in Marseilles, Nantes and Bordeaux; the prosperity
of Marseilles also gave evidence of profitable connection with
the Levant, a link established in the sixteenth century, when
France inaugurated a policy of friendly relations with the
Porte.

A glance at the map will show how these territories were so
disposed as to ensure conflict with the English. Thus, on the
North American continent it was obvious that, by linking the
upper reaches of the St. Lawrence with the Mississippi in the
area south of the Great Lakes, the English colonies would be
encircled and prevented from spreading westward. Hence the
strategic importance of the Ohio valley, and the determina-

tion of the colonists of Virginia, Maryland and Pennsylvania to expel the French from their strongholds. So too, as the Antilles proved to be the most prosperous sugar islands in the world, the powerful sugar interests in England were anxious to retain them at the conclusion of the Seven Years War, in preference even to Canada. On the west coast of Africa the English slavers had to face the rivalry of the French, who were subsidised by a premium for every slave exported; even more, in India the two nations were in bitter rivalry, which resulted in war. Geography, combined with the almost fortuitous circumstances of settlement, had decreed that these two powers would come into conflict, if only for the sake of their overseas trade and possessions.

In the seventeenth century the French colonies had been peopled by merchants and trading companies; in the eighteenth, they were under the nominal control of the Minister of Marine and a special department for the colonies created in 1710. As regards the slave population, the French planters were, in theory at least, guided by the *Code Noir* of 1685. This code imposed harsh penalties on the negroes for petty offences, but otherwise it was humanitarian in comparison with that of other countries. Masters had to educate their slaves in the Roman Catholic faith; they had to ensure that families were not divided when sold; that they were given a proper supply of food, and that, in cases of abuse, they could appeal to the magistrates. Concubinage with blacks was forbidden, and the marriage laws for the coloured population were the same as for the whites. In economic matters the French colonists had some special favours. They could refine their own sugar; goods sent to them from home were exempt from duty, and imports from them were protected from foreign competition. Otherwise, the French colonial empire was restricted, notably in its exclusion of Huguenots and Jews; and a meticulous control was exercised by the home government, by means of governors and *intendants*. Local initiative was discouraged. In contrast with the English, the French possessions were regarded as outposts of metropolitan France, an attitude of mind strengthened by the clergy, who were very powerful, especially in Canada.

English overseas development had lagged behind that of the other great powers. In North America there were 13 colonies on the narrow coastal strip stretching from Maine to Georgia, and bounded by the Alleghanies and the Appalachians. These settled colonies, each having its semi-autonomous legislature, were peopled mainly by settlers of British stock, with an admixture of Dutch, Scandinavian, German and Huguenot, but they were divided by a gap that has never been bridged—that between the northern colonies, where climatic conditions favoured an economy similar to that of England, and the southern colonies, where, in large plantations, negro labour was used for the production of cotton, tobacco and indigo. In the West Indies the most important British possessions were Jamaica, Barbados, the Bahamas, and Leeward Islands, all of them engaged in the production of sub-tropical materials, notably sugar, so much in demand at home. Slaves were obtained from the west coast of Africa, usually as one of the cargoes of a triangular trade which, beginning with the export of manufactured goods from England to Africa, continued with the transport of human cargoes by the dreaded middle passage to the West Indies, and ended there with the exchange of slaves for sugar, intended for shipment to England. To the north were the Newfoundland cod fisheries, valued because the voyage thereto provided a training in seamanship; and because the salted cod, together with English textiles, was traded for Mediterranean products. In India, Clive's victory at Arcot in 1751 inaugurated a period when the French were steadily ousted from their supremacy, and the East India Company undertook commitments which eventually led to the British empire in India. But in the East India spice trade the English never succeeded in dislodging the Dutch, though they obtained a footing in the trade with China, through the port of Canton.

The loss of the American colonies had serious political repercussions, but did not injure English trade. Moreover, the acquisition of Canada and military successes in India were serving as foundations for the second and greater British Empire—greater, because a sense of responsibility and even trusteeship displaced the old idea of profit and exploitation.

The attitude of eighteenth-century opinion to the colonies varied between indifference, criticism and cynicism. In his *Lettres Persanes*[1] Montesquieu alleged that their general effect was to weaken the mother country; only in negroes did the colonies have abundant population. Voltaire was sarcastic about the snowy wastes of Canada. Later in the century, in a book[2] purporting to be a history of European settlements in east and west, the Abbé Raynal vehemently condemned the exploitation of native labour and forcible conversion to Christianity, two evils which he dated from the Portuguese conquests in the east. Dr. Johnson's savage attacks on the colonies and the colonists are well-known. More relevant was the contrast drawn by Burke between the high moral principles with which many young Englishmen set out for the east and the corroded characters with which they returned. Josiah Tucker, dean of Gloucester, was a vigorous representative of the body of opinion which maintained that England would be better without her colonies. If such was the state of opinion among the educated classes, it cannot be expected that the statesmen (excepting the Elder Pitt) had much regard for the sentiment of empire, and it is not surprising that, in the wars with France, overseas possessions were regarded as useful makeweights for balancing losses and gains on European battlefields.

---

[1] Letter cxxii.
[2] G. T. F. Raynal, *Histoire Philosophique des Etablissements et du Commerce des Européens dans les Deux Indes*, Amsterdam, 1770.

II COMMUNICATIONS AND OVERSEAS TRADE

Exploration and settlement on the Atlantic seaboard had thus provided Europe with a frontier, the extent and resources of which seemed limitless, an unknown quantity which challenged the most active nations. In the eighteenth century these were the British and the French; the Atlantic had, as it were, a selective effect in singling out these two. The same applied to the Indian Ocean. Because of the great distances and the difficulty of access from Europe, the Pacific was not yet an important sphere of European trade. Secondary areas of potential rivalry were the Baltic and the Mediterranean. From ports on the southern shore of the Baltic, such as Danzig and Königsberg, were shipped great quantities of wheat, the produce mainly of Poland and Pomerania, while from Sweden and Russia were exported iron, copper, tar, pitch, hemp and the resinous woods used for the masts and rigging of ships, all of them essential for the expanding navies of England and France. It is true that England might have obtained her naval stores from the northern American colonies, but the Navy Board was conservative, and difficulties were put in the way by the New Englanders, who had more profitable markets in the West Indies. Access to the naval stores of the Baltic was thus essential for the maritime nations, and here the English and French were following the lead of the Dutch, who retained much of their supremacy in northern and European waters, but failed to develop their Atlantic trades. The Mediterranean, by contrast, was a source of supply for silk, wine, oil, dried fruits and a host of Levantine goods, paid for by fish, textiles and hardware, as well as by re-exported colonial products. In this contrast the Baltic and Mediterranean may be considered as complementary to each other; accordingly, trade between them with France, Holland and Britain was conducted on a vast scale.

Generally, therefore, we may consider Europe as the focus

of two oceanic trades radiating from the Atlantic and the Indian Ocean, the one supplying precious metals and sub-tropical commodities, while the other provided coffee, tea, spices, saltpetre and the more delicate fabrics then becoming fashionable in western Europe. Supplementing these trades was the interchange, by short voyages, of the products of the Mediterranean and the Baltic. The European nations had become dependent on their neighbours and on the outside world; accordingly an interruption of communication with her sources of supply might spell ruin for a nation. Hence the vital importance of sea power.

For participation in these world trades easy access to salt water was obviously essential; so also, at the receiving end, the ports and rivers were vital factors. From this point of view Britain was the most fortunate. In proportion to her size, she is well supplied with rivers and, in the eighteenth century, the navigability of many of them was improved. Later in the century the network of rivers was linked up by means of canals, to such an extent that few places of importance were more than a dozen miles from navigable water. Innumerable estuaries on the west coast provided good harbours for the new Atlantic trades, hitherto served mainly by Bristol; in the eighteenth century sugar and slaves brought prosperity to Liverpool, while Glasgow was greatly enriched by her tobacco imports. Nor did this impede the continued development of ports such as London, Newcastle, Leith and Hull, all con-veniently situated for the Baltic and continental trades; for voyages to the Mediterranean and the Far East the port of London still provided the main point of departure.

In comparison France was not so fortunate. The Pyrenees divide her coast line into two widely-separated areas, a handi-cap surmounted, only to a very slight extent, by the construc-tion of a canal linking Bordeaux and the Garonne with Sète on the Mediterranean. On the Channel coast only Havre could accommodate ships of 500 tons; La Rochelle served as a port of supply for the Newfoundland fisheries, for sugar imports and sugar refining as well as for the slave trade. Nantes and Bordeaux profited mainly from sugar imports; Lorient, founded by the Company of the Indies, maintained trading relations with China and India. The connections of Marseilles with North African ports and the Levant were strengthened after the treaty of Belgrade (1739), when French influence in Constantinople was revived. After about 1748 the expansion of French colonial trade can be described as spectacular, an expansion in which Havre and Marseilles played an increasingly important part. On the other hand, in the interior of France, transport was for long impeded by innumerable tolls, but the main roads were the best in Europe.

After the Union with Scotland (1707) which created the United Kingdom of Great Britain, all the rivers, from their sources to their estuaries and ports, were under the ultimate control of the government at Westminster. The same is true, though to a less extent, of France because, although she controlled nearly all the sources and all the exits of her great rivers, she had no power over the estuaries of several streams originating in France, such as the Scheldt, the Meuse and the Moselle. Much more handicapped in this respect was Belgium. Her chief river—the Scheldt—rises in France and reaches the sea in Dutch territory. Between 1648 and 1832 the Dutch maintained an almost complete closure of this river, lest Antwerp might rival Amsterdam. This policy was acquiesced in by England, determined that Austria should not become a maritime state (by her control of Belgium); accordingly, the Emperor Charles VI was obliged by diplomatic pressure to keep the Scheldt closed, and to suspend the operations of his Ostend East India Company.

Contrast this with the situation in Holland. The Meuse of France is the Maas of Holland; at its junction with the Rotter stands the city of Rotterdam, one of the international ports. The Dutch also control the mouths of the Rhine, and their shipbuilding industry was greatly helped by the fact that timber could be floated down from the Black Forest almost to their back doors, whereas in England it had to be carried over bad roads. As well as this the Rhine served as a two-way avenue connecting the North Sea with industrial centres in Holland, Belgium, Luxembourg, Westphalia, the Ruhr and Switzerland—the most enterprising areas in Europe—and so the Dutch were able to combine two things, oceanic trade and the tapping, mainly by rivers, of resources in districts far beyond their frontiers. Dutch prosperity was based not on herring bones, but on easy access to water, salt and fresh.

Until the opening of the Black Sea in 1774 the Danube, the second-longest river in Europe, was little more than an internal waterway, connecting Ulm, Ratisbon, Vienna, Buda-Pesth and Belgrade. Of these cities Ratisbon was commercially the most important, for it had prescriptive rights over the navigation of the river, and was the chief market centre of southern Germany, comparable in its importance to Cologne on the Rhine and Magdeburg on the Elbe. As the regions served by the Danube were mainly agricultural, and as it did not reach any great port, the river did not have the same amount of traffic as other waterways of less extent. Nevertheless, it facilitated the passage of French products into southern Germany, especially after the alliance of France and Austria in 1756, an intercourse that may have promoted a higher standard of living, especially in Bavaria. This suggestion is strengthened by the fact that much employment there was given to French architects and sculptors.

In contrast with the Danube, a river deriving special importance from its outlet is the Elbe which, rising in the mountainous border of Bohemia and Silesia, passes through Saxony, Brandenburg, Hanover and the city of Hamburg, to reach the sea at Cuxhaven. The two cities of Dresden and Magdeburg are situated on the Elbe, which thus provided an outlet for Saxon textiles and the minerals of Bohemia; moreover, as the river was linked with Berlin by the Spree, it proved of vital importance to Frederick the Great in his development of

Prussian industry. Hanover also benefited by her access to the Elbe, as she did also by her acquisition of Bremen on the Weser. With its predominantly south-east north-west course the Elbe, rather than the Rhine, may be regarded as the dividing line between western and central Europe—to the northeast were the great corn lands of Brandenburg, Pomerania and Poland, provinces where serfdom predominated; while to the south and south-west were the Rhineland and Bavaria, in which a newer, capitalist economy was gradually taking shape. Moreover, as a free, imperial city, Hamburg was not dominated by any of the greater powers; and, by the end of the century, it was the greatest of the continental ports, conveniently placed for all the points of the compass, providing access to and an outlet from the agricultural and industrial regions of western and central Germany.

Farther east is the Oder, another river which played an important part in the expanding economy of Prussia. Rising in Moravia the Oder, after passing through Silesia and Pomerania, enters the Baltic at Stettin, a port captured by Prussia in 1713 and confirmed in her possession by the treaty of Nystadt. With his acquisition of Silesia in the Austrian Succession War, Frederick was able to use the Oder for the export of Silesian minerals, linen and cloth; in effect therefore he converted the Oder into a Prussian river by conquest of territory near its source and at its mouth. The same is partly true of the Vistula, a Polish river, the lower reaches of which flowed through that part of Poland taken over by Frederick in the first Partition (1772), but the port of Danzig was not incorporated into Prussia until 1793. Outside the Baltic Frederick developed the outlying possession of Emden, from which a Prussian company traded with the east.

Except for local and Mediterranean trade, Spain did not make effective use of her ports until after the ending of the Cadiz monopoly; but in 1755 the Catalans formed a Catalan Company which brought American cotton to Barcelona and negro slaves to Puerto Rico. Already, in 1728, the Caracas

Company had been founded for trade with Venezuela. Lisbon, the European terminus for the Brazil trade, provided a strategic advantage to England when she was engaged in war with Spain. On the Adriatic the Habsburgs sought to develop the ports of Trieste and Fiume, in spite of the fact that neither is on a navigable river; they succeeded nevertheless in making Fiume the port for Hungary, from which there were shipments of copper and corn; while Trieste (created a free port in 1750) served as an outlet for the velvets, silk, lace and munitions of the Austrian lands. Trieste was active also in shipbuilding. Venice had an extensive trade in works of art, mirrors, porcelain and fancy goods; Genoa had long been a banking and financial centre of importance, and its merchant princes were trading in bullion. The most enterprising of all Mediterranean ports was Leghorn (Livorno), on the Tuscan coast, a free port, open to all races and religions, where Mediterranean, African and Levantine goods were exchanged for imports from England, France, Hamburg and the Baltic, activities encouraged by the Grand Dukes of Tuscany, who had no mercantile marine of their own. Leghorn owed much of its success to the fact that it had the best-equipped quarantine station in the Mediterranean, and so the risk of infection from plague was reduced to a minimum.

Generally, in the international trade of this period, the ideal was to exchange the raw material of a colony or possession for the manufactured goods of the home country, in such a way that some kind of balance was effected. Hence the maritime states might be classified according to the success with which this balance was achieved. The Dutch benefited greatly from their share in the slave trade and from smuggling goods into the Spanish empire, but there was no great exchange of Atlantic products for home manufactures because, in their heyday, they were essentially the carriers of other nations' goods; moreover, they had neither the population nor the natural resources for great industrial development at home. So in their case, the question of balance does not apply. No oes it apply to Russia, which aimed at self sufficiency and had large export balance in her favour, derived mainly from hipments of iron and naval stores, the return for which consted mainly in bullion and luxury goods, the latter intended or consumption by the aristocracy. But we can speak of mbalance when we consider the relations between Spain and Portugal on the one hand and their overseas possessions on he other, for here we are concerned with the economic links etween European states and their overseas possessions. Spain as abundant mineral deposits, but these were either worked y foreigners or not worked at all; neither she nor Portugal ad extensive industrial communities, with the possible exception of those in Catalonia. Still more, the import of great quantities of the precious metals appeared to obviate the ecessity of a return in home manufactures, with the result hat the Atlantic trades provided no industrial stimulus at ome. Portugal remained dependent on England for her textiles; as with Spain, what overseas trade she had was conducted mainly in foreign ships. An illustration of a trade in vhich Spain benefited little from her maritime commerce vas provided by the Philippines. From the port of Manila arge quantities of oriental and fancy goods were shipped to Acapulco, on the west coast of Mexico, where they were xchanged for Mexican silver, a trade in which Spanish manuactures played no part. Nor did the colonists in the Philipines directly benefit, because this trade was a monopoly, onferred on religious houses in Manila.

It was otherwise with England and France. Both, especially England, greatly developed their mercantile marines; their rades with the west increased three and four-fold in the ourse of the century; the disposition of their ports was djusted to conform with the new orientation of trade, and here was constant search for new "vents" or outlets for ome-made goods. Especially in England, the imports from he west were either re-exported or provided material for efineries and textile factories, all conveniently placed near a harbour or navigable river; home country and colony were one and indivisible in the sense that the negro slave, working among the sugar canes or in the cotton fields, was supporting home industry by wearing a shirt made in Lancashire from colonial cotton. The textiles, hardware, leather goods and mechanical instruments of England found a ready market in the American colonies, and it was mainly from the profits of this well-balanced, two-way trade that England was able to pay for her wars. This benefited not only the merchant and shipper, but also the landlord, and was reflected in the fact that more wheaten bread was consumed in England than in any other country, The old colonial system, much of it based on slave labour, provided good dividends for the home country.

III THE ARMED NEUTRALITY OF THE NORTH. MERCANTILISM. THE PHYSIOCRATS.

This interdependence of nation and colony and between the European nations themselves led to an increasing realisation of how serious was the threat of maritime war, since it might imperil not only a nation's trade, but even its existence. Accordingly, among the smaller nations, there was a keener appreciation of the advantages of neutrality. There existed no generally accepted code of international law, different principles being applied by the maritime nations; but, among the Mediterranean states, the *Consolato del Mare* provided the nearest approach to a system. In the earlier part of the eighteenth century the axiom of widest application was : free ships, free goods; enemy ships, enemy goods. But free ships were not allowed to carry contraband. In virtue of this principle the neutrals, particularly Swedes, Danes and Dutch, enjoyed great latitude when their powerful neighbours were at war, since they could trade with other neutral ports or with ports of belligerents, carrying neutral or enemy cargoes. These concessions however were not uniformly applied, and were some-times of limited duration. Meanwhile, with the development of British sea power, it became obvious that this latitude would stultify one of the main purposes of sea power—to cut off the enemy from the resources of his overseas possessions. For this reason, at the outbreak of the Seven Years War, England ap-plied a new set of rules, the general effect of which was to exclude neutrals from those trades in which they had not been engaged in peace time. France, deprived of access to her all-important West India islands, was using Dutch ships to bring home imports from the Antilles, and so the effect of this " rule of 1756 ", as it was called, was that England now treated these neutral Dutch ships as enemy vessels and confiscated their cargoes.[1]

Naturally, the Dutch resented this treatment, and insisted on the old principle : free ships, free goods, a principle em-bodied in several Anglo-Dutch treaties of the previous cen-tury. On their side, the English complained that the Dutch had not fulfilled their commitments under these treaties; in-deed, from the British point of view, the Dutch were now of little value as allies. The Hollanders were in a difficult posi-tion. A great part of their economy was based on the carrying trade, and this to such an extent that, during the War of the Spanish Succession, their merchants had insisted on trading with the enemy. But, in spite of protests by the neutrals, English policy remained unshaken, and the almost complete severance of France from her overseas possessions in the Seven Years War had disastrous effects on her economy. War was becoming " total ".

The trouble flared up again in 1780, this time with Spain as the alleged culprit and Russia as the complainant. Two Russian vessels were seized by Spanish warships in the Medi-terranean on the allegation that they were carrying grain to the besieged garrison in Gibraltar. The Empress Catherine

[1] For this subject see R. Pares, *Colonial Blockade and Neutral Rights 1759-1763* (1938).

made an indignant protest; a fleet was assembled at Cronstadt and, for a time, there was a chance that the Empress might combine with Britain in order to demand satisfaction from Spain. Catherine was persuaded by her minister Nikita Panin to make a public declaration on behalf of the neutrals. This declaration, promulgated early in 1780, was based on the axiom that all neutral ships should sail freely between the ports of nations engaged in war, an axiom to be maintained by force. Hence the name: the Armed Neutrality of the North. Later in the year Denmark, Sweden and Holland acceded to the Declaration, and were afterwards joined by Prussia, Austria, Portugal and the American colonists. The response of England, Spain and France was at least conciliatory, for they expressed general approval of the Declaration, and insisted that they had always respected the rights of neutrals. The testing time soon arrived. In December 1780 Britain declared war on the States General, on the ground that, for some time, they had been supplying the American rebels with stores and munitions, whereupon the Dutch appealed to the powers united in the Armed Neutrality. But the appeal was rejected on the ground that the Anglo-Dutch dispute was not within the scope of the Armed Neutrality. Until the conclusion of peace in 1783, this confederation of maritime powers constituted a serious menace to Britain, but conflict was avoided because in this war (the War[1] of American Independence) England did not apply " the rule of 1756 " in such a way as to provoke the neutrals.

Posterity, always anxious to sum up past conditions in a convenient generalisation, has used the word Mercantilism (a word coined in the 1880's) to describe the basic principles regulating the economic relations of European states in the seventeenth and eighteenth centuries. The term is now somewhat discredited. It was Colbert who had given concrete expression to the system—if it can be called a system—for he

[1] below, pp. 274-7.

mphasised the competitive elements between states, and
trove to regulate the commerce and industry of France in
uch a way as to make a maximum contribution to its power.
Attempts were made to set up factories under state control;
ndustry was encouraged even at the expense of agriculture;
oreign workers were brought into France in the hope of
cclimatising new industries. The economic life of the nation
vas regulated by codes and inspectors. All this was based on
ertain assumptions which, for long, were barely contested—
hat the precious metals constitute wealth; that every effort
hould be made to accumulate them, and that the gain of one
ation must be at the expense of another. In maritime trade
he ideal was to import raw materials to be worked up or
nanufactured at home, and to exclude, by heavy tariff or other
neans, the manufactured goods of foreign countries.

Clear expression to these principles was given in the Navigation Acts enforced by England after 1651, with amendments
nd additions after 1660. The English Acts had a number of
bjects, such as exclusion of foreign ships from the coast-wise
nd colonial trades, encouragement of the building of large
hips, suitable for the Atlantic crossing and for conversion
nto warships and, thirdly, the creation of a " corner " in such
ropical raw materials as tobacco, sugar, cotton and dyeing
voods, by enacting that these should be landed only in Eng-
and, from whence a considerable proportion would be re-
xported. By these Acts, England sacrificed immediate econ-
mic interest to a policy of large ships, long voyages and a
reference for the raw materials now in European demand.
Here was a direct link with the pursuit of power; indeed,
Adam Smith declared that, if the sole object of commerce
vas power, then the Navigation Acts were the wisest measures
ver conceived. But there are few laws that cannot be evaded,
nd the Navigation Acts, usually mitigated in war time, were
tultified on a large scale; indeed, there were stations in New-
oundland and St. Eustatius where smuggled goods could be

transhipped. Other maritime nations imposed restrictions on their overseas trade similar in spirit to those of the English Acts.

The system had its critics. One of the earliest and most convincing of these was Richard Cantillon, a banker of Irish extraction who had made a fortune from Law's schemes. He died in 1734, and his *Essai sur la Nature du Commerce en Général* was not published until 1755. Meanwhile, his *Essai* had circulated widely in manuscript, and was given publicity by reference to it in one of the most popular books of the century—*L'Ami des Hommes,* by Mirabeau the Elder, published in 1756. Cantillon, whose main concern was with population, contended that an abundant populace was necessary for national wealth. Land, he declared, is the true source of such wealth, and labour is the means by which it is produced. Accordingly, agriculture should be encouraged and luxury discouraged. These were not revolutionary doctrines but they showed a difference of approach—away from the old idea that wealth consists in bullion; also, there was now new emphasis on population and agriculture.

There is a direct link between these views and those of the Physiocrats, who were exercising a strong influence on French and European opinion after about 1760. The Physiocrats whose opinions were popularised by the *Encyclopédie* (1751-72) included Quesnay (Madame de Pompadour's physician), Gournay and Dupont de Nemours, all of them men of some intellectual standing; indeed the movement may be regarded as the economic aspect of the Enlightenment, having important social and moral implications. The name implies a special reverence for nature and, perhaps inevitably, its advocates invoked the old ideal of Natural Law or Natural Right. Briefly, their main tenets were that agriculture and labour are the true sources of wealth, to which commerce is subsidiary; that the security, property and liberty of the person should be the main object of legislation; that economic enterprise

[1] below, pp. 253-5.   [2] below, pp. 324-5.   [3] below, pp. 337-8.

should be free; that taxation should fall evenly on all classes, and that, as national wealth depends ultimately on that of other nations, there should be an economic solidarity among them, not lightly to be disturbed. On these bases other doctrines were grafted—opposition to serfdom and slavery; national education; national armies, all under the control of an enlightened autocrat. Like so many of their contemporaries, the Physiocrats were convinced that the evils of civilisation could be cured by the application of science and reason. For the purposes of this chapter their importance lies in this that, anticipating Adam Smith, whose *Wealth of Nations* was published in 1776, they demanded, if not Free Trade, then relaxation of those restrictions which hampered industry and international trade.

These doctrines made a profound impression on some of the more enlightened rulers of the century. They influenced Joseph II in the administration of his Austrian dominions (in contrast with his mother, who was more conservative), and they had some effect on the policy of Charles III of Spain. In France they inspired Turgot, whose reforms of 1776 were unfortunately set aside.

Nevertheless, it is possible that the old, restrictive system was undermined not by opinion, but by hard economic fact, namely, the great expansion of capitalism which, in its complete development, is essentially international. This was proceeding rapidly in the more enterprising countries, notably England. The Dutch were also progressive in their attitude to investment and public finance. They had never been dominated by mercantilist restrictions; on the contrary, they had often made great profit by breaking through the restrictions imposed by their neighbours. In the eighteenth century, with the beginnings of decline in their overseas trade, they turned to investment in foreign countries, notably England, as the best means of using their capital. The dividends received from this source added to the total of their national wealth, but the capital exported did not appear in the national balance sheets. In this way it was demonstrated that the true state of a country's financial position could no longer be assessed as a balance of imports and exports; no longer could the wealth of a state be expressed solely in terms of its holdings of the precious metals. In this way the basic principle of Mercantilism disappeared.

In the later decades of the century this process became manifest in other nations, including the Scandinavian countries, in spite of the fact that they did not possess great accumulations of capital. After 1756 the advantage of neutrality prompted several northern states to develop their overseas activities, with consequent increase of capital and, almost as a corollary, a relaxation of restrictions on trade. Elsewhere, these restrictions remained, notably in undeveloped countries, as in central and southern Italy, and in countries such as Russia under Peter the Great, or Spain under Philip V, or Prussia under Frederick the Great, in all of which states it was necessary to build up a national economy almost from the beginnings. After all, a new state or a pioneer colony, where there is little or no accumulated capital, needs protection against its wealthier neighbours and competitors. Accordingly, a word like " Protectionism " might be a more meaningful term than the now outworn " Mercantilism ".

Chapter IV

AGRICULTURE AND INDUSTRY

I AGRICULTURE

Eighteenth-century Europe was still predominantly agricultural, with wide-scattered industrial areas. Steadily increasing population made greater demands on the first of these, while the needs of large armies taxed the resources of the second, with the result that, as more man power was diverted to industry, the need for foodstuffs became even more imperative. In different degrees the nations lost their self-sufficiency and were obliged to expand their agricultural output. After about 1750 England became one of the corn-exporting countries; by 1779 Catalonia was importing wheat from Sicily, northern Europe and Canada. In France, strenuous efforts were being made to ensure free internal circulation of corn, in spite of local prejudice and opposition. Generally, the European states were devoting more arable to the production of cereals. With this increased demand for foodstuffs, there was stimulated a new, scientific interest in agriculture; and attempts were made, mainly by enclosures and fertilisers, to obtain a greater yield than had been possible under the old, self-sufficing economy.

In early settlements on the land, recourse had at first been made not to the most fertile soils, but to soil easily cultivable by the primitive implements in use. In practice, this meant lands on alluvial plains, near rivers and away from mountains, mineral deposits or populous areas; land which, from its geological structure, could easily be turned with the spade, and might serve for either arable or pasture. Usually there was a superabundance of such territory, and so marginal land did not have to be utilised until later in the century. These natural factors may account for the open field system, a system of which there were innumerable variations, all having this in common that they were worked by peasant communities, usually under the direction of an overlord, whose overseer or steward annually allotted to the peasant strips of land, long or short, sometimes an acre in extent, all of them scattered throughout the open fields. The peasant might have difficulty in finding his strips, and might have to cross those of his neighbours in order to reach them; as they were usually narrow, space had to be left at the ends in which to turn the plough. As they were separated, not by hedges but by balks of earth, they were open to the cattle. The system, obviously wasteful, recalls the exigencies of a primitive population, but at least it did provide some kind of holding for everyone. Essentially a method of subsistence farming, it was based not on owner-ship of land, but on access to it; and could not readily be combined with improved methods for increasing the yield.

This system prevailed throughout the greater part of Europe from east and centre to the midlands of England. It was not usual in the north or south-west of England, nor in the south-east; it appears to have been absent in Brittany, possibly because of the survival of a more ancient type of organisation; its absence in Holland, Belgium, Lombardy and Venetia may more confidently be attributed to greater density of popula-tion in these areas, with their semi-industrial character and their need for abundant wheat. But why, even within the same country, there should be areas of enclosed land often alongside the open fields is still one of the vexed problems of economic history. Some areas such as moorland were obviously unsuitable for open fields; equally, proximity to a town was bound to create a demand that could be met only by the more intensive cultivation characteristic of enclosed land. En-closure, after all, is little more than the substitution of private ownership for communal rights; in this sense, it was one of the " improvements " of eighteenth-century Europe. After

1760 it began to be carried out extensively in England, less extensively in northern France, and usually it was combined with more scientific farming—draining, fertilising, and the adoption of a system of rotation of crops. Inevitably, it meant some dislocation for the open fielders, many of whom were either forced into the towns, or obliged to become wage labourers. The demands of increased population were insistent, so this relic of the past had to go.

As well as this distinction between enclosed and unenclosed land there was the more radical distinction of free and unfree labour. In England the well-known Act of 1660 had not abolished all the feudal tenures, for copyhold tenure still remained and survived until 1925. A large part of the agricultural population of England held by this tenure, usually a holding of about thirty acres, subject to the control of the lord of the manor, who might restrict the tenant's use of timber on the holding, or prohibit his access to minerals. No rent was paid; but, on the death of the copyholder, the incoming tenant, usually the eldest son, had to pay to the lord a " fine ", or capital sum, generally assessed at three times the annual value. These copyholders were obviously quite distinct from landless labourers. They were free, by arrangement with the manorial lord, to dispose of their holdings, which might even revert to the widows on their death.

In France, the system was more complicated, and became more oppressive as the century progressed. There the manorial system was more intact; the seigneurs, many of them, lived in towns and had little interest in agriculture; accordingly, they were more dependent on bailiffs. In many cases the lord had, in effect, given up what we call ownership while still retaining the jurisdictional rights[1] pertaining to the manor; these were numerous and vexatious. Thus the peasant could be required, at intervals, to pay for the drawing up of a *terrier* or inventory of the land which he cultivated; he could purchase or exchange land only after paying *lods* and *ventes*—these sometimes

[1] above, pp. 20-1.

amounted to half the purchase price; exchange of land by purchase or inheritance gave occasion for other exactions—*rachat, mariage, quint* and *requint*. Many of the old *corvées* had, by the eighteenth century, been commuted for payments in money or kind—the former were the *cens* or *censives,* the latter was known as *champart* or *terrage*. There were also the *banalités*—the obligation of the peasant to take his grapes to the seigneurial press, or to make use of the seigneurial bull if he bred cattle; he usually had to resort to the lord's bake house in order to bake his bread, or to the lord's mill in order to grind his corn. These feudal dues often amounted to about a seventh part of the net produce of the land, and were nearly equal in amount to the direct taxes. Whereas the English landlords, with their profits from the more efficient cultivation of their lands, were not compelled to increase their monetary exactions from copyhold tenants, many French seigneurs, on the other hand, impoverished by their manner of life, were obliged to insist on the exaction of the last *sou* that could be wrung from the strictest interpretation of their manorial rights. Peasants holding by the *métayer* system appear to have suffered most from this seignorial reaction.

There were small communities of serfs in France, notably in Franche Comté and the Jura; these were *mainmortables,* that is, they did not have control over the disposition of their holdings. But these were a very small proportion of the population, and it remains true that many French peasants were in a comparatively favourable position, which improved with the rise in prices of agricultural products; but, for those who did not own their land, this was more than offset by the rise in rents.[1] They were not tied to the soil; they were vexed by the *taille*,[2] it is true, and by the resurrected minutiae of the dead

---

[1] After about 1770 the rise in rents was steeper than the rise in prices—C. E. Labrousse, *Esquisse du Mouvement des Prix et des Révenus au XVIIIème Siècle,* pp. 630-1. (Paris 1932).

[2] A tax levied during the Hundred Years War. Literally, a portion of revenue or property " cut off ".

medievalism but, essentially, they were free. About a quarter of the peasantry had possession of their holdings, though these might be subdivided among large families; probably about a half lived by the *métayer* system, in which the seigneur provided implements and seed, taking half the produce for himself; the remaining quarter were landless labourers. These conditions compared very favourably with those prevailing east of the Elbe, where the lord combined rights of ownership with jurisdiction, in which respects his powers were unlimited, and extended to the serf's children. " Parcels " of serfs might bo sold or transferred; they might even (as in Russia) be gambled away in a game of chance; otherwise, they were tied to the soil, and those in possession of a holding had neither security of tenure nor any guarantee that they would be allowed sufficient time for working their land. Money played little part in this almost medieval economy, in which the Junkers of East Germany had the worst reputation. There were, however, some attempts at alleviation. Frederick the Great decreed the emancipation of serfs on the royal demesne, but it is not certain how far this proved effective; in 1768 Maria Theresa set up a commission with the object of defining and limiting the *corvées* that might be imposed in the Austrian lands, but its findings were contested by the nobility and appear to have had little salutary effect. Enforcement of agrarian reforms in Hungary and Bohemia led to outbreaks of violence as the peasants objected to the payment of monetary dues in lieu of *corvées*. Eventually, colonies of foreign workers had to be introduced as nuclei of a free peasantry.

Agricultural conditions differed greatly in the European states and even in the same state. Owing mainly to geographical and climatic causes these conditions in Spain were more varied than elsewhere. Most of the interior is table land, about 2,000 feet above sea level; dry and hot in summer, cold in winter, producing mainly esparto grass. This contrasts with the northern regions where a more typically European vegetation predominates and with the southern coastal belt, where the vegetation is sub-tropical. The distinction roughly over-laps that between the arid and the rainy regions, the latter predominating in the north-west coastal areas and on the southern slopes of the Pyrenees, extending into Navarre, Aragon and Catalonia. In contrast, parts of central Aragon and southern Andalusia were little better than desert. In no other European state were there such violent contrasts. For long, Spanish economy had been subordinated to the *Mesta*, a privileged corporation of sheep farmers, and the annual migra-tions of millions of sheep from Estremadura to Aragon had seriously interfered with the cultivation of cereals. But, by the eighteenth century, Spanish wool, noted for its fineness, was losing its monopoly, with consequent decline of the *Mesta*; accordingly, more encouragement was given to arable farming, especially in the later decades of the century. Condi-tions among the peasantry varied enormously. As most of the nobility had vast estates, small properties were exceptional; but the Basque provinces were noted for their population of free and hard-working small farmers; similar conditions pre-vailed in parts of Catalonia and Aragon. In Castile leases were short and the *corvées* were heavy; shepherds and horse-breeders were favoured at the expense of wheat growers. In Andalusia the agents of the great landowners collected the workers from the towns at seed time and harvest to work in the fields for two periods of about two months each. Many of these workers were kept in a state of permanent indebtedness to their employers. Elsewhere, as round Seville, most of the farm workers were itinerant, as were bands of *gitanos* or gipsies, for whom there was more tolerance in Spain than elsewhere.

Agriculture in Spain was impeded not only by climate and geology but by human institutions. The great landowners, who seldom lived on their estates, left the task of management to overseers; there was similar neglect on the part of the clerical landowners, with the result that much of the land was left untilled. In Granada, which had been intensively cultivated in the early seventeenth century by the Moriscos, conditions were such that some contemporaries expressed regret that the " New Christians " (Moriscos) had been expelled. *Mayorazgos* or entails were common throughout Spain mainly because family pride insisted on the perpetual retention of an estate, however small, within the family. Such estates could neither be sold nor divided, and as there was seldom any capital available, these units could rarely be stocked, and so were uneconomic.

A sharp contrast with these conditions is provided by the Belgian Netherlands, where the change from Spanish to Austrian over-lordship proved beneficial. Progress was accelerated by Maria Theresa and her son Joseph. Between 1709 and 1794 the agrarian population of Belgium more than doubled, a population composed of independent farmers, assisted by their wives and children. Their *petites exploitations* were intensively cultivated; manure and lime were used, and the maximum of produce was extracted from the soil. The farms, mostly intermediate in size between the large units of eighteenth-century England and the small holdings of France, were subjected to an elaborate system of crop rotation; in addition to wheat—the exportation of which was free in normal times—flax and tobacco were grown. The potato provided food for human beings and the turnip a winter food for cattle. Belgium was perhaps the only country in Europe where tobacco imports from America were unnecessary. Similar conditions prevailed in the dairy farms of Holland; elsewhere in Europe there were " pockets " of fairly intensive cultivation, as in parts of the Rhineland and Lombardy. Switzerland and Luxemburg were prospering from a high standard of cultivation conducted by small-scale, independent farmers.

By the early years of the eighteenth century many of the Netherlands innovations in agriculture were being introduced into England, notably in the cultivation of the turnip and of the new grasses such as clover and sainfoin. Extensive cultivation of these crops led indirectly to a great change in the national dietary. Hitherto the cattle were killed off in the autumn and the meat salted down for the winter; this, together with pickled fish, had provided food for half the year. But, as the turnip provided a winter food for cattle, greater longevity was now possible, and experiments could be made in stock breeding, as by such pioneers as Robert Bakewell (1725-95) who greatly improved the breed of sheep and cattle, and introduced the Leicestershire longhorns. In this way the quantity and quality of meat were improved and the diet of Englishmen benefited. Increasing use of the potato helped further in this direction. There were other important advances. In 1733 a Berkshire farmer named Jethro Tull (1674-1741) published an account of his mechanical drill for the more regular sowing of seed and for breaking up the surface of the soil; he also advocated the use of lime for neutralising the acid which accumulates in heavily manured land. Tull's mechanical device and his principles of soil chemistry were adopted not only in many parts of England and Scotland but in those areas of the continent where agriculture was most progressive. At the same time there was much experiment in the rotation of crops, the most popular rotation being the Norfolk system. This was based on the assumption that clover prepares the way for wheat, wheat prepares the way for turnips; turnips for barley and barley for clover. Norfolk and East Lothian, where Tull's device had been generally accepted, were then among Britain's most advanced agricultural areas.

The rise in prices, maintained unevenly throughout the eighteenth century, enhanced the price of corn and helped to raise rents. To this process the English Corn Laws also contributed, since they gave bounties to landlords for corn exports whenever the price fell below a certain level and forbade export in times of scarcity. The general effect of these measures may have been to keep the price of corn fairly steady. But English agriculture was fostered by considerations of wider import. As nowhere else in Europe life in the English countryside was agreeable and popular; it was also socially desirable. It was not disfigured by small holdings; and, especially in the later years of the century, was beginning to assume something of its modern shape—with its regular pattern of hedges cutting across what had once been open fields; its large and well-maintained farms; its numerous "gentleman's seats", built not from rents, but from the profits of trade or government office. In other words, English agriculture had this advantage that it was backed by capital, much of it personally directed by shrewd landlords such as "Turnip" Townshend in the early part of the century and Coke of Holkham in the later. The other pillar supporting this structure was the large-scale tenant farmer. He usually paid a high rent, it is true; but the comparatively generous scale on which he lived was proof of partnership in his landlord's prosperity. Voltaire was only one of many foreign observers who were impressed by the well-being and even amplitude of existence enjoyed by the tenant farmers of England.

Although contrasted in many respects, France and England showed an increasing interest in agriculture during the eighteenth century. Local societies were formed for its encouragement; even the academies, which had previously concerned themselves only with abstract matters, now included in their agenda discussion of agricultural problems as when, in 1755, the Academy of Bordeaux devoted its attention to the causes of blight in wheat. The *Encyclopédie,* under the title *Agronomie,* devoted a long article to the processes of agriculture; at Ferney Voltaire, among his many activities, occupied himself with the management of a model farm. In Prussia and Austria agriculture was included in the curricula to be studied by aspirants for posts in the civil service. As never before, it was recognised by statesmen that, mainly in view of increasing population, there must be a greater yield from the land; that this object was partially achieved is attested by the fact that there were comparatively few periods of large-scale starvation.

After 1709 France had little experience of acute shortage. Nevertheless, during the Seven Years War and for some time thereafter thousands perished from starvation in Saxony and Bohemia.

From the point of view of agriculture, the century abounded in sharp contrasts—between the low level of cultivation in many parts of Spain, in southern Italy and in Sicily and that prevailing in the Netherlands, in some parts of France, in Lombardy, Switzerland and in many areas of England. There was also the contrast, even more fundamental, between those areas, notably in England, where there was large-scale application of capital to the land, cultivated by peasants who, though often over-worked, were free and those areas, in central and eastern Europe, where there was exploitation of the unlimited resources of cheap, servile labour. This contrast in the cultivation of the soil was paralleled by a contrast in political institutions, and there may have been some truth in Montesquieu's dictum : " lands are well cultivated in proportion not to their fertility but to their liberty ".[1]

II INDUSTRY

Over the entrance to the workhouse at Leipzig was a Latin inscription which may be thus loosely translated : " for compelling the idle and controlling the feeble-minded "—an inscription commemorating the old association between pauperism, lunacy and compulsion. This clearly indicates an attitude to labour very different from that prevailing to-day, when there is not only a high degree of specialisation among the different occupations, but a recognition (however nominal) of the dignity of labour and a secure position for those institutions, such as trade unions, which have the special duty of safeguarding it. In the *Ancien Régime,* communities were more self sufficient; their needs were simpler; there was

[1] Montesquieu, *De L'Esprit des Lois,* bk. XVIII, ch. 3.

nothing to be proud of in being a worker; apart from the gilds, there was no class consciousness among those who had to earn their living by their hands. What we call the workers were then called " the poor "—these were not an accredited class of society but a large and potentially dangerous community on its fringe. Outside the towns they had no status. Agriculture was not always a whole-time occupation for it often shaded off, by infinite gradations, into what are now specialised pursuits—a small farmer might employ his family in the spinning and weaving of raw materials provided by his own sheep or supplied to him by an entrepreneur, taking the product to one of the " cloth towns " where it was finished in a factory; or he might travel round the country, with his bales of wool, thus acting as a commercial traveller. In districts where there was open-cast mining he might smelt the ore in his own furnace as did the father of John Wilkinson, the inventor, at his farm in Cumberland. This variety of occupation, particularly true of England, did not apply so obviously to the vast corn lands of northern Germany and eastern Europe. By contrast, deep mining, whether for coal, as in Scotland, or for salt, as in parts of Germany, was a specialised, whole-time occupation, conducted by workers whose status approximated to that of the serf.

Before the Industrial Revolution the location of industry might be determined by a number of factors, such as proximity to a sea port, abundance of fuel, presence of metals and water supply, whether in the form of wells or of streams and waterfalls. Sugar refining, distilling and tobacco manufacturing are examples of activities conducted at or near a port; shipbuilding was necessarily conducted within easy reach of salt water. Otherwise, the sea coast was not favoured for industrial development, and most of the large enterprises were located far inland. The textile industries need soft water for their processes and running water in order to supply power, both of which are more likely to be found in the uplands of the interior than near the shore; moreover, the manufacturer of textiles has to draw his partly-finished material from communities of cottage workers spread out in a wide circle. Abundant supplies of water are obvious necessities in such enterprises as paper making, brewing, tanning and the tempering of steel; but water as a source of power was the paramount necessity, and here we often find the explanation of the selection of a particular site. As Professor Ashton has pointed out,[1] a stream, a bridge and a fulling mill may provide the nucleus of a village and then of a town. Supply of fuel was another obvious consideration. The timber resources of England, France and western Germany were being seriously depleted by the conversion of forests into charcoal, and it was usually shortage of timber that caused migration of metal industries, for example, the movement of the English iron industry from the Weald of Kent and Sussex to the midlands, where there was plenty of coal. Output of coal[2] greatly increased in the eighteenth century, England, northern France and Belgium being the main sources of supply; the proximity of coal and iron dictated the location of the " heavy " industries, first in England and later in western Europe. As early as 1709 Abraham Darby of Coalbrookdale in the Severn Valley was using coke for smelting, an innovation which started an iron industry in Shropshire and Worcestershire, but this new application of coal did not become widespread until later in the century. The continued use of charcoal and its high price serve to account for the fact that England imported the greater part of its iron from Sweden and later from Russia.

There was also the human factor. Before the end of the century there existed an abundant supply of cheap, servile labour, including female and child labour, everywhere in evi-

---

[1] T. S. Ashton, *An Economic History of England: the Eighteenth Century*, p. 95.

[2] For this see J. U. Nef, *The Rise of the English Coal Industry*, and T. S. Ashton and J. Sykes, *The Coal Industry in the Eighteenth Century*.

dence, from the iron and copper mines of the Urals to the vast textile industries of Saxony and Bohemia. In England, where long tradition had accustomed the poor to value their infant children as wage earners, the pauper population rose by leaps and bounds after about 1780, in consequence mainly of the so-called Speenhamland System, by which the justices paid a subsidy from the rates for each pauper child, whether legitimate or not. Consequently, more perhaps than any other country, England had a vast supply not so much of man power, as of juvenile and infantile power; and, as the Industrial Revolution developed in the north, there was a general shifting of population from London and the south to the north and north-west. Pauper children were sent off in " parcels ", of ten or twelve, to each of which the Poor Law authorities usually added one idiot child for good measure. In these days before factory legislation, the distinction between free and servile labour was nominal, and it is difficult to distinguish between the mentality of the Lancashire factory owner and that of the slave owner in the southern American states. On a higher level there was the labour force provided by those who had emigrated because of religious conviction, notably the Huguenots, who had come to England and Prussia in the later years of the seventeenth century, bringing with them their skills, particularly in silk weaving and the making of delicate instruments. The industrial reforms of Frederick the Great would have been barely possible without the help of his large population of Huguenots. England benefited also by the influx of Palatines and Moravians. Most of all, she derived great advantage from her Protestant Dissenters, many of them the products of Dissenting Academies (where " modern " subjects such as mensuration and foreign languages were taught);[1] these men were better qualified than their Anglican contemporaries for the requirements of a new, industrial age. The English Dissenters were almost driven into commercial and industrial pursuits by the fact that they

[1] below, p. 310.

were debarred, or at least severely discouraged, from entry into the liberal professions.

This expansion of population was matched by expansion of demand. There were the innumerable requirements of the much larger armies in the field—for uniforms, guns, muskets, spades, saddlery and boots—to which must be added the demands for luxury goods by many classes of society now familiar with the increased amenities of life. But the spread of industry was very uneven; by 1783 it was only in England that steam power was being used in industry, and that on a small scale. Of this greatly increased economic activity only a brief sampling can be attempted.

First, the luxury and semi-luxury trades. Here France was in the lead. This was the best period of French furniture making, in which a notable part was played by the Parisian gilds; skilled workmen were also employed in the making of tapestry and works of art at the Gobelins factory in Paris. Their products served as models for the craftsmen of Europe. Another luxury enterprise was the making of fine lace, in which the Huguenots were active; this highly specialised craft was also carried on in several Belgian towns, in Venice and at Honiton and other towns in England. Clocks and watches were made at Geneva and Nuremberg, and English time-pieces had such a high reputation that the names of famous makers like Tompion were often forged. English plate and silver ware reached a point of perfection that has never been surpassed. Of other barely essential goods, silk is an example of a luxury that has become almost a necessity. This industry had been established in the middle ages mainly in Florence; by the sixteenth century the wearing of silk was extending to many European countries.

In France the centre of this industry was at Lyons, which had a large export trade; other centres were Amsterdam, Antwerp and Berlin. Here again the Huguenots were in the lead. In England, as early as the 1720's the Lombe family (having obtained information from Italy) were producing silk in a factory at Derby, employing about 300 persons; power to drive the wheels was derived from the river Derwent. Linen was woven from flax at various places, notably in Flanders, Brittany, Holland, northern Ireland and Silesia. There was a world market for German, especially for Silesian linen; after 1783 the United States imported large quantities, and it was said that Germany paid for her colonial imports in linen.

In Europe the making of cloth was as common as the baking of bread, and there were nearly as many spinners as unmarried women. Young children, orphans, idiots, vagabonds and even soldiers in Prussian barracks—all of these might be compelled to serve in some branch of the cloth industry. It was becoming highly industrialised and capitalised, the manufacturers usually drawing their yarn from cottage workers spread out over a great area, and working it up in a factory. Some of these factories were large; that at Abbeville in northern France, founded by the Protestant immigrant Van Robais, employed several thousands of persons; elsewhere in France, notably in Champagne and Languedoc, there were extensive cloth enterprises. In Flanders there were such famous old cloth towns as Ypres, Ghent and Bruges, but these had lost much of their old pre-eminence. Saxony, Bohemia, Brandenburg and Silesia had many such textile centres, with a considerable export trade; but this was surpassed by that of England, where Somerset and the West Riding of Yorkshire were the most prosperous of the areas producing textiles from wool, while Lancashire was the home of cotton goods, and of fabrics made from a mixture of cotton and wool. Manchester, the centre of this industry, had the advantage that, as it was not an incorporated town, there were no gild restrictions, and so anyone was free to enter and set up his business. Cloth, in innumerable varieties, accounted for about half of the total volume of English exports, much of which was handled by the great trading companies. Practically every county or district produced its distinctive type, a fact attributable to differences in the quality and texture of the wool.

This advantage is accounted for mainly by British climate, with its great variations of rainfall over comparatively short distances, and serves to explain the prohibition of export of the raw material.

This prosperity of the English cloth industry also helps to account for the many mechanical inventions intended to speed up production of textiles. It has already been mentioned that England enjoyed a high reputation for her clocks and watches, and it is significant that some of the inventions before the coming of steam embodied clockwork devices. Among the best known of the inventors were Kay, Hargreaves and Arkwright. In 1733 John Kay of Bury in Lancashire took out a patent for a fly shuttle which, as the name implies, greatly accelerated the work of weaving, and about thirty years later James Hargreaves of Blackburn is said to have invented the spinning jenny, which made possible the spinning of wool, cotton or flax on a number of upright spindles, thus multiplying the number of threads handled simultaneously. A few years later Richard Arkwright of Preston (1732-92), in conjunction with Hargreaves and a clockmaker, succeeded in revolutionising the process of spinning by introducing rollers which were turned mechanically. By the 1770's this spinning frame was being widely used for cotton; soon it was applied to the weaving of woollen cloth. At first, Arkwright's source of energy was water power, but in 1790 he used a Boulton and Watt steam engine, and it is from this point that the factory system in England, with all its profits, benefits and evils, can be dated.

Except for the increasing use of silk and the import of delicate fabrics from the east, the enhanced importance of the textiles attests no more than the needs of a growing population and of larger armies. More clear evidence of the greater amenities of eighteenth-century life is provided by the glass and porcelain industries. Glass making had long been established in Bohemia, as had the blowing of ornamental glass on the island of Murano, near Venice. The making of small figures in fine porcelain appears to have started at Meissen, near Dresden, in the 1730's; the products were modelled on the works of J. J. Kaendler, the sculptor. This industry was stimulated by imports of Chinese porcelain, and keen competition among well-to-do amateurs encouraged the production of artistic pottery in many countries. Thus, glazed earthenware was called delft in Holland, majolica in Italy, faience in France and Germany. In England, Bow, Chelsea and Worcester were renowned for their products. Josiah Wedgwood (1730-95), the leader of this industry in England, opened a factory at Burslem (Staffordshire) in 1769, where he experimented successfully in such ceramics as cream ware, jasper ware and black basalt. Combining business enterprise with taste and vision, he built up a great industry from his centre at Etruria, the headquarters of a district now known as the Potteries. At this point, it may even be suggested that fine glass and porcelain helped to make possible a social revolution, for these objects were mounted in cabinets of mahogany, inlaid with satin wood, essential ornaments in the drawing-rooms now coming into vogue, and it was in the drawing-room that women, nearly emancipated, exercised their distinctive influence.

Lastly, the metallurgical industries. In spite of the use of coke for smelting made by Darby of Coalbrookdale early in the century, charcoal remained long in use for this purpose. But there was increasing resort to coal particularly where, as in the midlands and north of England, coal and iron deposits are found in close proximity. Birmingham—like Manchester, an open town—became the centre of a small arms industry, producing nails, scythes, pistols and sword blades, manufactured in small forges by immigrants from the countryside. On a less intensive scale a similar process was taking place on the continent, notably in Artois, Picardy and Belgium, where there were some large-scale enterprises such as the Anzin collieries (near Valenciennes) and the Le Creusot arms factory (near Autun in Burgundy). Another industrial area, dependent on coal and iron was the Ruhr, with its centre in Solingen. Among the arsenals where guns and ammunition were turned out on a large scale may be included Chatham, Cronstadt, Spandau, Liége, St. Etienne, Toulon and Rochefort.

The great European states were beginning to make more use of their mineral deposits. Russia obtained an increasing proportion of her iron and copper from the Urals which, as early as 1700, had attracted the attention of Peter the Great, who needed supplies for his wars. In the words of a Russian historian (Kliuchevskii) " Peter discovered the Urals ". A steady influx of escaped peasants from central Russia provided a labour supply for the foundries, where copper and iron were smelted with charcoal from the forests; soon the peasants were subjected to forced labour, and the Urals, with their centre at Ekaterinburg, became a source of supply for guns, bells and copper coinage. By 1722 the peasants engaged in the mines and foundries numbered about 5,000. In order to ensure a labour supply, Peter in 1721 issued an edict enabling merchants to buy serfs—a privilege formerly exercised only by the nobility—and in this way entrepreneurs might buy up a whole village and " ascribe " the inhabitants to a particular foundry. The foundry thus entered into the feudal system.[1] By 1745 there were 54 foundries in the Urals, and their period of greatest activity was from that date until the end of the Seven Years War.

But it was in Sweden and Britain that the greatest advances in metallurgy and engineering took place. In Sweden, where the mines were large and deep, technology was probably more advanced than anywhere else in Europe, as witness the numerous inventions of Christopher Polhan (1661-1751), who held an official position under the government as mining engineer. A designer of roads and canals, Polhan invented rolling mills for iron bars, hole cutting and file cutting machinery as well as a number of scientific instruments; indeed, he was a pioneer in the making of machine tools, and he appears to have anti-

[1] R. Portal, *L'Oural au XVIIIème Siècle* (1950), p. 47.

cipated some of the inventions of Watt. The career of James Watt (1736-1819) clearly illustrates how great inventions often originate from improvements of existing devices and how important is co-operation in the development of technology. As mathematical instruments maker to the University of Glasgow, Watt came into contact with Professor Joseph Black (1728-99), one of the most distinguished chemists of the century who, in 1761, enunciated his theory of latent heat.[1] From this point a new subject, that of thermal science, can be dated. Watt, perceiving the great practical importance of Black's theory, designed an improved steam engine fitted with a separate condenser. This alone meant an increase of power. In 1769 the invention was patented and, a few years later, in partnership with Matthew Boulton, Watt set up business at the Soho iron works near Birmingham, where the new, improved steam engine was produced in considerable numbers. Boulton provided the business acumen which was completely lacking in Watt. Another associate helped to increase the importance of the new inventions—John Wilkinson (1728-1808), who designed improved plant for the accurate boring of cylinders. As early as 1775, with the help of Wilkinson's devices, the Soho Works were producing cylinders more accurately bored than had been possible at any time in the past, and the same methods served to bore the cannon which afterwards played such a notable part in the Peninsular War.

The increasing preponderance of Britain in the eighteenth century was based largely on economic factors. Some of these were geographical or geological in origin, and reference has already been made to the unique advantages enjoyed by England from her rivers, estuaries, ports and great mineral resources, many of them in close proximity to coal. In the later part of the century these natural advantages were more intensively exploited, and it became obvious that in the northern half of the country conditions were specially favourable for industry, because the Pennine range, as it stretches roughly

[1] below, p. 283.

north and south, forms the watershed of streams flowing into the Irish Sea and North Sea, thus providing both water power and transport. Throughout England the numerous canals made up for the bad roads and linked remote areas with the coast. To these must be added the mineral wealth of Scotland, particularly in the industrial belt connecting the Clyde and Forth valleys. There was also the human factor. The sea-faring population, victimised though they were by the press gang, provided many of the best sailors in Europe; the artisans were distinguished for their high standard of workmanship; British inventors and technologists were noted for daring originality. Overseas trade, as nowhere else, was closely co-ordinated with industrial activity at home, the profits from the former often providing capital for the latter. There was no scarcity of capital; and, after 1714, the maximum legal rate of interest was 5%. Thrift, integrity and hard work were characteristic of many elements of the English population; indeed, they might have taken Robinson Crusoe as their bible, with its illustrations of how to "make do" on the most slender resources. On the whole, they were a God-fearing, Sabbath-observing people, convinced that idleness is a sin, and that material success is a proof of divine favour. Such were the natural and human advantages. They were not all to be found together in any other nation, and they help to explain not only why the Industrial Revolution began earlier in England than elsewhere, but why eighteenth-century Britain played an increasingly important part in world affairs.

Chapter V

DIPLOMACY: THE BALANCE OF POWER

I INSTITUTIONS AND PERSONNEL

" Wars give rise to treaties and treaties are the source of all wars " (Bielfeld). This is true of the group of agreements signed in the years 1713-15 and collectively known as the treaties of Utrecht. The general effects of these agreements were as follows. Philip V, grandson of Louis XIV, was confirmed in his possession of Spain and the Spanish Empire, but the Belgian Netherlands and the Italian possessions of Milan, Naples and Sardinia were conferred on Philip's rival, the Emperor Charles VI. Sicily was given to the Duke of Savoy, with the promise of a crown. The Elector of Brandenburg was awarded Spanish Guelderland and was confirmed in his title of king in Prussia. France undertook to recognise the Hanoverian Succession and ceded Hudson's Bay, Acadia and Newfoundland to England. Philip V renounced his claims to the French throne and France renounced her claims to that of Spain; in the treaty between Spain and Britain, Philip ceded Gibraltar and Minorca. The treaty between France and the Emperor, signed in March 1714 and known as the treaty of Rastatt, confirmed to France the territories of Alsace and Strasburg; and all conquests on the right bank of the Rhine, such as Breisach and Freiburg, were restored. By the Barrier Treaty of November 1715 the Dutch were given the right to garrison a number of fortresses in southern Belgium, including Ypres, Tournai and Namur (at the emperor's expense), and it was declared that the Scheldt was to remain closed. Not until 1720 did Philip and the Emperor come to terms.[1]

One broad effect of the settlement was to limit Spanish commitments in Europe, in itself a good thing, since it enabled the rulers of Spain to concentrate on the peninsula and the empire; moreover, the establishment of Habsburg rule in Belgium and in the Milanese brought a more enlightened government to these territories. By the acquisition of Gibraltar and Minorca Britain became a Mediterranean power, and this was strengthened by her old alliance with Portugal; in consequence, the English fleet might now hope to prevent the Toulon squadrons from joining with those at Brest and in Channel ports. So too, by her acquisitions in north America, Britain was preparing the way for her dominion in Canada—soon to be a cause of war with France. Another source of conflict, more immediate, was the dissatisfaction of Philip V and Charles VI. Philip was now excluded from the former Spanish possessions in Italy, and he had agreed (unwillingly) to surrender his contingent claim to the French throne; after 1715, when Louis was succeeded by an infant great grandson, the possible union of the thrones of France and Spain was a cause of considerable disquiet. Even more dissatisfied with the settlement was the emperor, who still regarded himself as the rightful heir to the Spanish possessions. Then there were the barrier fortresses in the Austrian Netherlands, which were supposed to provide the United Provinces with some kind of protection against invasion. The Dutch allowed these to fall into neglect. Lastly, two minor powers, Savoy and Prussia, emerge from the settlement. Of these Savoy, afterwards included in the kingdom of Sardinia, was to prove an important makeweight in European diplomacy; while Prussia, under Frederick the Great, was to revolutionise that diplomacy altogether. No human settlement could have imposed peace for long.

In spite of the constantly-changing face of international

[1] below, p. 131.

relations in the eighteenth century, there were certain traditions which still had some influence on the grouping of the powers. The old maritime rivalry between England and the States General had been fought to a finish in the preceding century, and the two countries had been closely associated since the accession of William of Orange to the English throne in 1689. Nominally, at least, the two countries had some common ground in their Protestantism; moreover, with the gradual decline of their navy and mercantile marine, the Dutch were no longer formidable as rivals; accordingly, the two countries are found in association, never very cordial, in the decades following the treaty of Utrecht. In theory, the Dutch were the most suitable of continental allies for England. But relations steadily became more strained. There were difficulties over the interpretation of seventeenth-century treaties between the two states; the Dutch were accused of failure to carry out their commitments, and they caused resentment among their allies by the persistence with which their merchants traded with the enemy. This ambiguous state of affairs between two potential allies degenerated into English seizure of Dutch ships carrying French cargoes during the Seven Years War, and into actual conflict in the War of the American Revolution.

There was also increasing ambiguity about another traditional alliance—that between England and Austria. Here there was little foundation for close association except that, as enemies of France, the Habsburg rulers of the Austrian lands appeared to be natural allies of England. In 1732 Horace Walpole declared in the Commons[1] that the "preservation of the imperial dominions entire" was necessary for maintaining the balance of power. But here again dissension soon arose. With the acquisition of Belgium, the Emperor Charles VI naturally hoped to develop the maritime potentialities of his new possession, for which purpose the Ostend Company was founded in order to trade with the east. But

[1] Cobbett, *Parliamentary History*, VIII, p. 878.

this aroused the jealousy of the maritime states, Britain, France and Holland; with the result that the emperor was forced by diplomatic pressure to suspend the operations of the company in 1727. Co-operation between England and Austria in the War of the Austrian Succession led to further difficulties. While Maria Theresa was anxious that her allies should concentrate against Prussia, for the recovery of Silesia, the English were intent mainly on the protection of Hanover and the war against France. This uneasy association was ended in 1756 when, by the Diplomatic Revolution, Austria became the ally of France.

With Russia, the Austrian alliance proved to be more durable. This was initiated in August 1726 by an offensive and defensive alliance between the two empires based on the similarity of their interests. Both powers wished to diminish French influence in Poland; they shared a common hostility to their old enemy the Turk and to their new enemy Frederick of Prussia. The two empires were united, in the Polish Succession War, in their support of the Saxon candidate for the Polish throne, Augustus III, against the French candidate Stanislas Lesczinski. In 1746 Elizabeth of Russia signed a convention with Britain for the defence of Hanover, at the same time renewing the Austrian alliance. This new alignment of forces was one of the causes inducing Louis XV to make peace in 1748. Thereafter, the Austro-Russian alliance stood the test of time, though it was seriously strained in the Russo-Turkish war[1] of 1768-74 and in the Bavarian Succession War[2] of 1778-79. This was the most consistent and enduring of all the eighteenth-century alliances.

More than any other state France was dominated by traditional policies, some dating from the sixteenth century, others from the seventeenth. In the course of the long struggle with the Habsburgs French kings had sought allies among the secondary powers, notably Sweden, Poland and Turkey; more-

[1] below, pp. 145-6.   [2] below, pp. 148-9.

over the marriage of Louis XV with a Polish princess Marie Leszcinska helped to confirm this tradition. Another ancient ally was Bavaria, whose dukes, the Wittelsbachs, appeared to be suitable alternatives to the Habsburgs as emperors; indeed, mainly by French influence, Charles Albert of Bavaria was elected emperor in 1742. Louis XV, constantly reminded of the great achievements of his predecessor, never quite adapted himself to the new order of things—for example he refused to take into account the emergence of Russia as a great power. In his view the Muscovites were too far off and too barbaric for association with Versailles. One consequence of this was seen in the Seven Years War when, although Russia was fighting against Prussia, one of the chief enemies of France, she was not regarded as a French ally.

Louis XV, who was not without courage, was restrained by a certain shyness from intervening directly in public affairs. Advantage of this was taken by a number of courtiers led by Prince Conti who, in 1748, encouraged the king to form a separate and secret diplomatic service to act independently of the ministry. Using a special cypher, the agents of this, the " secret du roi ", countermanded and thwarted the activities of French ambassadors abroad for a period of twenty-five years. The Duc de Broglie succeeded Conti as director of this organisation, the activities of which were directed mainly to Poland, where the official French policy was one of non-intervention, in contrast with that of the secret organisation, which sent funds to Poland for use against Russian intrigues. The resulting confusion of French policy in Poland gave Russia a free hand, and enabled Catherine in 1764 to secure the election, as king, of her nominee Stanislas Poniatowski. This proved to be one more stage in the progress towards the first Partition of Poland (1772); it also proved how the foreign policy of a great power might be stultified by a childish attempt to give its king a sense of power and initiative.

But this is not the only evidence of futility in the royal

foreign policy. In a remarkable set of instructions[1] drawn up in July 1757 for the Comte de Stainville (afterwards Duc de Choiseul), Louis made it clear that, in spite of the recent diplomatic revolution (the alliance with Austria) French policy had not really changed, for it was still directed, as in Louis XIV's time, to maintaining for France the leading rôle in Europe. By the treaty of Vienna[2] (1738), alleged Louis, France had won from the emperor the Two Sicilies and a part of the Milanese; by the treaty of Aix-la-Chapelle she had deprived Austria of Silesia and the duchies of Parma and Piacenza. For the achievement of these objects, according to the memoir, Louis had made use of the king of Sardinia in 1733, and of Frederick of Prussia in 1741, just as Richelieu had used the Swedes in the Thirty Years War, but with this difference that, whereas the Swedes had remained faithful allies, Sardinia and Prussia, both of them upstarts, had proved ungrateful. The memoir concludes with a condemnation of Frederick, who had usurped French influence in northern Europe and considered himself the equal of the king of France. Nothing could more clearly illustrate the mentality of Louis XV. He was claiming almost entire credit for the achievement of his allies in a manner so preposterous as to recall the imaginings of another monarch, George IV, who at times was convinced that he had played a distinguished part in the battle of Waterloo.

Another ruler who was still living in the preceding century was the Emperor Charles VI. For generations his ancestors had schemed, by secret treaties and family renunciations, to ensure that, on the failure of the line of Spanish Habsburgs, all the Spanish possessions would either descend to the Austrian branch of the family or would be divided with their

---

[1] *Instructions Données aux Ambassadeurs de France . . . (Autriche,* ed. A. Sorel), pp. 356 ff.
[2] below, p. 136. This treaty ended the Polish Succession war in 1735, but as it was not confirmed until 1738 the latter date is here given.

French Bourbon cousins, with the result that, for many years, Europe had been bedevilled by the schemings of these two great dynasties until, after the death of the last Habsburg king of Spain in 1700, the inevitable war had broken out. For long Charles had refused to accept the results of that war—the war of the Spanish Succession—and, after the death of his elder brother Joseph in 1711 and his own election to the empire, he continued to regard himself as the rightful ruler of Spain and its empire. Meanwhile, in 1703, in the lifetime of his father the Emperor Leopold, there had been effected a secret family arrangement which divided the Habsburg dynasty into two branches—the descendants of Joseph and the descendants of his younger brother Charles. By this arrangement the Austrian lands were to descend to the heirs of Charles, even if females, in preference to the daughters of Joseph I. This was made public in April 1713 when, in the presence of his privy council Charles promulgated a " publicum et perpetuum edictum ", known as the Pragmatic Sanction, whereby he decreed the indivisibility of the Austrian possessions, and their devolution to his descendants, male or female, provided that they were Roman Catholics.

As the years passed and the emperor failed to obtain a male heir, this meant that his daughter Maria Theresa would succeed. Charles now made it a main object of his policy to obtain the adhesion of the European powers to this instrument, though a little reflection might have taught him that, if his own ancestors and co-religionaries had failed to keep their word, jealous foreigners, some of them heretics, were even less likely to keep theirs. Charles was willing, in order to obtain acceptance of his Pragmatic Sanction, to make substantial concessions—for example his abandonment of the Ostend Company—and this use of the Sanction as a bargaining counter provides one of the few clues in the tangled skein of international relations during the years preceding the inevitable outbreak of the Austrian Succession War. Ironically enough, the only powers which, by any stretch of imagination can be regarded as having kept their word, included the heretic England and Holland and non-Catholic Russia. Otherwise, it would be unfair to denigrate the Pragmatic Sanction, because, after all, it did serve to hold the Austrian dominions together, and it strengthened the position of Maria Theresa in her heroic struggle to recover Silesia from the clutches of Frederick.

The above recital has necessarily involved an anticipation of events, but it may have elucidated some of the general principles underlying the many and confusing gyrations of European diplomacy in the first half of the eighteenth century. That diplomacy, no more immoral than that of other periods, gave abundant scope for the exercise of that finesse so characteristic of the age. Its negotiations and results were conducted almost entirely in French, a language which, by its suppleness and grace and frequent use of the subjunctive helped, for the time at least, to surmount difficulties that might have been more obvious in forthright languages such as English or German. The diplomatic negotiations of Prussia, Austria and Russia were conducted almost entirely in French, but Italian still served in communications with the Levant, and German or Latin was used by the German princes for negotiations among themselves. At the same time there was an increase of diplomatic personnel especially as, after the 1740's, Russia came into the foreground, and Constantinople became an active centre of intrigue. National departments of foreign affairs were enlarged and divided into specialised departments, particularly at Versailles and St. Petersburg; elaborate cyphers were devised; hosts of translators and copyists were employed; maps were assembled and archives classified; questions of ceremonial were regulated by experts. This development, most notable in France and Russia, was followed, at some distance, by other nations, including Austria and Sweden; but in England, the Foreign Office remained modest in size, and not until 1782 was there a Secretary of State responsible for foreign affairs. Before that date, this responsibility had been divided between the secretaries for the northern and southern departments.[1]

Diplomatic representatives were recruited almost entirely from the aristocracy; in practice, ambassadors were often members of the higher nobility. The ideal ambassador was a man of birth and breeding; a good linguist; able to keep his mouth shut at the right time, and endowed with such self control that he could allow the sovereign to whom he was accredited to beat him at a game of chess or cards. Beneath the ambassadors in status were papal nuncios, extraordinary and ordinary envoys; ministers plenipotentiary, *chargés d'affaires* and resident ministers. In the lowest rank were the internuncios, consuls and diplomatic agents. It was common for a young man of good family to be employed on the staff of an ambassador so that he could learn the rudiments of his profession. This continued to be the usual method of training, in spite of attempts to formalise education in diplomacy, such as were made by Torcy in France in the years 1712-1720; by Maria Theresa who, in 1746, instituted the Theresian Academy for the training of diplomats and civil servants, and by Frederick the Great who, in 1747, set up a " seminary of ambassadors ", composed of twelve men of good family. These experiments appear to have had little success.

As information was so essential for ministers and embassies, spies were frequently employed, and letters were opened in the post. The postmaster at Versailles was said, for a time, to have been in the employment of Prince Eugène and many of the Prussian couriers were reported to be in the pay of Kaunitz, the Austrian minister, who is also said to have had the key of the Prussian cypher. Behind the impressive façade of eighteenth-century diplomacy there was a vast underworld of espionage; but at least envoys were not murdered, as had occasionally occurred in the previous century. Information of a

[1] For a good account of this subject, see M. S. Anderson, *Europe in the Eighteenth Century* (1961), pp. 155 ff. See also D. B. Horn, *The British Diplomatic Service, 1689-1789* (1961).

supposedly secret character travelled far and quickly. Frederick the Great boasted[1] that he might learn from his agent at The Hague the truth about a plot hatched in St. Petersburg, or from his representative in Copenhagen about what was happening in Poland. There was also scope for ingenuity in the choice of representatives, having regard to the character or supposed character of the state to which he was accredited. Louis XIV had proved himself a master of this branch of diplomacy; he had an able successor in Frederick, who claimed that his envoys were selected on a definite system. Thus, when he was on bad terms with England, the Prussian ambassador to St. James's need be no more than a spy; but, when relations were good, he sent an "agreeable debauchee", who could hold his wine and make himself popular. At The Hague "a simple, solid man" was all that was required, because in Holland the important secrets of Europe were well known. Austrian diplomacy, alleged Frederick, was so dilatory and quarrelsome that the Prussian envoy in Vienna must be an expert in "stonewalling". Frederick was well served by his armies and his spies.

II 1716-40. THE POLISH SUCCESSION WAR

Frederick the Great maintained that the "balance of power" was a mere name, and that only by despising it could one achieve great things.[2] The part which he played in his wars illustrates the application of this maxim, and even serves to suggest that the year 1740, when he succeeded to the Prussian throne, provides a useful dividing line in the history of eighteenth-century diplomacy. The twenty-five years between

[1] This is stated in his "Political Testament" of 1762. See *Die Politische Testamente Friedrichs des Grossen*, ed. G. B. Volz (1920), pp. 54 ff.

[2] Frederick II, *Les Matinées du Roi de Prusse*, p. 18. This book appears to have been written in 1769 for his nephew, and was published, without date, later in the century.

the conclusion of the Utrecht settlement and the outbreak of the Austrian Succession War were marked by two series of events—the war in the Baltic, which did not end until 1721 and the efforts of both the emperor and Philip V to upset the Utrecht settlement in so far as it related to Italy and the Mediterranean. That there was no conflict on a grand scale was due partly to the war weariness of France and Britain, partly to the peace policies of Walpole and Fleury and the maintenance of a precarious balance of power which served, for the time, to curb the ambitions of such bellicose states as Spain, Austria and (until 1719) Sweden. Even more, this state of affairs can be attributed to a short-lived diplomatic revolution—the alliance between France and England. Louis XIV, who died in September 1715, was succeeded by a sickly child of five. The Duke of Orleans, contravening the terms of Louis XIV's will, established himself as Regent with full powers; but the succession to the French throne seemed precarious, especially as Orleans was suspected (unjustly) of having removed unwanted relatives by poison. In spite of his renunciation of 1713, Philip V of Spain claimed the Regency, and made no secret of the fact that he would repudiate his renunciation of the French crown. At the same time, another newly-established ruler George I of Great Britain had reason to fear deposition, because the Jacobite party was strong, and rose in rebellion in 1715. In these circumstances it appeared obvious that an alliance between the rulers of England and France would be the best answer to those who threatened to disturb the existing order of things. The initiative for this proposal appears to have been taken by the Abbé Dubois, formerly Orleans's tutor and now his secretary, whose acquiescence, and even participation, in the debaucheries of the Court commended him to the Regent. With the help of Stanhope, and in spite of the misgivings of George I, the Anglo-French alliance was concluded late in 1716, and was joined by the Dutch early in the following year. The compunction of George I may have been removed by the fact that the movement of Peter the Great's troops into Mecklenburg appeared to threaten Hanover.

By this unusual alliance the immediate threats to England and France were removed, but there were two trouble spots—the Mediterranean and the Baltic. By his first wife Philip V had a son who eventually succeeded to the Spanish throne in 1746 as Ferdinand VI; but, by his second wife, Elizabeth Farnese, niece of the Duke of Parma, he had two sons, Don Carlos and Don Philip. Elizabeth, who was the dominant partner of the royal pair, had an able and ambitious minister in her Italian compatriot Giulio Alberoni who had acted as agent for her marriage and was made a cardinal in 1715. This alliance of woman and priest proved to be a sinister one, for it was aimed at placing Philip on the French throne and securing possessions in Italy for Don Carlos and Don Philip which would restore Spanish influence in the peninsula. With these objects Alberoni made elaborate preparations. He strengthened the navy and, in concert with Jacobites, he stirred up opposition to the Hanoverian Succession; he encouraged the enemies of the Habsburgs in Hungary and Turkey, and even tried to induce Charles XII of Sweden and Peter the Great of Russia to sink their differences and combine in an attack on Hanover. In the summer of 1717 Spanish troops were landed in Sardinia and, by November, the island was in Spanish occupation. If they had had their way, Elizabeth and Alberoni would have provoked a European conflagration.

But the despised balance of power came to the rescue. The emperor, whose possessions in Italy were so obviously threatened, came out of his isolation to join the Anglo-French camp. In July 1718 he signed with the Turk the treaty of Passarowitz, by which Hungary was restored, and parts of Serbia, Bosnia and Wallachia secured for the Habsburgs; now that he was free from the Ottoman menace, he could turn his attention to the west. Events moved rapidly. Early in July 1718 a Spanish fleet landed troops in Sicily and soon the island was occupied. This brought together all the powers whose safety was menaced, and on August 2 1718 there was signed a treaty which provided that the House of Savoy should transfer Sicily to the emperor in exchange for Sardinia, and that Don Carlos should succeed to the Farnese possessions of Parma and Piacenza, with eventual succession to the Medici in Tuscany. The treaty also provided that the emperor should guarantee both the Hanoverian Succession and the contingent succession of Orleans to the French throne. Signed by England, France and the emperor, with the later adhesion of the Dutch, this was the Quadruple Alliance. Austrian troops at once invaded Italy in order to expel the Spaniards, and on August 11 Admiral Byng inflicted a decisive defeat on the Spanish fleet off Cape Passaro. Efforts then were made, mainly by Stanhope, to induce Philip to join the alliance, but even an English promise to restore Gibraltar failed to deflect Spanish policy. George I, threatened by a Jacobite invasion from Spain, declared war on Philip in December 1718, followed by France in January 1719. A French invasion of Spain and English attacks on Spanish shipping served to complete the discomfiture of Elizabeth and Alberoni, who lost a potential ally by the death of Charles XII of Sweden in December 1718. The Jacobite invasion of 1719 ended in failure; Spanish troops were expelled from Sicily and Sardinia; and, with the dismissal of Alberoni in December 1719, Philip had little choice but to accede to the terms of the Quadruple Alliance (in 1720). At long last the King of Spain and the Emperor Charles had come to terms; the first abandoned his claim to the French throne, and the second his claim to the Spanish monarchy and empire. But a woman's will eventually proved stronger than the combined forces of war and diplomacy for, by 1748, two Spanish-Bourbon dynasties were established in Italy—one in the Two Sicilies, the other in Parma and Piacenza.

This settlement of 1720 coincided roughly with that of northern Europe, where the menace of Charles XII was succeeded in December 1718 by the menace of Peter the Great.

Hanover was in danger from Russian invasion, and Peter's troops entered Swedish territory; on behalf of Sweden, an English fleet was sent to the Baltic on several occasions after the death of Charles XII, but was unable to follow the Russian ships into the Gulf of Finland. A confused welter of negotiations and double dealing, involving the emperor, France, Poland, England, Prussia, Sweden and Russia seemed, at times, likely to degenerate into full-scale war; but the co-operation of France and Britain provided a steadying factor, while French and English diplomats were actively engaged at the northern Courts. By the mediation of Carteret, envoy to Sweden, a treaty of November 1719 conceded Bremen and Verden to Hanover on payment of a sum of money; another payment confirmed Prussia in the possessions of Stettin and part of western Pomerania. At the same time, Denmark was detached from Sweden's enemies by confirmation of her rights in Schleswig. These arrangements were confirmed in September 1721 by the treaty of Nystadt, whereby Sweden ceded to Russia Livonia, Estonia, Ingria and Carelia, thus establishing Russian rule on the eastern coast of the Baltic. Finland was restored to Sweden. A revolution in Sweden had already created a limited monarchy for Ulrica Eleonora, Charles XII's sister who, in 1720, abdicated in favour of her husband Frederick I, formerly Landgrave of Hesse Cassel. These two pacifications, the one in the south, the other in the north, owed much to the co-operation of Great Britain and France.

The adhesion of Spain to the Quadruple Alliance in 1720, followed in the next year by the conclusion of the war in the north, served to create an appearance of peace, and in the years after 1724 two European congresses which met first at Cambrai and then at Soissons tried, somewhat ineffectively, to devise a settlement of outstanding difficulties. Of these, the most serious were those created by Elizabeth Farnese, who was impatiently awaiting the extinction of the Farnese and Medici dynasties in Italy in order that her sons might succeed, and was demanding the restitution of Gibraltar and Minorca. In this aggressive policy she was supported by the Dutch adventurer Ripperda, who was made foreign minister. On his side, the emperor, anxious to foster the Ostend Company, turned to Spain, and in April 1725, by a treaty usually described as the first treaty of Vienna, Philip V undertook to guarantee the Pragmatic Sanction and to support the Ostend Company, while the emperor promised the investiture of Don Carlos in the Italian duchies and also his support for the recovery of Gibraltar. Thus ended Spanish and imperial adhesion to the Quadruple Alliance. The reply of the maritime powers was prompt. In September 1725 England, France and Prussia joined in the defensive treaty of Hanover directed mainly against the emperor's support of the Ostend Company. Frederick William of Prussia speedily deserted this alliance and joined the emperor who, in 1726, secured another ally in Russia, whose sovereign, Catherine I, alarmed by English naval incursions into the Baltic, undertook to guarantee the Pragmatic Sanction. Now that she had the promise of imperialist support, with the possibility of Russian backing, Elizabeth and Ripperda proceeded to active measures, and in February 1727 the siege of Gibraltar was begun. This was followed by a short war between England and Spain. For the second time Elizabeth was risking a European war.

That it did not break out may be attributed to a number of fortuitous causes. In 1726 the Duc de Bourbon, French minister since Orleans's death in 1723, was succeeded by the aged Cardinal Fleury, who was determined to maintain the English alliance as the one guarantee of peace. His régime was described by a contemporary as a " convalescence "—a rare episode in the history of France. Then, in 1727, Catherine of Russia died, and as her successor Peter II was a boy, there was a break in the continuity of Russian policy. In Spain there was no enthusiasm for the bellicose ambitions of Elizabeth, who could now rely only on the emperor. He proved to be a broken reed. He had no money for a long campaign, and he was easily deterred when difficulties arose. So, in May

1727 there was one more revolution of the diplomatic kaleido-
scope when, by the mediation of Fleury, Charles undertook
to suspend the operations of the Ostend Company, and Spain
agreed to raise the siege of Gibraltar. These preliminaries
were ratified and extended in November 1729 by the treaty of
Seville, which drew England, France and Spain more closely
together and excluded the emperor altogether. By this treaty
Spain, for the time being, abandoned her claim to Gibraltar
and Minorca, and the signatories undertook to support Don
Carlos in the Italian duchies. If only temporarily, Fleury's
peace policy had prevailed.

In January 1731 the Duke of Parma died, and another crisis
arose. The emperor occupied the Italian duchies with his
troops in order to keep out Don Carlos : Elizabeth called on
her new allies, England and France, to intervene. The emperor
had now to be placated if Don Carlos was to succeed to the
duchies, and for this purpose the Pragmatic Sanction provided
a useful bargaining counter. By the second treaty of Vienna
(1731) the emperor came to an agreement with Britain, Holland and Spain, by which he consented to withdraw his troops
from northern Italy, and to admit Don Carlos into Parma and
Piacenza. He again agreed to suspend the Ostend Company
and to invest George II with Bremen and Verden. These were
substantial concessions. In return England and Holland
guaranteed the Pragmatic Sanction. Elizabeth Farnese had
won, but she was soon to win more.

Up to this point Italy, with its conglomeration of kingdoms, principalities and republics, had provided a reserve area
from which the more bellicose of western powers might hope
to recoup themselves. Another reserve was Poland which,
until his death in February 1733, was ruled by Augustus II,
Elector of Saxony. His son, Augustus III, was a candidate for
the succession; and, in return for a promise of Austrian support, he guaranteed the Pragmatic Sanction. But another candidate appeared on the scene—Stanislas Lesczinski, father-in-law
of Louis XV; so it appeared that Poland would now take the

place of Italy as a bone of contention for European potentates. To make matters worse, there were signs that the Anglo-French alliance was breaking down, owing to increasing colonial rivalry, and Anglo-Spanish relations were becoming even more strained, because of English smuggling in the Caribbean and the searching of English vessels by Spanish *guarda costas*. Most serious of all, there were signs that, after twenty years of peace, France was becoming bored; *La France s'ennuie*. Chauvelin, the minister of foreign affairs from 1727 to 1737, had little difficulty in stirring up the war spirit among his compatriots. This took the traditional form of opposition to the Habsburgs; on this occasion the emperor was to be deprived of his Italian possessions, for which purpose two allies were needed—the kings of Spain and of Sardinia. Meanwhile, by French influence and bribery, Stanislas was elected king of Poland in September 1733, an event quickly followed by a Franco-Sardinian and a Franco-Spanish alliance. There was a dualism in the motives accounting for France's engaging in war. On the one hand the king was anxious to enhance his own and his consort's prestige by obtaining a crown for his father-in-law, even if it was only the crown of Poland; on the other hand, the bellicose elements in the nation, wearied of peace, sought for a renewal of hostilities with the traditional enemy, the Habsburgs. The first of these objects met with no success, but the second did. In October Louis declared war on the emperor, and there began a short contest which, for want of a better name, is called the War of the Polish Succession. Britain and the United Provinces remained neutral.

The Polish Succession was soon settled. Russian and Saxon troops speedily expelled Lesczinski and placed Augustus of Saxony on the throne as the nominee of Russia and the client of the emperor. Now that Poland was gone, French diplomacy turned to another old prop—Turkey; but, with Christian compunction, Fleury hesitated to make a public alliance with the infidel, and Russia helped to save the cardinal's conscience by instigating a war between Turkey and Persia. Meanwhile the emperor, bitterly complaining that his traditional English ally had not come to his support, fared badly in the campaigns against France, conducted in the Rhineland and in Italy. In the Rhineland, the imperial general Prince Eugène, now in the decline of age, had to raise the siege of Philipsburg; in Italy the emperor's troops met with one disaster after another. Late in 1733 Charles Emanuel of Sardinia entered Milan; in May of the following year the Austrians were defeated at Bitonto in southern Italy, and in the following month the Franco-Sardinian troops defeated the imperialists at Parma and Guastalla. By the summer of 1735 Spanish troops were established in Naples, and in July Don Carlos was crowned king of the Two Sicilies. This, a humiliation for the emperor, was a great and probably unexpected triumph for Elizabeth Farnese.

A provisional peace, generally known as the third treaty of Vienna, was agreed upon in October 1735 and formally ratified in 1738. By this treaty, in which France, Spain, the emperor and Sardinia were the contractants, Stanislas renounced the throne of Poland and received in return the reversion to the grand duchy of Lorraine, which he was to hold for his life; on his death, it was to go to France. Stanislas died in 1766 and, in this roundabout way, Lorraine became a part of France. The treaty provided that the Milanese should be restored to the emperor, with the exception of Novara and Tortona, which were awarded to Charles Emanuel of Sardinia who, in return, signified his acceptance of the Pragmatic Sanction. Don Carlos, having restored Parma and Piacenza to the emperor, was given the largest prize of all—the kingdom of the Two Sicilies. In exchange for these important imperial concessions France accepted the Pragmatic Sanction. This guarantee was a poor exchange for the surrender of Naples and Sicily, and it was clear that the reputation of the emperor had suffered badly by his reverses in this war. Only in Poland had he succeeded, and that was a barren success; in Italy he retained only the greater part of the Milanese. Soon he was to experience further failure. His troops suffered reverses in the war against the Turk, conducted in alliance with Russia; and in 1739, with the help of Fleury's mediation, he had to accept the Peace of Belgrade, by which he lost nearly all that he had gained in the Treaty of Passarowitz.[1] These things may have hastened his death, which occurred in October 1740, at the age of 55.

The generation between the conclusion of the Utrecht settlement and the death of Charles VI was a period of diplomatic futility and inconclusiveness probably unmatched in European history. There was no stability in the numerous treaties and alliances, all of them designed for petty or dynastic motives, all changed or reversed within short spaces of time. The chief trouble maker—Elizabeth Farnese—was the only ruler to whom a consistent policy can be attributed, a policy pursued ruthlessly and crowned with success; contrasted with this was the vacillation of Russia, where palace revolutions and frequent changes of ruler destroyed any possibility of continuity, and the opportunism of such minor princes as the King of Sardinia, anxious to pick up the scraps left by more powerful combatants. Territorial gains in Italy and acquisition of the worthless crown of Poland; exclusion of the emperor from the ranks of the maritime states; paper guarantees intended to ensure the devolution of the Austrian lands to the descendants of Charles VI, such were among the objects of petty intrigue and pretentious diplomacy. That no great war broke out may be attributed to the link between Britain and France, a link steadily becoming more frayed, for in these years Walpole and Fleury were fighting a losing battle against the warmongers. The War of the Austrian Succession aroused the giants from their short slumber, and proved to be one more stage—an inconclusive one—in the long struggle between the two great adversaries of the century. These contestants were speedily joined by a third giant—Russia; and so, in the years after 1740, the destinies of

[1] above, p. 130.

Europe were in the hands of rulers far more menacing than the petty princelings and decadent potentates who had dominated the scene in the preceding generation. The age of power politics had dawned.

III 1740-1763. THE DIPLOMATIC REVOLUTION.

The Pragmatic Sanction had been guaranteed by Spain in 1725 (first treaty of Vienna), by Russia in 1726, by England and Holland in 1731 (second treaty of Vienna), by Augustus of Saxony in 1733, by France and Sardinia in 1738 (third treaty of Vienna). Of those powers which had *not* accepted the Sanction, the most important was Charles Albert of Bavaria, who derived his claim from an ancestor who had married a daughter of the Emperor Ferdinand I in 1546; it was this Charles Albert who was emperor from 1742 until his death in 1745. Among the powers which had accepted the Sanction, the first claimant, on the death of Charles VI, was Augustus III of Saxony and Poland, who derived his rights from his father's marriage in 1719 to Maria Josepha, elder daughter of the Emperor Joseph I—and this in spite of a renunciation. Among claimants to at least part of the possessions were the King of Sardinia and Charles, King of the Two Sicilies, both claiming in respect of ancestral connections. Even more ominous for the future was the ambiguous attitude of Fleury. Distinguishing between the empire and the Austrian lands, he contended that the French guarantee could not be urged against the rightful claims of a third party—France, it now appeared, had made no promise regarding the succession to the empire and, as for the lands, action must be suspended until it was clear who had the best claim. What with genealogical research and the elaborate casuistry of a reverend octogenarian, things might have ambled along in a leisurely way in the months after Maria Theresa was proclaimed Archduchess of Austria and Queen of Hungary and Bohemia, had not a

unexpected and dramatic event occurred in December 1740—
Frederick's invasion of Silesia. With this sudden irruption a
new era in European history had begun.

Frederick's conquest of Silesia was consolidated by his victory over the Austrians at Mollwitz in April 1741. These
events acted as a catalyst which fused together a number of
simultaneous reactions. Among these one can distinguish the
English war against Spain, which had begun in 1739; the two
wars by which Frederick established himself in Silesia; a
Russo-Swedish war 1741-3 in which the Swedes were badly
defeated, a war instigated by France; the efforts of Charles
Albert of Bavaria to secure both the empire and the Austrian
lands—again at the instigation of France; and, lastly, the
struggles of Charles Emanuel of Sardinia and of Elizabeth
Farnese to extend their possessions in northern Italy. It
would have been surprising if the last-mentioned potentate had
kept out of this mêlée. In the background there was being
contested a more momentous struggle—that between England
and France, conducted in Europe, in India and in Canada.
This war proved to be the last of the contests between France
and Austria until the Revolution; it also marked the end, for
all practical purposes, of the Anglo-Dutch and the Anglo-
Austrian alliances. Frederick's timing of his invasion was
almost perfect, because the death of the emperor had been
quickly followed by that of the Empress Anna of Russia, and
as she was succeeded by an infant, there was the prospect of a
long minority. So, at least, reasoned Frederick, who lived in
dread of Russia; and he proved to be right, for Russian intervention in the west, when it came, was too late. The war was
ended by the treaty of Aix-la-Chapelle (1748) which was no
more than a truce.

In the years immediately following the treaty of Aix-la-
Chapelle two new factors had to be taken into account by
European diplomacy—the size and efficiency of the Prussian
army, controlled by a ruler who had proved himself devoid of
scruple, and the unrealised potentialities of the Russian Em-

pire. Maria Theresa never reconciled herself to the loss of
Silesia; she hated Frederick with a womanly intensity, and
was convinced that England would do nothing to further her
interests. To her it was clear that the real danger came, not
from the old enemy France, now weakened by divided counsels, and controlled, to a large extent, by Madame de Pompadour; but from Prussia, an upstart and heretic power, completely detached from the more moderate and " gentlemanly "
traditions which hitherto had had some weight in European
diplomacy. The minister who gave direction to these pre-
possessions was Count Wentzel-Anthony Kaunitz (1711-
1794), one of the most astute and successful diplomats of the
century, an exponent of the older opinion that success could
be won as much by ingenuity as by force. From his point of
view there were circumstances pointing to the need for a
radical change in Austrian policy. Austria had something to
offer for French assistance in the recovery of Silesia, namely,
acquisitions in Belgium, that Cinderella of the Habsburg possessions; equally, from the French point of view, there were
serious objections to the continuance of the Franco-Prussian
alliance, for Frederick always played a lone hand, and was
quick to desert his allies as soon as his objects had been
gained. Also, and this weighed heavily with Maria Theresa,
he was a heretic. There was of course the danger that the
ostracism of Frederick might throw him into the British camp,
but this did not interrupt the negotiations which Kaunitz, as
Viennese ambassador, conducted at Versailles in the years
following the conclusion of the treaty of Aix-la-Chapelle.

Why not an Austrian alliance with France, the bulwark of
Catholicism in the west? In his mission to Versailles in 1750
Kaunitz had some difficulty in convincing the ministry of the
pacific intentions of his imperial mistress, but he succeeded
better with the king himself, who was supported by Madame
de Pompadour and by one of her creatures the Abbé Bernis
The Pompadour may have been influenced by the fact that

in her letters, Maria Theresa addressed her as "My dear Sister". All this was reinforced by Bernis, who pointed out that Austria was still a powerful force in Germany and no longer a menace to France; an alliance between the two would also strengthen the Bourbon interest in Spain and Italy. On his side, Frederick had now less regard for France as an ally; and he was justifiably alarmed by the fear that England, after her defensive treaty of September 1755 with Russia, would join in an Austro-Russian bloc directed against himself. As for George II, the danger which he dreaded in Germany was a Prussian attack on Hanover; but, as relations between France and England in north America became more strained in the years before 1756, it appeared that Hanover might have more to fear from France than from Prussia. This solicitude of George II on behalf of his continental electorate helped to counterbalance the bad relations which had existed since 1748 between Britain and Prussia. So, in Vienna, Versailles, Berlin and London there was much talk of a fundamental change in alliances. These were among the considerations which led, in 1756, to what has been called the Diplomatic Revolution.

The first step in that revolution was taken in January 1756 in the Convention of Westminster, by which George II and Frederick agreed to exclude Germany altogether from the Anglo-French hostilities which, in effect, had already begun. The Convention of Westminster also annulled the Anglo-Russian subsidy treaty of 1755, a treaty prompted by George II's solicitude on behalf of Hanover. In view of this proposed neutralisation of Germany, it might have been in the interests of France to avoid continental campaigns and concentrate on the naval and colonial war with England, a policy which had some support among those who directed French affairs. But at Versailles there was now a feeling of resentment. Frederick, by the Convention of Westminster, had deserted an ally, and not for the first time; accordingly, it was partly in order to punish him that in May 1756 France and Austria agreed to the defensive treaty of Versailles. In this compact Austria undertook to take no part in the hostilities between France and England, while France promised not to attack the Netherlands or any Austrian possession. The treaty did not commit either party to hostilities against Prussia, but Kaunitz regarded the treaty as the first step in that direction. France was still free to refrain from continental campaigns.

On the last day of December 1756 Russia declared her adhesion to the treaty of Versailles, and was promised a French subsidy, to be paid not directly, but through Austria. There was thus the basis of an understanding between France, Austria and Russia, but the last-mentioned power retained her peaceful relations with Britain. Not until the signing of the second treaty of Versailles on May 1, 1757, did Maria Theresa and Kaunitz achieve their object, because this compact was directed against Frederick, whose kingdom was to be partitioned. France undertook to pay an annual subsidy to Austria and to put a large army in the field; she was now committed to a European war, to be conducted mainly in the interests of the Habsburgs from whom, in the event of success, she could hope to obtain only a part of the Netherlands. In return she had, in effect, to abandon her old allies, Poland, Sweden and Turkey. It was a heavy price to pay. As well as this, there was the war with England, and so the second treaty of Versailles may be regarded as the crowning act of folly committed by the government of Louis XV. This reflected the inertia of French foreign policy in the years after 1748 and the over-confidence engendered by French naval and military successes at the beginning of the Seven Years War.

Even thus, the Diplomatic Revolution can hardly be regarded as the direct cause of the Seven Years War. Kaunitz had assembled all the ammunition necessary for a triple barrage against Prussia; only a spark was needed to set it off. Frederick applied the spark by his invasion of Saxony in August 1756. This may well have suited the designs of Maria Theresa and Kaunitz since what they wanted was a continental war for the recovery of Silesia. Into this France was dragged. The Franco-Austrian alliance appeared to be cemented by the marriage in 1770 of the Dauphin, afterward Louis XVI, with Marie Antoinette, daughter of Maria Theresa and sister of the Emperor Joseph II, but *L'Autrichienne* embodied for France the increasing dislike with which the Habsburgs were regarded. Weakened and discredited by the disasters of the Seven Years War France abdicated her rôle of leading partner in the European comity of nations, a decline relieved only by the triumph of French diplomacy in July 1772 when Vergennes, Louis's minister in Stockholm, helped Gustavus III to restore the royal authority and thereby to save his country from dismemberment. But the same year had already seen the partition of Poland, another French ally, of which France was no more than a distant and disturbed spectator.

On the other hand the Diplomatic Revolution proved of benefit to Italy, since the two allies no longer contested their claims there, with the result that the peninsula enjoyed peace until the Revolution. But it was otherwise in central and eastern Europe; for, as France receded into the background, Russia and Austria assumed a dominant position, with Prussia at hand as the most powerful military state in Germany. A new and somewhat perverted balance of power, seeking for compensations, no longer in Italy but in Poland and Turkey was substituted for the old, with complications arising from acute differences of religion—Orthodox Greek, Catholic, Protestant and Mahommedan—and of race—Teutonic, Slavonic and Ottoman. The dominant factors included the decadence of Turkey, the chronic anarchy of Poland, the ineffectiveness of French diplomacy, the far-seeing astuteness of Frederick, the obtuse cleverness of Kaunitz and the supreme a-morality of Catherine of Russia.

IV 1763-83. THE FIRST PARTITION OF POLAND.
THE BAVARIAN SUCCESSION WAR

A new era was ushered in by the death in October 1763 of
Augustus III of Saxony, king of Poland. This brought together two ex-enemies, Russia and Prussia, for whom Poland
so long as it retained its *liberum veto*, with its guarantee of
anarchy, was a potential zone of influence. To the north was
Sweden whose king, by the constitution of 1720, was as helpless as his Polish colleague; to the south was Turkey, ener-
vated by a long period of peace and threatened by religious
disaffection in Greece and the Danubian lands. Inevitably
these weaknesses must redound to the advantage of well-armed
and ambitious neighbours. One of Frederick's political
maxims was to ally, if possible, with your most dangerous
neighbour; accordingly, in April 1764, he entered into a
defensive alliance with Catherine II of Russia, an alliance
renewed in 1769. This was the most important of the continental alliances between the end of the Seven Years War and
the French Revolution.

Its first result was the agreement to establish Stanislas
Poniatowski, nominee of Catherine, on the throne of Poland.
Religious differences served to intensify Polish disunion since
the Orthodox Greek minority, persecuted by the Catholics,
naturally looked to Catherine as their protector; while the
Lutherans, suffering from similar disabilities, turned to Frederick. At that time there were three French agents in Warsaw,
two of whom were in the *secret du roi*, making, as Sorel[1]
pointed out, five cabals in all. They were extinguished by the
election of Poniatowski in September 1764. At Constantinople
French diplomacy, led by Vergennes, was less impotent; but
efforts to incite the Porte against Russia and Austria were

[1] In what follows the author has made considerable use of an old
classic, which has not yet been superseded—A. Sorel, *La Quéstion
d'Orient au XVIIIème Siècle*, 4th ed. 1902.

countered by Russian and Austrian agents engaged in stirring up the Christians in Greece, Montenegro and elsewhere against the rule of their Mahommedan overlords. Even these subversive activities Vergennes was able to turn to some account, particularly as they were paralleled by similar enterprises in Poland, and he even prevailed on the Porte to indite a remonstrance against the undermining of Polish independence. So, for a time, Turkey came forward as the advocate of constitutional principles, while in Poland Russian troops massacred Catholics in the name of toleration.

A more concrete result of French diplomacy was the Turkish declaration of war on Russia in October 1768, the beginning of a conflict which lasted until July 1774. Russia was the first to take advantage of this war, for in 1768 she seized Cracow, on the northern frontier of Galicia, a city which at one time had been the capital of Poland. In February 1769 Austria followed suit by taking over the province of Zips, on the Hungarian border, with the excuse that it had once been part of the Hungarian monarchy. Not to be outdone, Frederick ordered researches to be conducted in the Berlin archives for " proofs " of Prussian claims to Polish territories. A more practical measure was his drawing of a *cordon sanitaire* between his territory and Polish Prussia in order to prevent the spread of plague, from which thousands of Russians and Poles perished.

Another event occurring in December 1770 helped still further to clear the way for partition. This was the dismissal of Choiseul. For some time he had been sending large sums to Vergennes in Constantinople in order to bolster up Turkish resistance to Russia; with his removal there disappeared the one European statesman who might have offered resistance to the partition of Poland, for he was the chief obstacle to the entente between Russia and Austria. So the path of the triumvirate—Catherine, Frederick and Joseph—was now more clear.

In the smoothing of that path the Poles themselves gave

their assistance. Persecution united the Catholics in the Confederation of Bar, one of the unions maintaining an almost independent political existence; at the same time (1768) a treaty between Catherine and Poniatowski confirmed the *liberum veto*—a necessary preliminary to partition. But, before this could be effected, there were serious difficulties raised by the Russo-Turkish war. By their capture of Azov and Taganrog the Russians were penetrating to the Black Sea; more serious, by their occupation of Moldavia and Wallachia, they were occupying a substantial part of the lower Danube. Once they crossed to the right bank there was a danger of war with Austria. As the Russian successes continued the situation became more tense, reaching a climax in July 1770, when the Turkish galleys were destroyed at Tchesmé, on the coast of Asia Minor. Frederick now regarded his Russian ally with even greater fear and distrust; Kaunitz, having decided not to take the French alliances of 1756-7 too literally, felt that he had a free hand for an entirely new situation, a situation in which the choice seemed to lie between war and partition. By the beginning of 1771 there was taking shape the idea of some kind of triple alliance between Russia, Prussia and Austria from which two advantages might be expected—the peaceable partition of Poland and removal of the threat of a Russo-Austrian war. The latter object was to be effected by inducing Russia to surrender her conquests of Moldavia and Wallachia in return for a substantial slice of Polish territory. Frederick, now anxious for peace, was consistent in his contention that the partition would obviate a war which, if it broke out, must do infinite damage to Germany. Kaunitz, clever as always, tried to double cross his two associates by negotiating with the Porte, in the hope of obtaining better terms than the proposed partition afforded; but in this he may have been over-ruled by Maria Theresa and Joseph. Russian successes continued in the year 1771 and, for a time, peace among the triumvirate hung on a very delicate balance, particularly as Catherine made it clear that, if she were attacked by

Austria, she would summon her ally Frederick to her aid. Fortunately, however, the Russians did not cross the Danube.

As the danger of a Russo-Austrian war receded, the question of Poland again came into the foreground. England did not favour its partition and withdrew her naval help to Russia after Tchesmé, but she did not interfere. Louis XV was powerless to help either Poland or Turkey, and he had removed the one minister who might have obstructed the partitioners. Catherine was intent on partition as the logical outcome of Russian infiltration and as a means of facilitating access to the west, though her minister Panin was against it, as it entailed too close proximity to Prussia. Frederick wanted to incorporate West (Polish) Prussia in order to consolidate his dominions; Joseph and Kaunitz regarded Galicia as compensation for the loss of Silesia. For Maria Theresa a decision had proved painfully difficult. She still hated Frederick and distrusted Catherine; as a pious Catholic she was dubious about the whole transaction. How she was won over to acquiescence is not quite clear. Frederick stated the question in a letter to D'Alembert : " Catherine and I are brigands, but how did the Empress Queen manage to square her confessor?"[1] The answer may be that the confessors who ministered to the spiritual needs of the Habsburgs were notoriously compliant where matters of high policy were involved; and it was noted that, when the partition actually took place, the dowager empress, in spite of her tears, demanded all that she could expect to obtain. " We have acted in the Prussian manner " she confessed " and at the same time have tried to retain the appearance of honesty . . . We regret the loss of our reputation." For Austria it was peace with dishonour.

The treaties of partition were signed at St. Petersburg on 25 July 1772. Poland surrendered about one third of its territory and nearly one half of its population. The three powers took over territories adjacent to their own dominions, so that Russia obtained a broad strip on her western frontier

[1] Quoted in Sorel, *op. cit.*, p. 232.

comprising what had been formerly known as White Russia; Austria's share consisted mainly of Galicia, on the north-east frontier of Hungary; to Prussia was given Western or Polish Prussia, to the exclusion of Danzig,[1] the smallest of the three in area, but the most valuable strategically, since this joining of West with East Prussia consolidated Frederick's kingdom. This extension of Prussian hegemony to the Vistula and of Austrian to the lower Danube increased the proportion of the Slav element in both states, a fact which may have accentuated their dissociation from the civilisation of Western Europe. The intangible but essential elements of that civilisation had never penetrated deeply into Russia; the rulers of Austria and Prussia, on the other hand, may have been corroded by the partitions, since they had acquired great areas without striking a blow. After all, partition is like blackmail; the first success is bound to be followed by others, and the mere threat of force may achieve results otherwise attainable only by war. Here was the first consequence of the intrusion of power politics. Diplomacy had never been moral; now it was becoming sinister.

An illustration of how precarious was the balance of power in the decade preceding the Revolution was provided by the War of the Bavarian Succession, which brought into conflict two partners of the Polish Partition—Frederick and Joseph. On the death in 1777 of Maximilian Joseph of Bavaria, father-in-law of the Emperor Joseph, the heir—Charles Theodore, Elector Palatine—created an unusual diplomatic situation by expressing his unwillingness to leave Mannheim for the more spacious capital of Munich. To Joseph and Kaunitz this appeared an opportunity for extending Habsburg rule into Bavaria and so creating a great Habsburg *bloc* in central Europe by concessions, if necessary, in the Netherlands. Accordingly, early in January 1778, Charles Theodore agreed to a treaty by which he partitioned Bavaria with the emperor, and Austrian troops took possession. But the dividers of the spoil

[1] In Polish possession since 1577; acquired by Prussia in 1793.

soon found that they had to reckon with Frederick, who now came forward as defender of the balance of power, and guarantor of the Germanic constitution. Maria Theresa was desperately anxious to avoid war, but Joseph and Kaunitz were prepared to go to extremities.

Frederick insisted that, before the proposed partition could take place, the consent of Charles Theodore's heir—the Duke of Zweibrücken—was necessary; and, as the duke refused his assent, here, it appeared, was a cause of war. So two Prussian armies, one under Frederick, the other under his brother Henry, set out to march on Vienna. They were opposed by two Austrian armies, one under Joseph, the other under Loudon; but there was little actual fighting, and the losses were almost all from privation and disease. Meanwhile, Maria Theresa, now supported by Kaunitz, conducted secret negotiations with Frederick, at the same time invoking the mediation of France and Russia, while Joseph demanded military aid from France in terms of the second treaty of Versailles. To this Vergennes replied that the treaty did not cover such an unconstitutional act as Joseph's occupation of Bavaria. As Catherine of Russia refused to intervene, the position of Joseph soon became untenable. Accordingly, he was obliged to give way, and in May 1779 the Peace of Teschen was signed, the main terms of which were that Charles Theodore's renunciation of Bavaria was annulled, and Joseph restored the lands that he had seized, with the exception of a small area of about 200 square miles between the Danube, the Inn and the Salzach. Frederick benefited by the acquisition of Anspach and Baireuth. All this helps to account for the emperor's embittered protest : " the least move and I am suspected of upsetting the balance of power ".

From the military point of view there can be no comparison between the War of the Bavarian Successsion and the War of the American Revolution.[1] But both occurred almost simultaneously, and they provide material for an interesting con-

[1] below, pp. 274-7.

trast. The first was a dynastic contest of the traditional type, intended to prevent the consolidation of Austrian supremacy in central Europe; to contemporaries this threatened consolidation seemed like the revival of an old bogey—the empire of Charles V. The bogey was promptly dispelled by Frederick. The second war, that of the American Revolution, was fought not in land-locked Europe, but in the open spaces of the west where, for perhaps the first time in history, professional soldiers suffered defeat at the hands of amateurs. More important, the first of these wars was fought for causes in which only calculating monarchs were concerned, whereas the second was contested for the vindication of principles vitally important for the future of humanity.[1] For the time being France had surrendered her hegemony of Europe in order to be free for a war of revenge against England which bestrode the world like a Colossus. In alliance with the American colonists she won her war of revenge, thereby gaining laurels in the west which she had sacrificed in the east. Here was the real Diplomatic Revolution of the eighteenth century—this appeal to the New World for restoration of a prestige lost in the Old. But the French have a saying that revenge is a dish *qui se mange froid,* and this association of an ancient monarchy with successful rebels was followed, within a few years, by the era of revolutions, in which the throne of France was the first to be overturned.

[1] above, pp. 72-3.

Chapter VI

THE AUSTRIAN SUCCESSION AND THE SEVEN YEARS WARS

There are three great strategic bands of Europe: the northern, stretching from Belgium through lower Germany to the Vistula; the central, extending from the Rhine through Bavaria and the Danube basin to the Black Sea, and the southern, consisting of the area bounded by the Alps, the Adriatic and the Mediterranean. In the west, these three bands terminate in easy avenues of access into France, a fact evidenced in the Napoleonic Wars. In the southern of these three bands northern Italy, particularly the Milanese and the Po valley, were of importance in the wars of the Polish and the Austrian Succession, as exemplified by the battles of Parma and Guastalla in 1734 and Piacenza in 1746; the battle of Bitonto (near Bari) in 1734 won the two kingdoms of Naples and Sicily for the Spanish Bourbons. In the central band the valley of the Danube provided a battle area in the long struggle between Austrian and Ottoman, in which the former, under Prince Eugène, scored their most brilliant successes at Peterwardein in 1716 and at Belgrade in the following year. Both cities are in the Danube basin.

Of these three strategic areas the most important in this period was the northern, mainly because of the aggressions of Frederick the Great. At the western end Belgium was the scene of victories won for France by the maréchal de Saxe—Fontenoy, (1745), Raucoux, (1746) and Laufeldt, (1747). These were the most important of French successes in the War of the Austrian Succession. Belgium has always been ideal for military operations because of its contiguity to great states and because transport was facilitated by road, canals and rivers; there was also abundance of food and fodder. To the east of Belgium, Westphalia and the territory between Rhine and Weser were vital for the defence of Hanover, especially after the French victory over the Anglo-Hanoverians at Hastenbeck in southern Hanover (1757); two years later Hanover was saved by the victory of Ferdinand of Brunswick at Minden. Farther east, the Prussian district of Neumark was the scene of the indecisive battle of Zorndorf in 1758—the most fiercely contested battle of the Seven Years War. Most important of all was Saxony, which might be described as the centre of central Europe, crossed by routes leading to all parts of Germany. Dresden, its capital, commanding the passage of the Elbe at the point where it descends from the mountains, was occupied by Frederick in December 1745, on his successful conclusion of the second Silesian War; near by was the fortress of Pirna, where the Prussian king received the Saxon surrender in October 1756. Control of Saxony was vital to Frederick for two reasons—because its northern frontier is only a few miles south of Berlin, and because it provided entry into Bohemia and Austria. Invaded in the Austrian Succession War and devastated in the Seven Years War, Saxony was the scene of the most important campaigns and battles of the century, a rôle which it had already played in the Thirty Years War and was again to play in the Napoleonic Wars. It was at Rossbach, between Naumburg and Merseburg, that Frederick won his great victory over the French in 1757, a victory commemorated by the erection of a triumphal column, afterwards destroyed by Napoleon. Farther east, Silesia was the site of some of Frederick's victories over the Austrians in two successive wars—Mollwitz, 1741, Leuthen, 1757 and Liegnitz, 1760. In mountainous Bohemia the Prussian king was not always so fortunate. He failed at the siege of Prague in 1757, and his defeat at Kollin in the same year obliged him to evacuate Bohemia. The ruler of Prussia was so situated that he had a convenient front door for access to Saxony and Silesia, but he was justifiably apprehensive about his back door—East Prussia—through which the Russians could penetrate into Germany.

I ARMIES AND NAVIES

Such were the main geographical factors influencing the conduct of war. As regards the human factor, there was no great advance in military science during this period.[1] The size of armies had already been greatly increased in the reign of Louis XIV, an increase maintained, at an uneven pace, in the eighteenth century, and most marked in the Prussian and Russian armies. In 1713 the Prussian forces numbered about 38,000 men; in 1786 about 200,000; during this period the number of Russian troops advanced from about 130,000 to over 450,000. France put over 200,000 men in the field in the Seven Years War, of whom 150,000, under Soubise, crossed the Rhine in 1757 to join with the Imperialist, Swedish and Russian troops, making a total of 400,000 men, against whom Frederick had little more than 150,000. Some military leaders criticised the use of such large armies on the ground that they were difficult to manœuvre, a difficulty increased by the fact that they were not arranged in divisions.

How were such large bodies of men brought together? They were recruited in a variety of ways, from voluntary enlistment to kidnapping, such as was extensively practised by Frederick's emissaries in various parts of Europe; moreover, troops in conquered territory, such as Saxony, were forced into the Prussian ranks. Deserters from the enemy provided an-

[1] For a good account of this subject see chapter viii of *The New Cambridge Modern History* (1957), by Eric Robson. For naval history, reference should be made to the works of Sir Julian Corbett and Admiral Sir Herbert Richmond.

other source of supply. After the middle years of the century a greater degree of compulsion was used in obtaining recruits, but there was no systematic conscription in the modern sense, for it was held that all who contribute to the prosperity or well-being of the state should be exempt, and that service should be imposed only on those with whose lives the state might well dispense. Of all the armies of the period only that of Russia could, in any sense, be described as national, for it consisted of Russians drafted into the forces by a definite state system. In effect therefore the ordinary soldiers were collected mainly from the criminals, vagabonds and ne'er-do-wells, misfits of all nationalities, fighting not for a cause, but for their daily bread. In peace time, as in war, one of the main concerns of the officer was to prevent his men from deserting; but in spite of heavy penalties the losses from this source were very high. More men died from disease, especially typhus and malaria, than from wounds.

By contrast the officers were drawn mainly from the nobility, except in specialised or semi-civilian branches such as the artillery, in which the middle classes predominated. Officers alone, in the eyes of contemporaries, had the monopoly of honour; the only virtue demanded of their subordinates was that of obedience. In England commissions under a certain rank could be bought and sold; in most countries a regiment was regarded almost as the property of the colonel, who arranged for the men's clothing and equipment, on which he usually drew a commission. In France the system was reformed to some extent by Choiseul, who was minister of war and marine after 1758, for he brought the regiments more directly under the control of the state. But he did not succeed in altering greatly the unduly high proportion of officers to men—about one in fifteen—the highest of all in European armies. This proved a serious impediment to French military success because, even in war time, the officers were accompanied by servants and hangers-on, all of them accompanied by baggage, so heavy as to be a serious encumbrance.

There was little change in military weapons in this period. The rifle, which was lighter to carry and easier to load, was already displacing the musket; in 1740 a ramrod of iron displaced the old wooden rod, and facilitated the process of loading. The speed of fire—one shot per minute at the beginning of the century—was steadily improved to three shots per minute; the bayonet, *l'arme blanche,* was in almost universal use. For long the artillery had been a separate establishment; but, after the War of the Austrian Succession its importance was more clearly recognised, and the reforming Choiseul linked it with the conventional forces. In the Prussian armies this reform had made such headway that a battalion became a " moving battery ", and Frederick even introduced portable cannon, of from three to twenty-four pounds' weight. The artillery duel tended to take the place of the old hand-to-hand fighting.

Tactics were still conducted on conventional principles and the order of battle was not unlike that of the parade ground. When action was joined the infantry was arranged in long parallel lines, usually three in depth, so disposed as to promote rapid rifle fire. The danger of this formation was that the flanks might be turned; accordingly, in choosing their position, commanders tried to rest the flanks on some natural obstacle, such as a cliff or stream. An alternative to this, tried several times with success by Frederick, was the oblique order in which the aim was to destroy one flank of the enemy before the main body could get into action. This method was successfully applied by Frederick at Leuthen in 1757, Zorndorf in 1758 and at Torgau in 1760, but it failed at Künersdorf in 1759. Generally, there were two schools of thought, one favouring the *ordre mince,* or thin battle line; the other preferring the *ordre profonde,* in which a dense mass of troops depended on weight and speed for the momentum required to break the enemy line. But, as far as possible, actual combat was avoided by eighteenth-century commanders, even Frederick describing a battle as a disagreeable emetic, to be resorted to only in emergencies. In his earlier days, the Prussian leader had depended on speed and dash in order to keep the enemy on the move, preferably in territory outside Prussia; but, in later years, he became more cautious. There were other limitations on warfare. Campaigns could normally be conducted only in the summer months, and never far from supply bases, sieges were more common than battles and were conducted with elaborate ceremony, nor were armies inspired by the religious fanaticism of earlier or the nationalist fanaticism of later periods. War was more leisurely and more gentlemanly. By judicious marching and counter-marching combat could be avoided altogether. But not always. The prince of Hildburghausen, commander-in-chief of the combined French and Imperialist armies, was an old and quarrelsome Saxon, who seldom got up before noon. His main concern was to assert his superiority over Soubise, the French leader. He acted on the simple principle of advancing when the Prussians withdrew, and turning to the right-about when they advanced. Not surprisingly, he was soundly defeated by Frederick at Rossbach, in 1757.

In these circumstances it is understandable that the military profession was regarded with disfavour. Voltaire and Turgot despised it; Rousseau preferred citizen armies. One great general, Marshal Saxe, advocated compulsory military service; a German patriot J. J. Moser made a similar recommendation in 1770. The Physiocrats,[1] unimpressed by military glory, emphasised how, in modern conditions, success in war is dependent not only on leadership, but on the economic resources at the disposal of the combatants. In this respect France, with its large population and great potentialities of wealth, appeared to enjoy the most favoured position, but she was easily outdistanced by England, where facilities for government credit existed and where an expanding overseas trade could be maintained, even in war time, by powerful fleets. In contrast, Frederick the Great, unable to conduct his

[1] above, pp. 96-7.

wars on Prussian resources alone, had to supplement these by subsidies and loans—not always repaid—as well as by ruthlesss exploitation of conquered territories.

Like all great wars the War of the Austrian Succession and the Seven Years War brought about a quickening in the tempo of national life. Innumerable industries benefited by the demand for clothing and all kinds of equipment; the engineers were stimulated to devise new methods of building roads, bridges, reservoirs; for convenience of transport rivers had to be made more navigable. Demands such as these led to the setting up of military and technical academies; expert training now supplemented the inborn valour of the aristocratic officer class. All this was linked with the development of administrative machinery for handling the many problems that arose behind the lines—the settlement of conquered provinces, exchange of prisoners, handling of refugees, schemes of afforestation for supplying the shipyards with timber, the construction of great arsenals for national supplies of armaments and munitions. Arrangements had also to be made for accommodating the sick and wounded in houses near the battlefields, as there were no organised medical services other than those provided by the surgeons, and the civilian hospitals were either non-existent or unable to cope with the demands arising after a battle. In consequence, many of the wounded were left where they fell, often to be robbed and murdered. All these difficulties, however inadequately surmounted, and however unspectacular they may appear, provided training for administrative departments and personnel.

Warfare at sea had some close parallels with that on land. In both there was the same unwillingness to engage in combat and the same hesitation in following up a success. Indeed this conservatism was even stronger at sea than on land, for warships of the line were sometimes large vessels of as much as 2,000 tons, having crews of about 1,000 men, both of them difficult and expensive to replace. Already, in the late seventeenth century, Admiral Torrington had popularised the conception of "the fleet in being" as a justification for refusing to engage the enemy unless assured of his own superiority in force, and the court martial of Admiral Mathews in 1747 for his failure to destroy the French ships escaping from Toulon served to inhibit the initiative of English naval commanders who, moreover, were held, as in a straitjacket, by the official Admiralty Instructions. These had been formulated by Admiral Rooke (1650-1709). Obtaining the weather gage (i.e. the windward position) and maintaining unbroken line of combat—these were the cardinal maxims of English tactics; it was in defiance of these maxims that Rodney, breaking through the enemy line, won his victory at The Saints[1] in 1782. His failure to follow up his advantage (for which he was criticised) can be attributed to the imperfect signalling arrangements of the time. So too with other naval successes of this period; for example, the British triumphs at Lagos and Quiberon Bay in 1759 were chase actions, not line actions. It is not surprising that two of the decisive defeats of the century—that of the Spaniards at Cape Passaro in 1718 and that of the Turkish galleys at Tchesmé[2] in 1770—were between fleets unevenly matched.

By contrast, French tactics were less circumscribed than the English. Except in confined waters, French commanders usually preferred the leeward position, as they could more easily break off combat and escape with a following wind. Their aim was to disable the enemy ships by firing at the rigging, for the hulls of English oak were not easily penetrated. Nor were the French fleets bound by rigid orders. They avoided actual combat as much as possible, because their strength lay in the *guerre de course* and in privateering—attacks on British merchantmen by fast cruisers. This had been France's main policy ever since her defeat at La Hogue in 1692, just as, in the war of 1914-18, Germany concentrated on submarine warfare after the indecisive battle of Jutland. In both cases British losses were heavy, because so many targets were provided; moreover,

[1] A passage off Dominica.   [2] On the coast of Asia Minor.

unlike France, which was largely self supporting, England was dependent for survival on her sea-borne trade. It should be added that the French excelled in naval architecture, and designed ships that could be described as streamlined; indeed they served as models for English builders when they were captured. The French were also more advanced than the English in their recognition of the need for training officers in hydrography and seamanship.

The dominant factor in the naval wars of this period was the supremacy of the British Navy, and this in spite of periods of neglect, such as occurred in the régime of Walpole. Much of this superiority was due to Admiral Anson (1697-1762), whose return to England in 1744, after his great voyage round the world, was followed by a number of reforms in which he took the initiative. Naval officers were provided with a distinctive uniform; more latitude was allowed in the interpretation of Admiralty Instructions; the rating of ships was standardised, and their stability was improved by lowering the centre of gravity without lowering the centre of buoyancy. Consequently, English ships were more "stiff" in a breeze, and their ports on the lee side were less likely to be submerged—an important asset when a squadron was to windward of the enemy. Generally, the British Navy could face the combined navies of France and Spain with some hope of success, a fact which prompted many Englishmen to maintain that Britain should avoid continental warfare, and limit herself to attacks on enemy shipping and protection of her sea routes and colonies.

For the recruitment of sailors there was a greater degree of compulsion than in the recruitment of soldiers. In the French maritime districts the sea-faring population was registered in classes on the general principle that, while one class was free to serve in the mercantile marine, another was drafted into the navy. But in war time this system of registration usually broke down; so urgent was the demand for manning the ships that all the sea-faring population had to be pressed into service, and

even landsmen were forced aboard ship. In England th
system of pressing was notorious. Incoming merchant ship
were deprived of their crews by the press gang and crowde
into hulks before despatch to the fleet, where they had to serv
for long periods on inadequate pay and wretched food. Sho
leave was usually forbidden because it would have led
wholesale desertion; cramped in inadequate accommodatio
between decks the sailors, especially on long voyages, wer
decimated by disease and privation. Things were worst o
the West India station, where England maintained permaner
establishments at Jamaica and Antigua, for there the climat
the rum and the unsuitable food reaped a heavy toll. Tho
sailors who managed to survive a long period of service wer
usually ruined in health. Not until after the Mutiny of th
Nore (1797) was any improvement effected in the lot
England's seafaring men.

Considering the many thousands of men who were engage
on active service in this period, it is a matter for regret ho
few of them recorded their experiences. There were plenty
manuals of strategy and tactics; Frederick the Great wro
voluminously on military operations; but, so far as the ordina
soldier and seaman were concerned, there is an almost co
plete silence. Diaries may have been kept, but they have n
been forthcoming. Consequently, there is a certain unreali
and even aridity about the records of pre-Napoleonic wars, n
dispelled by the turgidity of Thomas Carlyle. But an exce
tion must be made in favour of Tobias Smollett (1721-177
who, as a young man, served as a ship's surgeon in Vernon
combined operations against Carthagena in the spring of 174
In his *Roderick Random* (1748) he recorded a graphic a
authentic account[1] of the bombardment of Bocca Chica;
well as this he described, from his own recollections, the di
ficulties and tragedies confronting the surgeon on board a sh
engaged in combat. Although he does not appear to have ha
personal experience of land fighting, Smollett's account of th

[1] *Roderick Random*, chs. xxxii and xxxiii.

vicissitudes of military life in his *Adventures of Count Fathom* (1753) has the same ring of verisimilitude that one appreciates in Defoe, even when he is describing something of which he had no personal experience. Otherwise it may be said of the great wars of the eighteenth century that, in regard to the human element, they are among the eloquent silences of history.

II THE WAR OF THE AUSTRIAN SUCCESSION

The War of the Austrian Succession was one of enemies not always willing to engage in combat and of allies who were usually at cross purposes. It included four struggles which sometimes overlapped—the maritime contest between England and Spain; the war between Frederick and Maria Theresa for the possession of Silesia; the hostilities conducted in Europe, north America and India by England and France, including the Jacobite rising of 1745; and, lastly, the attempts of Charles Emanuel of Sardinia to obtain territorial gains in northern Italy with Spanish help. In few wars have there been so many misunderstandings and resentments. England, willing to assist Maria Theresa by subsidies and moderate military activity, pressed her to yield to Frederick's demands; having got what he wanted, Frederick had no further use for his French allies while Britain, intent on defeating France, was irritated by George II's immobilisation of an army for the defence of Hanover; France, led by such warlike spirits as Belle Isle, was divided between two ambitions—to humble Austria, no longer a serious enemy, and to humble England, whose strength was not yet realised. This incertitude extended to all the participants. The Dutch, still anxious to maintain neutrality, provided inadequate support for the Anglo-Austrian armies; Russia, having completed a successful war against Sweden, remained in the background as a potential ally of Austria and enemy of Prussia; Charles Emanuel, having got Franco-Spanish troops into Italy, was always on the verge of going over to an Austrian alliance. In all this medley of confused ambitions the only figure cast in a mould that could be described as heroic was Maria Theresa, who emerged from the war stronger than at the commencement of hostilities.

Of the military leaders the most active (in addition to Frederick) were the maréchal Belle Isle and the maréchal Maurice de Saxe, the latter an illegitimate brother of the Elector of Saxony. Of the diplomats the most energetic was John Carteret, afterwards Earl Granville, who had distinguished himself by his part in the pacification of the northern powers (1719-1720) and was a secretary of state from 1742 to 1744; his strenuous support of George II's Hanoverian policy brought him trouble from his colleagues. Among the areas invaded were Bohemia, of which Maria Theresa was Queen; Bavaria, ruled by Charles Albert who was emperor[1] in the years 1742-1745; Saxony, whose Elector Augustus II, king of Poland, declared first for France and then for Austria; the Milanese, Savoy and Provence where Franco-Spanish troops fought on behalf of Charles Emanuel against the Austrians.

Prolonged negotiations having failed to settle the rival claims of England and Spain for depredations committed in the West Indies, war was declared between the two nations in October 1739. But for the peace efforts of Fleury, France might have become involved because of her commitments in the Atlantic trade, but it was not until 1744 that she declared war on England. With instructions to destroy the Spanish settlements in the West Indies Admiral Vernon captured Portobello in November 1739, and in the spring of the next year he laid siege to Carthagena. A landing was effected under Wentworth; but acrimonious disputes between general and admiral ruined the enterprise, and the expeditionary force had to be withdrawn. There was a similar failure at Cuba. More successful was Anson's circumnavigation of the globe, in the course of which he caused a diversion of Spanish naval

[1] The empire was vacant in the years 1740-2.

forces and captured the Acapulco galleon with its load of
Mexican silver *en route* for Manila. Thereafter English naval
activity in the West was limited to attacks on Spanish shipping
and dislocation of enemy trade, to the great advantage of the
smugglers, who used the Dutch West Indian islands as their
bases. After 1744 the naval contest was mainly one between
France and Britain, having for its object the crippling of the
prosperous French sugar trade of the Antilles. For this purpose the permanent English bases at Jamaica and Antigua
proved of great value.

The war might well have been limited to this naval contest
involving only England, France and Spain but for the intervention of Europe's chief trouble maker—Frederick of Prussia.
The rich province of Silesia lay close at hand, linked with the
Prussian port of Stettin by the Oder; its wealth in minerals
and textiles would greatly add to the resources of Prussia; and
its population, as it included a large proportion of Protestants,
was likely to welcome release from Habsburg oppression.
Frederick's invasion of Silesia in December 1740 was followed
by his triumphal entry into Breslau, the capital, where he
issued a proclamation announcing that he had taken this step
so that it should not be taken by another. This was no more
than a subterfuge. Meanwhile Britain announced that she
would assist Maria Theresa with a subsidy and 12,000 men,
but only as an auxiliary; Fleury adopted a similar reserve, for
he brought in France only as an auxiliary of Charles Albert of
Bavaria, promising to support both his candidature for the
imperial crown and his ambition to acquire sufficient Austrian
territory for the support of the imperial dignity. Then came
Frederick's victory over the Austrians at Mollwitz (April
1741), a victory which encouraged Belle Isle and the war
party in France to demand a more vigorous French policy, such
as was foreshadowed by a Franco-Prussian treaty signed in
June. This alliance was an uneasy one, for Frederick, who
wanted the French to strike at Vienna, was soon disgusted by
the dilatoriness of the French commander, the Duc de Broglie.

Nevertheless a Franco-Bavarian-Saxon army invaded Bohemia and took Prague. Another success for the opponents of Maria Theresa followed in June 1742 when, mainly by French bribery and threats, Charles Albert was elected emperor. Meanwhile Maria Theresa had not been idle. Her forces, augmented by Hungarian cavalry, expelled the French and Bavarians from Upper Austria, and then invaded Bavaria where they captured Munich, the capital of the newly-elected emperor.

Elated perhaps by these successes, Maria Theresa now hoped that her English auxiliary would co-operate with the Dutch in more vigorous action against the French. But King George, to the disgust of his subjects and ministers, persisted in immobilising a large force in Hanover, and the Dutch never even declared war on France. Unaware of the difficulties confronting English and Dutch policy, Maria Theresa now decided to dispose of one enemy before dealing with the other; and so, in June 1742, she consented to the Preliminaries of Breslau whereby Frederick was confirmed in possession of the greater part of Silesia. The Austrian Archduchess regarded this as no more than a temporary expedient. Thus ended what has been called the First Silesian War; thereupon Frederick promptly deserted his French and Bavarian allies. France's main concern was now to extricate the armies of Belle Isle and de Broglie from their perilous position in Bohemia. At the same time, Augustus of Saxony, having defected from the French, was added to the allies of Maria Theresa.

Already she had secured another ally of equally slender resources and equally slender fidelity. This was Charles Emanuel of Sardinia, who promised his support in return for the cession of the Milanese which, like that of Silesia to Frederick, was regarded by Maria Theresa as no more than a temporary concession, extorted from her mainly by English diplomatic pressure. Nor was the king of Sardinia the only candidate for Italian territory at the expense of Austria. Elizabeth Farnese, bellicose as ever, had communicated something of her enthusiasm to her lethargic spouse, whose younger son Don Philip had still to be provided for. So the imperialist territories of Parma and Piacenza were again demanded on his behalf. Nor was his elder brother Don Carlos, king of the Two Sicilies since 1735, prepared to remain quiescent, for he expressed willingness to join the Spanish forces in northern Italy against the Austrians. But, as in 1718, the trouble makers had reckoned without the British fleet. In 1742 the appearance of an English squadron before Naples had induced Charles to adopt a more conciliatory attitude, and British command of the Mediterranean made it impossible for Spain to send troops to Italy by sea. So the position in the peninsula became, for the time, one of deadlock, and Germany remained the scene of European warfare.

British military intervention did not take place until the summer of 1743, when a mixed army of English, Austrians and Hanoverians was formed in the Netherlands under the command of George II. This was the "Pragmatic Army". Advancing into Germany, this force defeated the French at Dettingen on the Main in June. The Pragmatic Army was strengthened by a Dutch contingent; and, as the Austrians had advanced into Bavaria, it seemed that now was the time for an invasion of France. But Britain had not yet declared war on France; nor could she rely on Dutch support, so the project had to be abandoned. English diplomatic pressure was still applied in order to induce Maria Theresa to make concessions, and in September 1743 Britain, Austria and Sardinia joined in the treaty of Worms, in accordance with which Italy was to be partitioned—Naples was to go to Maria Theresa; and Sicily, with part of the Milanese and Piacenza, to Charles Emanuel. The signatories guaranteed the Pragmatic Sanction, but made no mention of Silesia. The reply to the treaty of Worms was a Franco-Spanish agreement of October 1743 whereby Louis undertook to aid Philip V in the conquest of Gibraltar, with a promise of Parma, Piacenza and Lombardy for Don Philip. In this way the quarrels of a generation before were grafted on to a war which, at times, seemed no more than a sweeping up of petty rivalries and ambitions, set in the foreground against the determination of Prussia to retain Silesia and of Britain to assert her maritime supremacy over both France and Spain.

Thus far, the War of the Austrian Succession had been marked by no spectacular achievement other than the occupation of Silesia; there had been much negotiation, but the leading powers had not yet come into the open. The only rulers who really knew their own minds were women—Maria Theresa, determined to recover Silesia and, if possible, to add Bavaria to the Austrian dominions, and Elizabeth Farnese anxious, as always, to extend the Spanish-Bourbon possessions in Italy. But, in the early months of 1744, events took a more serious turn. The Jacobites were again on the move, this time on behalf of the young Charles Edward, the " Young Pretender ", and an expedition under the command of Saxe was despatched from Dunkirk in order to make a landing in Scotland, but a storm drove it back. Meanwhile, in February the combined Franco-Spanish fleet, having emerged from Toulon, was engaged in an indecisive action by Admiral Mathews and managed to escape, with the result that for a time there was a danger of invasion of the south coast of England. These events encouraged Louis XV to declare war on Britain in March 1744 and on Austria in the following month. Meanwhile Frederick was again on the war path. Disturbed by the successes of the Austrian troops in Bavaria and anxious about the future of Silesia, he entered into the Union of Frankfort in May 1744 with France, the Emperor Charles VII and a number of German princes with the nominal objects of restoring Bavaria and establishing the new emperor. In the following month Louis arranged with his allies that he would invade Belgium and the emperor undertook to hand over Bohemia to Frederick as soon as he (Frederick) had conquered it. Such were the preliminaries to what has been called the Second Silesian War.

Invading Saxony and Bohemia, Frederick set out for Prague in August, but a formidable mass of Austrian and Saxon troops was concentrated against him, and his projected conquest of Bohemia ended in failure. He had received little or no support from his French allies, who now deserted him as he had deserted them in 1742. The death of the Emperor Charles VII on January 20, 1745, removed one of Maria Theresa's most serious enemies and paved the way for the election of her husband Francis Stephen of Lorraine to the imperial throne, but meanwhile her cause suffered serious reverses in the Netherlands, which were invaded by Saxe. His brilliant victories over the Austrian, British and Dutch troops at Fontenoy (1745), Raucoux (1746) and Laufeldt (1747) were accompanied by an occupation distinguished by the absence of atrocities. Nor did French success end with the occupation of Belgium for, in 1748, Saxe invaded the United Provinces, capturing Bergen-op-Zoom and Maestricht, thus creating a situation not unlike that of 1672, when Louis XIV had poured his troops into Holland. The reaction of the Dutch in both instances was similar, namely, to strengthen the hands of the Orange dynasty against its republican opponents. So William IV became stadholder of all seven provinces, with greatly enlarged powers, but the danger to the Dutch was averted in 1748 by the end of hostilities.

The conquest of the Netherlands and the capture of Madras were the only successes achieved by France in the War of the Austrian Succession. Elsewhere, in Britain, in Canada and in nothern Italy she suffered serious reverses which, at the peace settlement, were weighed against her success in Belgium and India. In the summer of 1745 England was menaced by the landing of Prince Charles Stuart in the west Highlands, followed by a march into England which penetrated as far as Derby, causing the government to withdraw troops from the continent. This was followed by the Convention of Hanover in August whereby George, abandoning the cause of Maria Theresa, guaranteed the maintenance of Frederick in Silesia.

But the Jacobite threat was short-lived, for Prince Charles was supported by only a handful of rebels in England, and his retreat to the north was ended by the utter defeat of the clans at Culloden in April 1746. Meanwhile, Maria Theresa, deprived of English military support, was relieved by the absence of French troops from Germany, and so had now to deal only with Frederick; but that wily monarch, by a series of brilliant victories over the Austrians in the summer and autumn of 1745, culminating in an invasion of Saxony, obliged Maria to agree to the treaty of Dresden in December, a treaty which secured Silesia to the Prussian king. She was obliged to make this concession not only by the defeats of her own armies, but by the successes of her Franco-Spanish-Sardinian enemies in northern Italy.

In June 1745 France suffered a great loss by the capture of the Canadian fortress of Louisburg, controlling the entrance to the St. Lawrence, a capture effected by troops from New England, assisted by a British squadron. This was the first occasion when colonial troops achieved a distinct success on behalf of the mother country against the French enemy. Two years later France experienced defeats at sea, when Anson fought two actions off Finisterre, scattering the armed escorts of convoys, one bound for Quebec, two others for the East and West Indies. In India, on the other hand, the French had better fortune. At first it was thought that the sub-continent would be excepted from the Anglo-French war, but events proved otherwise. Both powers had settlements and factories in India under the direction of their East India Companies, the chief English settlements being at Calcutta, Madras and Bombay, while the French were in occupation at Surat, Pondicherry, Masulipatam and other stations on the eastern coast. The arrival of a British fleet in the Indian Ocean dispelled any hopes that these settlements would be excluded from the scope of hostilities; whereupon Dupleix, commander of the French forces in India, summoned to his aid La Bourdonnais, supreme commander of France's eastern empire. This was folowed by a period of inactivity on the part of the English eet which enabled the French to capture Madras in September 746. English naval reinforcements arrived too late to reverse his loss, which offset the British capture of Louisburg in the revious year. Not until the Seven Years War was French ominion in India seriously contested.

The War of the Austrian Succession had thus proved to be series of separate contests, never co-ordinated with each ther, and all pursued with varying degrees of success or ailure. By the spring of 1748 it was clear that operations in Europe, in the West Indies, in Canada and in India had reached stalemate. Frederick of Prussia had retired altogether from the contest; neither England nor France had achieved anything in Germany, though France had occupied the Netherlands; Maria Theresa, who had more than held her own, had not won back Silesia, nor had she made any headway in northern Italy against the Franco-Spanish armies. In such circumstances it was very difficult to make any balance sheet of losses and gains, but some such attempt was made by the peace of Aix-la-Chapelle (October 1748). This settlement, or rather truce, was based on the principle of return to the *status quo*. Britain, to the disgust of the New Englanders, restored Louisburg in exchange for Madras; Charles Emanuel received a part of the Milanese, and Don Philip was established in Parma and Piacenza. At long last Elizabeth Farnese was satisfied; both her sons had now been provided for. The real struggle—that between England and France—was merely deferred.

III THE SEVEN YEARS WAR

The eight years between the peace of Aix-la-Chapelle and the outbreak of the Seven Years War were years of undeclared war between England and France in North America and in India. In both areas the English had a better strategic position and more resources in men and money at their disposal, for the French colonists in Canada did not number more than about 60,000, as contrasted with the two million settlers in the thirteen American colonies. French colonial ambitions in the west were dependent on linking the St. Lawrence with the Mississippi through an ill-defined area south of the Great Lakes. Accordingly, under their governor Duquesne, they began a systematic penetration of the Upper Ohio region intended ultimately to link Montreal with New Orleans; Fort Duquesne was built in 1753, and there began a series of skirmishes between the French expansionists and the English colonists, the latter aided by small contingents from England. In 1754 the young George Washington had to retreat from one of these border forays. There were also seizures of ships in the St. Lawrence. The climax came in June 1755 when Boscawen attacked a convoy taking supplies to Canada; he captured two French warships. Similar conditions of " cold war " prevailed in India where, with the help of the ports of Calcutta and Bombay, the wealthier English company was maintaining superiority over her rival. War was declared between England and France in May 1756, and was followed within two months by the English loss of Minorca and Calcutta.

Between the extremities of east and west are the Straits of Dover, on the control of which the security of the first British Empire depended. To England it seemed vital that no great foreign power should have bases east of the Straits. Hence British insistence on the dismantling of Dunkirk; hence the old alliance with the Dutch; hence also the demand that the emperor should not develop the maritime resources of Belgium. But the French persisted in rebuilding Dunkirk; the Dutch allowed the barrier fortresses to fall into decay, and made it clear that they would not come to the help of England unless she could prove that she was not the aggressor. As for Belgium, that province had been occupied by the French in the years 1744-8, and might easily again be occupied. The restoration of Louisburg to the French in 1748 may be regarded not

aly as the equivalent for the restoration of Madras but as the
rice paid by England for removal of the threat that Antwerp
ad the Texel would become sites of French naval bases.
here was also Hanover; on its security ultimately depended
ae defence of the seaboard from Holland to Denmark. As for
liances, Sweden and Denmark were more likely to declare
ar France than for Britain; Russia might well adhere to her
ustrian alliance; as for Spain, the accession of Charles III
(formerly Don Carlos) to the Spanish throne in 1759 was
ollowed by a family compact with France which led to hosti-
ties against England in 1762. Hence the strategy[1] of the
even Years War was world-wide; events in the colonies were
aterlocked with events in continental Europe, and successes in
ne area might have to be offset against losses in another.
ortunately, in the elder Pitt Britain possessed a statesman
apable of thinking in global terms, having the intuition for
electing the right leaders, irrespective of seniority or family
onnection; endowed with sufficient imagination to realise the
ast potentialities of the empire and determination to use all
ae resources of sea power, even at the risk of offending
eutrals. It was an accident of fate that in Frederick of
russia Pitt had the one continental ally capable, by his mili-
ary genius, of inflicting defeat on the French.

In these circumstances Britain and France might well have
mited themselves to the maritime and colonial struggle thus
voiding continental entanglements; indeed, this was the
olicy advocated for England by the " blue water " school, a
olicy supported by Pitt himself when in opposition. As
ritain had never been a considerable military power, the de-
ision to intervene in the continental campaigns with only
Frederick as an ally was a gamble that ought to have failed, for
t involved conflict with the armies of France, Austria and
Russia, the three greatest military nations in the world. In-
vitably, the brunt of the fighting had to be borne by Freder-

[1] For this see Sir Julian S. Corbett, *England in the Seven Years
War*, I, pp. 18 ff.

ick who, but for the death of the Tsarina Elizabeth in January 1762, might well have been obliged to give up the struggle. The British cause was helped by another able leader—Ferdinand of Brunswick, who succeeded the incompetent Duke of Cumberland as commander of the combined British and Hanoverian forces. But the success of Pitt's continental gamble can be attributed as much to the weakness of his enemies as to the genius of his ally. The Austrian generals were often dilatory and seldom followed up their successes; the Russian impetus was steadily weakened by knowledge that the death of the Tsarina Elizabeth would be followed by a reversal of policy; the French armies were led by generals whose incompetence was notorious, even in that age.

Events were precipitated by Frederick's invasion of Saxony late in August 1756. As usual, he could quote justification for his action—he was obviating an attack from Russia and Austria by anticipating it; "proofs" would be found in the Dresden archives. Events then moved rapidly. Dresden was captured; Pirna was besieged; in October the Saxon army capitulated and was incorporated among Frederick's troops. In May 1757 the second treaty of Versailles united France and Austria against Prussia, and at the same time an offensive alliance was signed between Austria and Russia. The Emperor Francis Stephen imposed the Ban of Empire on Frederick; and Ferdinand of Brunswick, commanding British and Hanoverian troops, took up position in Westphalia, which was threatened by a French army of 100,000 men under the Maréchal d'Estrées. By the summer of 1757 the situation in east and west Germany had become critical, for the Russians invaded East Prussia; and the Duke of Cumberland, in command of the army for the defence of Hanover, was obliged, after his defeat by d'Estrées at Hastenbeck, to sign the Capitulation of Klosterseven (September). Frederick had now to face assaults from the Russians in the east, the Austrians in the south, the Swedes in the north and the French in the west. As he could deal only with one enemy at a time his armies, diminishing with each year of hostilities, were kept continually on the march from the Oder to the Elbe and from the Elbe to the Weser. Badly defeated by Daun at Kollin in Bohemia (June) Frederick was kept going by three things, an English subsidy, reduction of pressure on him by Pitt's policy of raids on the French coast, resulting in withdrawal of enemy troops from Germany and, thirdly, the presence in Westphalia of Ferdinand of Brunswick's army. Even thus, his position throughout a great part of 1757 was desperate until relieved by his great success at Rossback in November. This was followed a month later by his victory over Daun and the Austrians at Leuthen. These successes drove the Austrians from Saxony and Silesia.

But the odds were still heavily against the Prussian king. His enemies greatly outnumbered him; his scattered territories were difficult to defend; his armies, never more than about 150,000 men, were being constantly thinned by casualties, disease and desertion. Even his victories, as in August 1758 over the Russians at Zorndorf, did little to relieve the situation, for in that year the Swedes invaded Prussian Pomerania, and in Saxony he was defeated by the Austrians at Hochkirch (October). What Frederick dreaded most of all was a junction of the Austrian and Russian armies. This was effected in the summer of 1759, the Austrians under Loudon (their best general) and the Russians under Saltikov, with the result that, greatly outnumbered, Frederick was completely defeated at the battle of Künersdorf, near Frankfort-on-the-Oder (August 1759). Next month the Austrians recaptured Dresden. But these victories were not followed up, and Prussia was saved from annihilation by the dilatoriness of the Austrians and the increasing concern of the Russians about what was taking place in St. Petersburg. This uncertainty may account for the withdrawal of Russian troops into Poland.

Nevertheless there were certain less tangible things operating in Frederick's favour. One of these was his refusal to accept defeat. " I have been saved by despair and self esteem ", he afterwards wrote; " by the fact that I would rather see my kingdom in ruins than yield. My obstinacy has plagued the world ".[1]

Meanwhile in 1757 the Newcastle-Pitt administration had been formed in which Pitt, as secretary of state, was the leading spirit. He was ably assisted by subordinates and colleagues. Through his brother-in-law Temple he had practical control of the Admiralty, and there he had the help of Anson,[2] who was First Lord from 1757 until his death in 1762. Anson's reforms in naval administration and in the dockyards were such that he has been called the Father of the Navy. Refusing, on Newcastle's solicitation, to make political appointments, he secured the devoted loyalty of such admirals as Rodney, Howe, Hawke and Boscawen. For the army similar services were performed by the Huguenot Lord Ligonier,[2] a veteran of the Spanish Succession and the Austrian Succession Wars, who acted as commander-in-chief in England. These two, Anson and Ligonier, co-operated as informal chiefs of staff. Pitt provided the mainspring of the ministry, communicating to it something of his energy and determination. The capitulation of Klosterseven was repudiated; a large subsidy was paid to Frederick, and the army of Ferdinand of Brunswick for the defence of Hanover was strengthened. In 1758 Louisburg was again captured; Fort Duquesne was taken and re-named Pittsburg. The following year (1759) proved to be " the year of victories ". In August the French fleet was defeated by Boscawen at Lagos and in November at Quiberon Bay by Hawke, two victories which prevented the junction of the Toulon and Brest fleets. These French naval disasters had their results in different parts of the world. In the Channel they disrupted the preparation for invasion of England, an invasion planned by Choiseul, who had succeeded the pessimistic Bernis as minister of war late in 1758. In Canada Montcalm had to be left in isolation, deprived of naval support from

[1] *Les Matinées du Roi de Prusse* (n.d.), p. 28.
[2] For Anson see S. W. Pack, R.N., *Admiral Lord Anson* (1960); for Ligonier, see Rex Whitworth, *Field Marshal Lord Ligonier* (1958).

France; and in September he was attacked by Wolfe, who had ascended the Heights of Abraham. The English leader was slain; Montcalm died of wounds, and Quebec passed into British hands.

These events had their parallel in India where Clive, a young cadet of the East India Company, won his great victory at Plassey over Suraj-ud-Dowlah in June 1757, followed by Sir Eyre Coote's success at Wandewash. Soon the French were cleared out of Bengal; and thus, by 1760, French rule in Canada and India was practically at an end.

At the same time fortune favoured the British cause in western Germany. Hanover was saved in August 1759 by the victory of Ferdinand of Brunswick over the French at Minden. This victory, occurring less than a fortnight before Frederick's disastrous defeat at Künersdorf, provided an illustration of how delicately balanced was the final decision in this war. Meanwhile, under Choiseul's more intelligent administration, there was a cooling off in French relations with Austria. By the third treaty of Versailles (March 1759) Choiseul cut down the Austrian subsidy and revoked the French guarantee for the restoration of Silesia. Maria Theresa, with what help she might obtain from the Russians, would now have to deal as best she could with Frederick.

For Frederick the year 1760-1 was a year of desperation, when it seemed only a matter of time before he would be forced to yield. The Austrians were in Silesia and still held Dresden; there were the same ups and downs of fortune which Prussian resources could not much longer sustain—Frederick's defeat at Landshut in June, followed by a victory over Austrians and Russians at Liegnitz in August 1760. Invading Brandenburg, the allied enemies of Prussia occupied Berlin for a few days in October, and this alternation of victory and defeat, advance and retreat continued throughout 1761. Frederick was indeed saved by his obstinacy, and by lack of co-operation among his enemies; indeed, for some time he had been aware that the succession of the Tsarina's heir, her nephew Peter, would be in his interests, and that this fact accounted for a lessening of impetus in the Russian onslaught. The death of Elizabeth early in January 1762 was speedily followed by a complete reversal of Russian policy. Peace was made with Frederick by Peter III in May; all conquests were restored; at the same time Sweden withdrew from the war. At the eleventh hour Frederick had been saved. But, even before the conclusion of hostilities, he was secretly plotting with Russia for the dismemberment of Austria and Denmark; his lust for conquest was unappeased.

In the west the situation had been altered by the accession of the young George III to the British throne in October 1760 and the rise of his favourite Bute. The alliance of Charles III of Spain with Louis XV in August 1761 caused Pitt to demand an immediate declaration of war on Spain; on George III's failure to comply, Pitt resigned in October, and thereupon the subsidy to Prussia ceased. By January 1762 Britain and Spain were again at war, and with disastrous consequences to the partners in the Family Compact. From Spain England captured Cuba and the Philippines; from France, several West Indian islands, including Martinique, Grenada and St. Lucia, conquests which can be attributed not to the initiative of George III or Bute, but to plans made by Pitt before his resignation. Peace negotiations culminated in February 1763 when the treaty of Hubertusburg (a village in Saxony) was signed by Austria, Prussia and Saxony, followed by the treaty of Paris, between Britain, France, Spain and Portugal. The effect of the first of these was to restore the *status quo,* which meant that Silesia finally became Prussian territory. Seldom have so much blood and treasure been spent on the acquisition of a territory of comparable size. Saxony was evacuated; the Dresden archives were restored, and Frederick promised to give his vote for Joseph, son of Maria Theresa and the Emperor Francis Stephen, as King of the Romans— the preliminary step to his election as emperor.

The treaty of Paris was more complicated. With the exceptions of the islands of St. Pierre and Miquelon, and the retention of French fishing rights off Newfoundland, the whole of Canada passed into British dominion. In the West Indies England retained St. Vincent, Dominica and Grenada, but restored Martinique and Guadaloupe. France received back Goree and Belle Isle; in exchange for the latter, Minorca again became British, and Senegal was added to English possessions in West Africa. Both powers retired altogether from continental campaigns, the French undertaking to dismantle Dunkirk. In India, where their military power had been destroyed, the French were allowed to retain only a few trading factories. In the west, the greater part of Florida was ceded to England, and Cuba was restored to Spain. From France, Spain received New Orleans and the lands to the west of the Mississippi—this marked the final stage in the abandonment of French ambitions in the north American continent. The Philippines, captured by an English fleet during the peace negotiations, were restored to Spain on condition that a ransom should be provided. The money was never paid.

Like so many peace settlements this one satisfied nobody, and created resentments that had to be avenged. Austria emerged with some credit from the war, stronger and better organised than in 1756; but Maria Theresa, who never abandoned her hope of recovering Silesia, felt that she had been betrayed by England in two wars. Frederick, indignant that his subsidy had been stopped, was equally convinced of England's " perfidy ", and remained for the rest of his life an implacable enemy.[1] Even in England the settlement was unpopular, for it seemed that the brilliant achievements of Pitt and British arms merited better returns, and the wastes of Canada appeared to many a poor substitute for the prosperous sugar islands of Martinique and Guadaloupe. Russia, who had made her peace with Prussia in May 1762, took no part in the final settlement; thereafter she remained elusive and

[1] For this see F. Spencer, " The Anglo-Prussian Breach of 1762 " in *History*, new series, vol. XLI (1956), pp. 100-112.

enigmatic. France had already, after the defeat of Rossbach, been described by a witty Frenchwoman as "Madame Job". Her military leaders, many of them appointed by the influence of Madame de Pompadour and the banker brothers Pâris, had publicly proved their incompetence; her most energetic statesman, Choiseul, had been completely thwarted by the double dealing of his royal master in his secret diplomacy. Most ominous of all, Louis XV showed complete indifference to the disasters which overwhelmed his country. This was not interpreted by his subjects as an indication of strength of character; nor could Frenchmen help contrasting it with the solicitude and even anxiety on behalf of his kingdom which Frederick of Prussia had shown throughout his campaigns. Neither the defeat of Rossbach nor the loss of Canada seriously disturbed the pleasures of the French court, a royal indifference which completed that long process of disillusionment whereby France lost faith in her monarchy.

PART TWO

THE EUROPEAN STATES

SCIENCE AND THE ARTS

THE ENLIGHTENMENT

Chapter VII

THE SCANDINAVIAN COUNTRIES AND RUSSIA

I DENMARK-NORWAY AND SWEDEN

The Union of Kalmar (1397) had united the three kingdoms of Sweden, Denmark and Norway but, in the fifteenth century, Norway came under the overlordship of the Oldenburg kings of Denmark and, in the sixteenth century, Sweden achieved her independence under the Vasa dynasty. Two of the Vasa kings, Gustavus Adolphus and Charles XII, brought Sweden into a European prominence not justified by her natural or human resources; thereafter, decline was inevitable. In 1721 the treaty of Nystadt imposed an uneasy peace on the Scandinavian kingdoms by which Denmark-Norway benefited at the expense of the defeated Sweden; but this treaty did at least establish more permanent frontier lines between the two kingdoms, and enabled both of them to enter on a period of recuperation after years of devastation and war. Thereafter, as secondary powers, Sweden and Denmark were subjected to diplomatic pressure by the leading monarchies, and a new element of instability was introduced by the fact that Russia became a great European state.

Economically, the twin kingdoms of Denmark-Norway were, to some extent, interdependent. Foreign wheat was excluded from southern Norway; Norwegian iron and glass were given preferential treatment in Denmark. Otherwise, the two were sharply contrasted. In Norway only the coastal strips were cultivable, but there was abundance of timber and the naval stores so much in demand by the maritime powers;

in consequence, the population of Norway consisted mainly of foresters, lumbermen, and small, independent farmers. Less primitive conditions prevailed in Denmark, where agriculture was not yet rivalled by the cattle industry; but, despite the efforts of such well-intentioned kings as Frederick IV, the Danish peasant remained, for the most part, a serf, entirely dependent on the owner of the estate, usually an absentee noble or a burgher. As so many peasants escaped to the towns or took refuge in vagabondage, a decree of 1733 required that they should be tied to the soil for 22 years after their fourteenth birthday, this being the period when they might be called up for military service. Otherwise, Danish agriculture was progressive. As in other countries, enclosures displaced the open fields; new inventions, such as Tull's mechanical drill, were introduced, and the potato took its place as a domestic crop. Much waste land was brought under cultivation, and the government conducted extensive surveys in order to promote agricultural yield. As well as this, there was an increase in Danish shipping and overseas trade, greatly advantaged by neutrality in the wars. Companies for overseas trade were formed; these were active in the east and in the Mediterranean.

One of the many dangers threatening the stability of the northern kingdoms was the power of the old nobility, a class large in numbers and still half medieval in spirit. In this respect there was a contrast between Denmark and Sweden because, in the previous century, the powers of the Danish nobility had been greatly diminished; whereas, in Sweden, they retained their predominance throughout the eighteenth century. Accordingly, Denmark-Norway benefited by the benevolent despotism of their Oldenburg rulers, who favoured the rise of a new, semi-official nobility and the emergence of a burgher class. These rulers were Frederick IV (1699-1730), Christian VI (1730-46), Frederick V (1746-66) and Christian VII (1766-1808). Of these, the first was characterised by efficiency, the second by rigid piety, the third was considered dissolute and the fourth, Christian VII, a ruler of unbalanced mind, was suspected of a design to restore the royal absolutism which, in the course of time, had been considerably modified by the initiative of ministers and councils of state. Some of the most efficient of these ministers were natives of Holstein, but in 1771 Christian VII appointed, as first minister, his favourite and physician J. F. Struensee, a Prussian.

This appointment was followed by a short period of precipitate changes, intended to increase the power of the crown and to destroy social and administrative abuses. In order to secure the first of these objects, the privy council was abolished, and King Christian resumed many of the ancient prerogatives of his ancestors. The second object was achieved by a number of reforms in finance, industry and penal legislation, all intended to "modernise" Denmark. The privileges of the nobility were further curtailed; they were forbidden to consign their creditors to prison; parents were no longer allowed to keep erring children in confinement; torture was abolished, and the burdens imposed on the peasantry were mitigated. As Struensee knew no Danish, his edicts were promulgated in German, a fact which may have diminished their effectiveness. A palace revolution, headed by the dowager queen, consigned the minister to prison; and, on the accusation of illicit intercourse with the young queen Caroline Matilda, sister of the British George III, Struensee was executed in April 1772.

In Sweden the death of Charles XII in 1718 was followed by a long period of reaction against royal absolutism. This began in 1719 with the trial and execution of Baron Goertz, who had acted as minister of the late king. Charles's sister Ulrica Eleonora was then elected queen by the Diet, but she was soon induced to abdicate in favour of her husband Frederick of Hesse Cassel, styled King Frederick I of Sweden who, in 1720, accepted a constitution which practically nullified the royal powers and transferred them to the Diet and the Council of the Estates. The Swedish Estates were four in number, consisting of nobility, clergy, burgesses and peasants. Each Estate deliberated and voted separately, an unwieldy system which impeded the work of legislation; indeed, in the period 1720-72 Sweden's internal weakness arose from the fact that there was neither a clearly-defined nor powerful executive. The Council of the Estates had been altered in 1720 to this extent that many of the old heads of colleges or departments holding office for life had been displaced by officials responsible to the Diet, and so it appeared that the principle of ministerial responsibility had been established. Moreover, as the composition of the Council was now influenced by changes in the balance of parties within the Diet, it seemed that the Swedish constitution after 1720 was similar in character to the British, since the Diet resembled a parliament, while the Council, whose members were responsible to the Diet, appeared to be the counterpart of an English Cabinet. But this interpretation is based on the assumption that the British system was one of Estates—an assumption which is untenable.[1] Still more, the Swedish constitution revealed in an exaggerated form the defects inherent in a system of Estates. The four component parts were bitterly divided. The preponderant Estate, that of the nobility, caused much resentment by insistence that its members should have a monopoly of high office; the clergy, distrusting the nobility, frequently allied with the burgesses, and all three were prepared, if need be, to combine against the Estate of the peasants who, in their dislike of petty tyrants, naturally turned royalist in sympathy. Inevitably, much executive responsibility passed into the hands of a secret committee, in which the nobility were supreme, and the peasants not represented at all.

Nor was this irreconcilable element among the four Estates the only source of instability in Sweden; there was another cause, namely, the dynastic claims of the House of Holstein Gottorp. These claims extended not only to Denmark and

[1] above, pp. 62-3.

weden but to Russia, where there were no settled rules for
the succession to the throne. This matter had remote origins
and is not easily capable of simplification. In the fifteenth
century Christian I of Denmark had raised Holstein to the
level of a duchy, stipulating that it should be under separate
administration. This king had two grandsons, of whom the
elder was an ancestor of the Oldenburg rulers of Denmark,
while the younger acquired the territories of Holstein Gottorp.
This younger, or Ducal family as it was called, split into two
branches, of which one was among the ancestors of the Russian
Tsars from the accession of Peter III in 1762, while the other
—that of Holstein-Gottorp-Eutin—were ancestors of those
kings of Sweden who ruled from 1751 to 1818. In Sweden,
the House of Holstein had acquired its claim to the throne by
the marriage of Frederick of Holstein-Gottorp-Eutin with
Sophia, elder sister of Charles XII; a nephew of this prince,
Adolphus Frederick, succeeded to the Swedish throne in 1751,
mainly by Russian influence. He was followed twenty years
later by his son Gustavus III, who could at least claim that he
was a Swedish-born king.

There are no quarrels like family quarrels, and in the eight-
enth century it appeared at times as if the Oldenburg-Hol-
stein-Romanov disputes would provide a counterpart to the
Bourbon-Habsburg quarrels of western Europe. The fate of
Sweden, and, to a less extent, that of Denmark was not uncon-
nected with the outcome of palace revolutions in Moscow or
St. Petersburg. Generally, there was a fear that a Russo-
Swedish entente would be directed against Denmark, with a
threat of war, but the pacific policy of the Danish kings
Christian VI and Frederick V prevented a clash, though the
latter was saved only by the death of Tsar Peter III in 1762, as
the death of his predecessor Elizabeth had already saved
Frederick the Great. These were not the only occasions when
an unexpected death had solved a problem of Scandinavian
politics. Some kind of settlement of the Schleswig-Holstein
question was reached in 1773 when, by arrangement with

Catherine the Great, the King of Denmark, by payment of
sum of money and interchange of territory, acquired full
control over Schleswig and Holstein. In this way Denmark
avoided partition, but the threat to her Swedish neighbour
was more serious, because of her unstable constitution and the
great power of her nobility.

As a secondary power Sweden was dependent on foreign
alliances, and there was division of opinion whether these
should be with Britain, France or Russia. For about 20 years
after 1720 Count Arvid Horn, President of the Chancery, succeeded in maintaining some kind of unity, mainly by association with the Anglo-French entente and with the help of pro-
French families. His policy of peace and freedom from foreign entanglements recalls that of his near-contemporaries
Walpole and Fleury, but inevitably it brought on him the
accusation of cowardice, with the result that in 1738 there
came into existence a formidable opposition party known as
the Hats. A "youth movement", unaware of the privations
which Charles XII's aggressions had brought on their ancestors, the Hats, who were in power until about 1765, made no
secret of their ambition to win back the Baltic provinces from
Russia, by war if necessary. For the most part an urban party
having close links with the aristocracy, they favoured commercial interests, particularly the profitable export of iron, in
which, for a time, Sweden had almost a monopoly. Their
opponents, less aristocratic and less bellicose, were dubbed the
Caps, or Night Caps, implying that they were timorous old
men. The Caps favoured a more liberal economic policy than
the strict mercantilism advocated by the Hats; only in regard
to agriculture were they in agreement, for both parties favoured a free farmer class, emancipated from the restrictions of
tenancy imposed by the crown and private landlords.

The impetuosity of the Hats, together with complications
arising from the succession to the Russian throne, served to
bring Sweden into the Austrian Succession War. A series of
palace revolutions resulted, in November 1741, in the acces-

on to the Russian throne of Elizabeth, daughter of Peter the Great. Meanwhile, mainly by French influence, Sweden had been induced to declare war on Russia, for the alleged object of freeing the Tsardom from the yoke of German favourites, in return for which Elizabeth had given a promise that, if she succeeded to the imperial throne, she would restore the lost Baltic provinces to Sweden. This unusual and over-subtle arrangement suggests that, at this time, Sweden was little more than the cat's paw of Fleury and Frederick of Prussia, both of them anxious to detach Russia from the supporters of Maria Theresa. The plan succeeded only to the extent that Elizabeth was placed on the throne but, once securely established, she showed herself unwilling to fulfil her promises, and so the mock war with Sweden became a serious one. Sweden and Finland fared badly in the hostilities that followed. In 1743 the treaty of Abo restored peace on two conditions—that Sweden sacrificed to Russia a portion of southern Finland and that she accepted as prospective heir to the Swedish throne Elizabeth's nominee Adolphus Frederick of Holstein-Gottorp-Eutin. On the death of Frederick I in 1751, Adolphus Frederick succeeded and reigned until 1771. All this proved the gullibility of the Hats, and the discredit which they incurred helped to restore the fortunes of the Caps. But Adolphus Frederick married Louisa Ulrica, a sister of Frederick the Great, a queen who made no secret of her intention to restore absolute monarchy, an ambition which caused her at first to ally with the Hats, and then to lead a revolutionary party of her own. The failure of this attempt brought the throne into disrepute.

The ambition to regain the whole of Pomerania induced the Swedish Diet to favour Sweden's entry into the Seven Years War on the anti-Prussian side. This intervention proved to be as unfortunate as that in the Austrian Succession War. In 1762, when Frederick was at last free from his Russian adversaries, he directed his forces against Swedish Pomerania, and the Swedes were obliged to sue for a separate peace. This was granted on the basis of return to the *statu quo*. The Hats, now out of favour, were displaced by a younger generation of the Cap party, which advocated a number of reforms, such as freedom of the Press, relaxation of mercantilist restrictions, limitation of the privileges of the nobility and promotion of a vigorous agricultural policy. But in the nine years after 1763, with an increasing realisation that neither faction nor propaganda could take the place of effective government, it became obvious that the constitutional experiment of 1720 had broken down, and that the country was approaching a state of anarchy. The Estates had delegated their powers to the Council which, for lack of information, had been obliged to transfer its duties to provincial bodies. The Hats, it was reported, were very weak, but they were even more opposed to the restoration of royal authority than the Caps.

With the death of Adolphus Frederick in February 1771 and the accession of his son Gustavus III it was clear that a fundamental change in the constitution was necessary if Sweden was to be saved from the partition which was then threatening Poland. Accordingly, the traditional French alliance was renewed, and Vergennes was sent to Stockholm, with assurances of substantial subsidies. In August 1772, by a *coup d'état*, Gustavus annulled the existing constitution and restored to the crown many of its ancient privileges, mainly at the expense of the nobility; reforms of justice and re-establishment of order speedily followed on this re-instatement of executive authority. These events had some international repercussions. A strong, unified Sweden, backed by France, appeared to be both a menace to Denmark and a stumbling block in the path of aggressive Prussia; for a time indeed there was talk of war. But Frederick, anxious to enjoy in peace his Polish acquisitions, was conciliatory, in which attitude he was assisted by British diplomacy; on her side Catherine of Russia, preoccupied by her war against Turkey, was guided by the moderate counsels of her minister Panin. This coincided with the peaceful settlement of the territorial claims of the Holstein-Gottorp family, with the result that Denmark was appeased. Gustavus III proved to be an enlightened monarch, a patron of art and letters, the founder of an Academy in Stockholm. But eventually the Swedish nobility proved too strong for him, and in March 1792 he was assassinated. Even before that event Frederick of Prussia had declared: " what a terrible thing it is to be king of Sweden ".

After the conclusion of hostilities in 1721 the Scandinavian countries made considerable advances in the arts of peace. In Sweden there already existed a strong native tradition in favour of technology, particularly in mining and metallurgy;[1] in Denmark the increasing importance of the cattle industry is reflected in the study of veterinary science; there was also an advance in medicine and surgery, and in 1736 a college of surgery and anatomy was established in Copenhagen. Norway had a scientific society in 1766. At the same time more attention was paid to the vernacular languages. Hitherto Latin and German had served for purposes of literary expression, but these were gradually displaced by Swedish and Danish, for which languages grammars and dictionaries were provided. Societies were founded for the promotion of linguistic studies. In art, the style commonly known as the Baroque was responsible for edifices some of which were more symmetrical and dignified than many of the examples of that style to be found in western Europe; examples are the royal palace in Stockholm, the work of the Tessin family; the Riddarhuset or Hall of the Nobility, and the Charlottenburg palace in Copenhagen. After about 1770 in Scandinavia, as elsewhere, there was a revival of classical taste.

For a time the progress of the Humanities, especially in Denmark, was impeded by the iron grip of Pietism. This creed may be dated from 1675 when the Alsatian P. J. Spener pub-

[1] above, p. 116.

lished his *Pia Desiderata*. Halle became the headquarters of the new movement which, in revolt against formal Lutheranism, insisted on the personal element in faith and the necessity for good works. The northern wars, with their consequent epidemics of disease and near-starvation, as they demonstrated the wrath of God, proved favourable to the growth of Pietism, with the result that, to many, even such innocent pastimes as the theatre and folk dancing became anathema. Of this attitude Christian VI of Denmark (1730-46) was the most thorough-going exponent and, in his day, the Copenhagen Sundays were indeed days of gloom. The Enlightenment, when it came to the north, was a revolt against Pietism.

In literature foreign models were followed. The Dane Ludwig Holberg (1684-1749) familiarised his readers with English and French thought, particularly as represented by Locke and Bayle. As a university professor he knew from experience the excessive pedantry of the older traditions; these he ridiculed in his plays and in his " Subterranean Journey of Niels Klim ", a satire which owed much to Montesquieu's *Lettres Persanes* and Swift's *Gulliver's Travels*. In this imaginary descent to the centre of the globe he professed to find a civilisation providing amusing similarities and contrasts to that on the surface. Holberg, who has been hailed as the first Danish philosopher and even as a precursor of Ibsen, was obliged, in a pietistic age, to convey his message under the cloak of irony and sarcasm. A similar rôle was played in Sweden by Olaf Dalin (1708-83). One of the many continental admirers of Addison and *The Spectator,* he modelled his " Swedish Argus " on the latter, thus introducing to northern readers that spirit of moderation and compromise so refreshing when first experienced, but so insipid for many of us to-day. Like Addison, Dalin had two special antipathies— religious excess and academic pedantry.

II RUSSIA

The early history of Russia was a long contest against the forests and the Tartars; not until the fourteenth century can we speak of a distinctive Russian civilisation; nor was the Tsardom securely established in Moscow until the sixteenth century. On that civilisation Tartar institutions, such as they were, appear to have left little impression, though the admixture of Asiatic blood may have added elements of stolidity and endurance to the European stock. Important administrative influences were derived from Byzantium, and the national religion was that of the Greek Orthodox Church. It was not until the eighteenth century that Muscovy took its place, a somewhat ambiguous place, in the European comity of nations; at the same time there began an imperialist policy of expansion, notably in the Baltic lands and in the south east.[1]

About 90 % of the Russian population consisted of peasants, the remainder being made up of clergy, merchants, and nobles. In the Orthodox Church, which was characterised by a rigid distinction between Regular and Secular, the great monasteries were not only places of seclusion, but also landed and financial institutions, in which respects they served as outposts of Russian civilisation in the north east. Contrasted with them were the secular clergy, many of them illiterate, often sharing in the activities of the peasants, and handing down their parishes from father to son. In these circumstances it can well be understood why the church in Russia did not produce the administrators and educators who played such an important part in the development of western civilisation; herein is one of the many factors distinguishing Muscovy from the rest of Europe. Another contrast is presented by the nobility. As in the west, they originated from the military necessities of the state, but it was not until the sixteenth century that the crown began to grant estates on conditions of military

[1] above, pp. 52-3.

service. These were measured not so much by acreage as by the number of serfs ascribed to them—at first, a holding of 1,000 serfs was common but, by the time of Catherine the Great there were grants of as many as 100,000 serfs. Moreover, in the course of the eighteenth century, the nobility gradually divested themselves of the obligation to perform service, except in war time; accordingly, the duty of military service in peace time, as in war, fell exclusively on the peasants. This concession to the nobility illustrates how the Tsardom was coming to be dependent on a powerful aristocracy; indeed even the succession to the throne was often determined by the nobility acting through the Imperial Guard.

The peasantry consisted of state peasants, who had some control over the disposition of their holdings, and the serfs who populated the lands granted to nobles by the crown. Both classes paid a poll tax; indeed, this was one of the main sources of royal revenue. Usually, the serf worked for three or four days a week on the lord's demesne and, for the rest of the week, on his own holding; but this was subject to the caprice of the noble landowner, to such an extent indeed that there were cases where the serf could work his own plot only on Sundays. Serfdom had come comparatively late to Russia—probably not before the granting of military fiefs in the sixteenth century, when there already existed a slave class. There then followed a process by which the two classes were, in effect, assimilated; the slave was " promoted " to the serf status so that he was obliged to pay the poll tax, while the serf was reduced to a condition bordering on slavery. This steady degradation of the great majority of the population is one of the most striking characteristics of the history of Russia in the eighteeenth century. It extended even to the state peasants because, if the land which they inhabited was given to a noble, they automatically became serfs. In 1765 a *ukase* empowered landowners to sentence serfs under 45 to hard labour in Siberia; two years later the right of appeal against harsh treatment by the lord was taken away. The nobles exercised jurisdiction over their serfs, the only limitation being that they could not impose the death penalty. Barely distinguishable from the negro slaves of the southern United States, the Russian serfs could be sold by public auction. Nor was this state of things limited to the land, because, in the new workshops and foundries[1] established in the time of Peter the Great, the labour supply consisted of serfs.

In theory the Tsars were responsible to God alone; in practice, they were often at the mercy of the nobility. After the death of Peter the Great's grandson in 1730, Russia was ruled until 1796 by a succession of Tsarinas; nor was there any clear rule about the succession. Peter had himself enacted that the Tsar or Tsarina should nominate the successor, but he did not exercise this power. After his death in 1725 he was succeeded by Catherine I (1725-7) his widow; Peter II (1727-30) his grandson; Anna (1730-40) his niece; Ivan VI (1740-1) the son of Anna's niece; Elizabeth (1741-62) daughter of Peter the Great; Peter III son of Charles Frederick of Holstein Gottorp and Anna Petrovna, daughter of Peter the Great and, lastly, Catherine II, daughter of the Prince of Anhalt Zerbst and widow of Peter III. Peter the Great was unfortunate in his male descendants. His son Alexis died in prison in 1718 on a charge of *lèse majesté*; Alexis's son Peter II died from smallpox at the age of 15. Of the other Tsars Ivan VI succeeded at the age of three months and, for a time, the regency was exercised in succession by the German Biren and the mother of the infant Tsar. But late in 1741 Elizabeth was induced, mainly by French influence, to come forward as a candidate for the throne; and, in consequence of a palace revolution, she became Tsarina. She began by disavowing her promises to Sweden[2] and placed the infant Ivan in confinement, where he was murdered in 1764 because, by then, he was the centre of plots against Catherine II. Meanwhile,

[1] above, p. 116. [2] above, p. 187.

Tsarina Elizabeth made public her nomination of Peter of Holstein Gottorp as her intended heir, a fact of some consequences in the course of the Seven Years War because Peter was known to be an admirer of Frederick of Prussia. But the most extraordinary succession was that of Catherine II, or the Great. Married in 1744, she detested her husband Peter, a man of infantile mentality who loved to play with toy soldiers. On good terms with the Palace Guard (some of the officers were among her lovers) she had no difficulty in arranging a *coup d'état* in the summer of 1762 whereby Peter was forced to abdicate. Shortly afterwards, by the connivance of his wife, he was murdered. The widow then ruled as Tsarina, having no other claim to the throne than her (voluntary) widowhood.

Even by the time of the treaty of Nystadt (1721) Russia was by no means a homogeneous state, for there was a large German element in Livonia and Estonia; the Ukraine had not yet been assimilated; in the south and south-east the Cossacks remained almost independent communities, and the lands bordering the north coast of the Black Sea were inaccessible until 1774. These facts give some significance to the attempts made by Peter the Great, who ruled from 1682 to 1725, to unify and modernise his country. Endowed with shrewd intelligence and almost epileptic energy, having learned much from his travels in the west Peter, with the help of able foreigners, created a structure of improvisations and borrowings, a patchwork of veneers over the rough timber which it scarcely concealed. With his boyish curiosity he was interested, not in the abstract achievements of western civilisation, but in its tangible things—soldiers, ships, guns, mechanical devices of all kinds. He encouraged foreign artisans and technicians to settle in his kingdom, and young Russians were sent abroad for training—to Holland for shipbuilding, to France and Austria for military training, to Germany for medicine, to England for the arts and crafts. Numerous Swedish prisoners of war after his victory at Pultava in 1709 supplied the nucleus of a civil service, and in the German Ostermann he ad a skilful minister of foreign affairs. In 1711 St. Petersburg, founded in 1703, became the new capital, but there was return to Moscow by some of his successors.

Peter believed that his country was superior to all others in natural resources, and that these could be exploited only by the state and by force if necessary. He envisaged a future period when Russia, like China, would be able to turn its back on the world. One of his first steps was to enlarge the number of taxpayers, for which purpose he brought the peasants within fiscal control, enacting that their lords should be responsible for their taxes. Numerous industrial companies were established, carefully regulated and subsidised, all under the general supervision of the College of Manufactures, a measure which suggests Colbertian influence. In 1721 the directors of factories and workshops were empowered to take over whole villages of serfs in order to utilise their man power. As well as this Peter set up schools of medicine, navigation, mathematics and gunnery, also elementary schools in the chief towns and garrisons. Idleness was accounted the chief social crime. In public finance he taxed as many things as possible in the hope that some of them would give satisfactory results; from the head tax alone, which fell almost entirely on the peasants, he raised about half his total revenue. Like Frederick the Great after him he wanted money with which to support a large army, an object in which he succeeded, as the yield of the taxes during his reign was trebled. Dissenters from the Orthodox Church had to pay extra, but they were not persecuted.

As regards administrative measures most of Peter's reforms were tentative or impermanent. In 1718 he abolished the old *prikazi,* or government departments, substituting colleges or administrative boards, on the Swedish model, for justice, foreign affairs, revenue, trade, admiralty, mines and manufactures. These were mainly consultative institutions, each composed of eleven members, including some foreigners. But the system was too complicated; moreover the colleges were not linked with local bodies, and so were not informed of local conditions; on the other hand, they were assisted to some extent by the Senate, which supplied official explanations of imperial decrees and dealt with questions referred to its decision. In time the colleges took over much of the work of the Senate, leaving that body to act as the chief adviser of the sovereign. In 1719 a provincial administration was introduced when the country was divided into fifty provinces, each under a governor who was assisted by a tax collector and officials responsible for supplying the troops and managing the forests.

In accordance with his ideal of a secular state, Peter abolished the Patriarchate in 1721, and its place was taken by a synod which included lay members. A number of monasteries were dissolved and much of the property of the church was sequestrated. The Tsar tried hard to establish a system of secular education and to break the monopoly of the Slavonic Greek-Latin Academy in Moscow, for which purpose he instituted a number of elementary schools; but, even in his lifetime, these declined, and their place was taken by church schools. With the nobility his reforms were equally radical and equally impermanent. By a *ukase* of 1714 he decreed the indivisibility of noble estates, his intention being that, as the property would fall to only one heir, the landless sons would be obliged to enter the army or civil service. The period of service, whether in a military, naval or civilian capacity, was for 25 years from the age of 15. In this way the army became national, and was based on a system of conscription, by which every twenty peasant households had to supply one man. A hierarchy of ranks was introduced into the military and civil services in 1722, each of them divided into fourteen grades, Peter's object being to ensure that promotion should be by merit alone. On reaching the eighth grade (from the top) in one of the forms of service, a title of nobility was acquired. For the administration of justice there were ten circuits, each having its superior court; at the same time the criminal law was codified. This imposed harsh penalties, even for minor

fences; according to the nature of the crime, there were
several different methods of inflicting death.

In the towns the merchants were regimented and divided
into two gilds which distinguished between the industrialists
and the artisans. Townspeople were conscripted into administrative service in the government stores of wine and salt and
in the levying of customs duties. The merchants represented
only a small proportion of the population—according to some
authorities about 3%—and it should be recalled that they
handled no more than a fraction of the commerce of the
country, as much of this was in the hands of agents, notably
English agents. Mainly for this reason there was no middle
class in Russia, a deficiency accentuated by the steadily increasing degradation of the peasants. It was Peter who began
this process for, by his assignment of a large proportion of
the peasantry to the judicial and personal control of the nobility, he was responsible for the creation of a great mass of
servile labour. This was accompanied, after Peter's death, by
steady enhancement of the privileges and powers of the
nobility. Many of them travelled to western Europe, bringing
back some of its culture and vice; the requirement that they
should entertain lavishly caused many of them to adopt a
luxurious mode of life, with consequent accumulation of debt.
In effect therefore Russia knew only two classes—a small
minority of the eighteenth century and a great majority of the
fourteenth.

Peter died in February 1725, leaving no instructions about
the succession, a circumstance which enabled a powerful group
of nobles acting through the palace guard to choose the successor. This is how Peter's widow Catherine came to the
throne. Her short reign of two years was followed by that of
Peter II, grandson of Peter the Great. His death from smallpox in January 1730 was followed by a division of opinion in
the Supreme Privy Council, of which advantage was speedily
taken by one of the leading nobles, Dmitry Golitsyn, to offer

the crown to Anna, the widowed duchess of Courland, one of Peter the Great's nieces. Golitsyn drew up a scheme of constitutional reform on the Swedish model, imposing strict limitations on the prerogative and, as these were accepted by Anna, she came to Moscow as the prospective Tsarina. There she was crowned as Anna I but, as it was made clear to her that a large section of the nobility was opposed to any diminution of the imperial prerogative, she tore up the charter of limitations with her own hands. Returning to St. Petersburg she appointed Christopher Münich (or Munnich) as commander-in-chief of the army. Münich, who had served under Prince Eugène, had proved himself a successful general in the wars against the Turks, but his tenure of imperial favour was contested by E. J. Biren (or Bühren) a Courlander of German origin, who filled the household offices with his Teutonic friends, leaving the direction of civil affairs to the Chancery which was controlled by the German Ostermann.

This strong German element in the new régime caused much resentment among the nobility, but Anna dealt with opposition and criticism by old-fashioned methods—death, torture and exile—to such an extent that she is known in Russian annals as Anna the Bloody. Human beings and animals she treated with sadistic cruelty. On her death in October 1740 there followed an interval of 13 months when the infant Ivan VI was nominally Tsar, an interval ended by another palace revolution, engineered by France and Sweden, which placed Elizabeth on the throne.[1] Her accession was followed by the exile of Münich, Biren and Ostermann, the last of whom was replaced by Bestushev, whose duplicity made even more impenetrable the recesses of Russian foreign policy in these the early days of the Austrian Succession War, when France, by direct means and through the intermediacy of Sweden, was striving hard to detach Russia from the supporters of Maria Theresa. Failure to effect this object served, for a time, t

[1] above, p. 187.

scredit French diplomacy in the north. Elizabeth died early
January 1762.

Her reign had at least been more moderate than that of her
edecessor, and was of some importance in the cultural his-
ry of Russia. The Academy of Sciences (founded in 1725)
:tended its activities by organising geographical expeditions
.d preparing the first scientific map of the empire. In 1755
.e university of Moscow was founded; in the following year
state theatre was established in St. Petersburg. Beginning in
.e middle decades of the century, a number of semi-scientific,
:mi-popular journals were published, and the reading public
.as increased in number. The lead in these movements was
.ken by M. V. Lomonosov (1711-65) whose encyclopedic
.arning recalls that of Leibniz, except that he was not a
.athematician, his interests being mainly in natural science,
.iman history and philology. He had studied in Germany,
.d was distinguished for his patriotism. Among his contem-
.raries French influence predominated, and the classics of
.e late seventeenth century, particularly Boileau's *Art Poét-
.ue,* had considerable influence on Russian poets and versi-
:rs.

Elizabeth's successor Catherine II (1762-96) provides an
:xample of that small class of comparatively obscure persons
.ho, coming from outside, have given direction and unity
. peoples alien in religion, language and political thought
. themselves. This at least proved a supreme measure
f adaptability. As well as this, she was a natural-born
:tress, able to perform convincingly in any rôle, and never
.cumbered by considerations of integrity. Endowed with a
.ore than usual amount of sexual passion, she had over
.venty male favourites in the course of her reign; but, like
.lizabeth I of England, she was able to throw a lover aside as
.on as he had served her purpose; indeed, she recalls the
.ler of Elizabethan England in her freedom from religious
. moral convictions, and her ability to co-operate with

ministers very different in temperament from herself. Supreme optimism and an unfailing belief in herself often blinded her to the true state of things among her subjects, but these personal qualities gave her a driving force enabling her to surmount, or more often, to dodge difficulties and dangers more formidable than any confronting her royal contemporaries. There was a certain theatrical element in her rule. On the one hand she wielded the strongest and harshest autocracy in Europe, never hesitating to utilise her authority to the full; on the other hand she was the greatest blue stocking of the century, maintaining an animated correspondence with Voltaire and giving hospitality to Diderot. A keen student of Montesquieu, whose opinions she modified to suit the requirements of her prerogative, she was admired by Frederick the Great, who saw in her a kindred spirit.

The earliest of Catherine's reforms involved an increase in the powers of the Senate and the beginnings of a process of decentralisation, whereby local administration was placed more directly under the Senate's control. Measures for these purposes were enacted in 1763 and 1764, and at the same time the salaries of officials were increased so as to diminish peculation. Catherine's predecessor had considered projects for colonising desert areas by settling them with foreign immigrants: this policy was put into effect, with the result that by 1768 over 100 colonies, consisting of about 23,000 inhabitants, were established, mainly on the lower Volga. The foreign immigrants were mostly Germans and Serbians. At the same time, the process of secularising church lands, inaugurated by Peter the Great, was completed, in spite of Catherine's assurance to the Orthodox clergy that she was their friend. By decree of 1764 many monasteries were abolished, and although their lands were not given directly to the nobility, this confiscation enabled the empress to be even more lavish in her grants of crown lands.

These were all practical measures. But there was much less practicability in Catherine's scheme for a drastic revision of Russian law and the promulgation of an idealist code of laws.[1] The matter was referred to a large commission, consisting of about 600 deputies representing nobles, state peasants, towns and Cossacks, for the guidance of whom Catherine busied herself with the drawing up of an " Instruction ". She must have enjoyed this literary task, since it enabled her to display an extensive knowledge of the most advanced opinion of western Europe, particularly that expounded by Montesquieu and Beccaria.[2] Montesquieu's condemnation of tyranny she adroitly evaded by a justification of her own autocracy. Russia, she declared, was a European state, and its great extent necessitated the vesting of absolute power in the ruler. Penal legislation, she declared, should be not only preventive in its object, but also moral and educational; for, under a wise system, the guilty party will be convinced of the error of his ways. Frequent application of the death penalty has never mended the morals of a people; the use of torture is contrary to reason; the certainty of even a small but inevitable punishment will prove a stronger deterrent than an uncertain possibility of death.

With such exalted precepts for their guidance, the commission started its proceedings in 1767. The deputies were provided with instructions from those who had elected them, similar to the French *cahiers* of 1789. Of these there were about 1,400. There was general agreement that more decentralisation should be introduced, and that the provinces should be better supplied with doctors and educational facilities. Many deputies insisted that the taxes were too heavy. Class interest was shown in some of the demands; for example, the nobles claimed exemption from the death penalty and from torture; that the penalties for slandering them should be increased, and that they alone should have the right to own land and serfs. The merchants demanded limitation of com-

[1] For this and Catherine's reforms generally see P. Milioukov, C. Seignobos and L. Eisenmann, *Histoire de Russie,* vol. ii, ch. xi.
[2] below, p. 240.

merce to themselves; the state peasants wished to have the privilege of owning serfs. A few members of the commission deplored the misery of the unfree population, but a majority maintained that, without serfdom, the prerogatives of the crown would be endangered. The lesson was not lost on Catherine. She did not codify the findings of the commission, but she utilised them in her edicts, notably that of 1775 which reformed local administration. Her prerogative, she now realised, must rest on the institutions of serfdom and a powerful nobility. Not until 1861 was serfdom abolished in Russia.

Catherine's first war with Turkey and her part in the first Partition of Poland have already been referred to.[1] Her gains in the war were substantial, as they enabled Russia to penetrate to the Black Sea and to the south-east, but they might have been greater had it not been for a serious crisis at home. This was the revolt of Pugachev (1773-4) which, beginning as a Cossack rising, rapidly extended to the Urals, the Volga basin and the south-west of Siberia. Many of the serfs who joined in this revolt believed Pugachev's claim that he was the Tsar Peter III, and had miraculously escaped from assassination. This was the most serious peasant revolt of the century. With the conclusion of the Turkish War in 1774 Catherine had more troops available, and the revolt was crushed with merciless severity. Pugachev, a man of some character and ability, was executed in Moscow.

The lesson derived by the empress from this revolt was the need to strengthen local administration so that dissatisfaction could be dealt with promptly. For the purpose of giving effect to this object, she studied the proceedings of the commission of 1767-8; and, from her reading of Blackstone's *Commentaries* in a French translation, she became enamoured of the English system, with its lord lieutenant and deputy lieutenants for each county, assisted by justices of the peace for the maintenance of law and order. The result was the edict of 1775. Russia was divided into local governments, each of 300,000-

[1] above, pp. 145-8.

400,000 inhabitants under the control of a lieutenant general, who was endowed with vast powers and was responsible only to the Senate. In each government there were four colleges, two for justice, one for finance and one for general administration; subordinate to the colleges of justice there were separate tribunals, for nobles, merchants, artisans and free peasants. Each government was divided into districts of about 20,000-30,000 inhabitants, under the control of a Captain of Police who was chosen by the nobles. The edict provided for committees in each district to supervise education, hygiene and public assistance, and there were arrangements for representation of the people by deputies in the local administration. This system, complicated and costly, lasted until 1860, and proved of benefit only to the free; it also ensured that trouble among the unfree could be dealt with on the spot.

Consistently with her general policy, Catherine promulgated a Charter of the Nobility in 1785. This was a codification of all the privileges granted to the nobility, including trial by peers, exemption from public service and taxes, the right to establish factories and to export their products and, lastly, freedom from corporal punishment. As well as this, some kind of corporate organisation was introduced by the institution of corps of nobles in each government, with the exclusive use of hospitals and schools. Catherine followed this up with an edict of 1786 which attempted to establish a system of state education. For this, the model was that set by Austria, where a scheme of public instruction had been inaugurated in 1774. The Russian plan envisaged the establishment of elementary schools in the towns, open to all classes; by the end of her reign over 300 such schools had been founded. But the nobles objected to the mingling of classes and, as the great majority of the population lived outside the towns, this measure did little for the peasants. So Catherine continued to rule over an illiterate Russia.

Chapter VIII

AUSTRIA, PRUSSIA AND GERMANY

I AUSTRIA

The greater part of central Europe was occupied by the lands of the Habsburgs,[1] of which the core was the Grand Duchy of Austria, with its dependencies of Styria, Carinthia and Carniola. In the sixteenth century two kingdoms had been added by the termination of earlier dynasties—Hungary and Bohemia—the crowns of which, nominally elective, were actually hereditary in the Habsburg family. Transylvania, formerly an appendage to Hungary, was subjected to Austrian rule in 1699 and became a Grand Duchy in the reign of Maria Theresa. To these were added the Milanese, Sardinia, the Belgian Netherlands and Naples, all acquired by the treaty of Utrecht; in 1720 Sicily was taken over in exchange for Sardinia, which went to Victor Amadeus of Savoy. On the extinction of the Medici family in 1737 Tuscany passed to Francis Stephen of Lorraine, husband of Maria Theresa, and so into Habsburg possession.

A glance at the map will show how these territories, scattered though they were, provided at least the nucleus of a maritime state. The Austrian Netherlands had a seaboard on the North Sea; there was access to the Adriatic through the ports of Fiume and Trieste; Naples, Sicily and Tuscany border on the Mediterranean. But the jealousy of the maritime powers prevented the Emperor Charles VI from utilising the potentialities of the Belgian coast though Ostend, even without its Company, was a considerable port. The defeat of the

---

[1] For the Holy Roman Empire see above, pp. 48-50.

imperial forces in the Polish Succession War obliged Charles to surrender the Two Sicilies to the Spanish Bourbons in 1735. As for the Tuscan ports such as Piombino and Orbitello, they were unenterprising, and were easily outdistanced by the free port of Leghorn. There remained Antwerp but, ever since 1648 it had been kept very nearly closed. In effect therefore Ostend, Trieste, Fiume and Leghorn were the only sea outlets for the vast possessions of the Habsburgs, which thus became very nearly land-locked states. Access to the Black Sea was not obtained until after 1774. All this accounts for a certain reorientation towards the east, and helps to explain the attempts to exchange outlying Belgium for centrally-situated Bavaria. Favoured by England in the earlier part of the century as a makeweight against France, Austria veered towards Russia as her diplomatic partner, with the result that a vast dominion which, but for diplomatic pressure and military defeat, might have had some maritime importance, became a great territorial and militarist state.

Of the three personages who in succession ruled the Austrian dominions in this period Charles VI, a lover of art and music, was dominated by his confessors, and showed an intolerance of heresy more characteristic of the seventeenth century than of the eighteenth. His object was to extirpate Protestantism from all his dominions, and even in Hungary Roman Catholicism was declared the religion of the state. This showed a certain obtuseness or duplicity in Charles's character, since he earnestly demanded and accepted subsidies and troops from heretic England and Holland in order to safeguard his territories and if possible extend them; perhaps he was assured by his confessors, as his father had been, that heretics might safely be used for such purposes, in the same way as one uses beasts of burden. His daughter Maria Theresa had a better grasp of realities. Steeled by the adversities of war, she had enough commonsense to realise that Austrian defeats were due mainly to the outworn medievalism of the administration, and so she inaugurated a number of conservative reforms which, in spite of the loss of Silesia, at least enabled the Austrian Empire to survive. In sharp contrast to his mother and grandfather Joseph II, though a sincere Catholic, was a fierce anti-curialist or anti-papalist, a crowned revolutionary, a tireless devotee of the principle that reform must come quickly, not from beneath but from above.

There was no possibility of unity in such a ramshackle confederation of states as the Austrian Empire, held together, as it was, by nothing stronger than the Pragmatic Sanction. In the east, there was always the threat from the Turk, with its inevitable penetration into Hungary; indeed, in consequence of repeated invasion, much of the central part of that kingdom had been laid waste, and had to be re-peopled, mainly by Austrians, Germans and Rumanians, with the result that less than half the population consisted of Magyars. Hungary, which still retained her old traditions of independence and was outside the Customs Union of the other Austrian territories, was never really incorporated into the Habsburg possessions, and had to be given special concessions. In order to conciliate Magyar opinion, and as a reward for Hungarian help in the War of the Austrian Succession, a royal palace was built at Pesth; nor were the Hungarian Estates obliged to make a substantial contribution to the imperial exchequer; indeed, only the use of force would have obliged the local nobility to do so. There was similar lenience with the Belgian Netherlands and the Italian dependency of Milan, where old institutions were left practically untouched, and control was exercised through viceroys, most of them conciliatory and even benevolent. It was otherwise in Bohemia, where Czech nationalism, religion, language and literature had been crushed after the initial success of the imperialists in the Thirty Years War. Bohemian lands became a happy hunting ground for Court favourites, who were rewarded with large estates, and in 1752 the Bohemian nobility as a distinct institution was abolished. Accordingly, an alien aristocracy exercised a despotism over its peasantry, harsh even on the standards prevailing east of the Elbe, the cause of at least one serious rebellion. Moreover, as Bohemia was the borderland between Prussia and Austria, she suffered more than any other state in the great wars of the century, when outbreaks of famine obliged workers in the fields to live on roots. Bohemia was the Ireland of the Habsburg dominions.

This infiltration of Austrian and German population into Hungary and Bohemia was matched by foreign immigration into Vienna, so that the capital became composed of elements drawn from almost every country in Europe. In the earlier part of the century the most distinguished example was Prince Eugène of Savoy (1663-1736), grandson of a duke of Savoy, the greatest leader of the Austrian armies in this period. One of his ablest successors, Laudon or Loudon, was of Scottish extraction; Daun, another notable general, came from the Rhineland. This cosmopolitan character was reflected in the capital, where French, Italian and even English served as supplements to German. There was no anti-Semitism in this polyglot society, indeed it was the Jew administrator Sonnenfels who did much to secure the abolition of torture.

Vienna was the headquarters of an administration that can be described as cameralist in the sense that control was directed by highly trained officials who provided the staffs of new departments for justice, education and finance. The essence of cameralism is simply that it regards the work of administration not as the province of the amateur, but as the monopoly of the expert. The university of Vienna had a special faculty to provide the required training; so had the university of Halle, for the supply of Prussian civil servants. Increase of population, elimination of exemption and privilege, regulation of the rights of seigneurs over their serfs, greater efficiency and uniformity in the raising of taxation—these were among the objects of the new cameralist school. The success of their application may account for the delay of revolution in the Austrian lands until 1848.

Maria Theresa, one of the few Habsburgs who could learn

from experience, aimed at doing for Austria what Frederick was doing for Prussia, namely, creating on the basis of a re-formed economy, a well-filled treasury and a highly-trained army. For the latter purpose she established a military academy at Wiener Neustadt; regular training as well as a code of military discipline took the place of the old haphazard system; moreover, the monopoly of the nobility in the higher com-mands was greatly diminished. In order to raise more revenue the control over taxation previously exercised by the Estates was reduced to a minimum, and in 1749 Chancellor Haugwitz introduced a number of fiscal reforms which resulted in a larger yield. Colonies of foreign workers were introduced and an attempt was made to lighten, or at least to regulate, the *corvées* with which the peasants were burdened; an agrarian commission was set up in 1768; but reforms, such as they were, had to be forced over the heads of the landowners. Nor did reform always conciliate the peasants, because commuta-tion of labour services for fixed payments caused discontent and even rebellion among them. Maria Theresa had more success in her encouragement of commerce and industry. Roads were improved, silk and porcelain industries were deve-loped, and schools of industry were established. A strict mer-cantilist policy limited imports; with the opening of the Black Sea to navigation, the Danube provided a wider avenue for export of Austrian products, as well as for the corn and copper of Hungary. Trieste, site of the headquarters of the Austrian Levant Company, maintained an active trade with Adriatic and Mediterranean ports.

The Italian and Belgian possessions were to some extent outside this system; of these the former is treated elsewhere.[1] After four years of occupation by the French in the years 1744-8 Belgium enjoyed peace and a large measure of pros-perity. Of this the basis was agriculture. As nowhere else the soil was subjected to an intensity of cultivation such as enabled the population of the countryside to survive economic

[1] below, ch. ix.

rises.[1] It was otherwise with industry, in which there was
little development in this period, so the prosperity of the
villages contrasted with the poverty of the towns.[2] Nominally
subject to a Netherlands Council in Vienna, the Belgian Low
Countries were administered by a local viceroy. Of those
who acted in this capacity the most notable was Charles of
Lorraine, brother-in-law of Maria Theresa, whose rule lasted
from 1744 to 1780. Cosmopolitan and easy of access,
an advocate of the use of French as the spoken language, he
helped to make the government of the Habsburgs more acceptable than in any other part of the Austrian dominions. The
prosperity of the country, especially after the middle of the
century, enabled the Netherlands Estates to make substantial
contributions to the Viennese Treasury. After 1749 the
Austrian government refused to pay for maintaining the
barrier fortresses, which speedily fell into decay; they had
served not to protect the Dutch, but to enable them to prevent
the Belgians from building new roads or improving transport.
The Scheldt remained closed, in spite of the efforts of Joseph
II to have it opened; not until 1832 was the river opened for
shipping.

Because of his harsh edicts against Protestants Charles VI
had never been popular in the Netherlands, but these edicts
were not consistently enforced and, in practice, dissent was
rarely penalised. Nevertheless the church, represented by the
university of Louvain and the Jesuits, provided a barrier
against intellectual development. Of all the eighteenth-century
universities that of Louvain was probably the most reactionary;
and the only institution which, in any sense, provided for
cultured taste was the Opera House in Brussels. There were
also many lodges of freemasons on the English model and,
after the expulsion of the Jesuits, their buildings and churches
were mostly converted into colleges and schools. Generally,
the best that can be said for Austrian rule in Belgium in this

[1] above, p. 105.
[2] H. Pirenne, *Histoire de Belgique,* vol. v, bk. iii.

period is that no attempt was made to Germanise the stat possibly because it was thought in Vienna that this remo province was unlikely to remain for long in Austrian posse sion.

For a great part of the forty years between her accession i 1740 and her death in 1780 Maria Theresa ruled the Austria dominions with the help of a Council of State, which wa assisted by three central councils—for war, finance and con merce. The Empress Queen, who was described by Frederic the Great as the wisest of his enemies because she could contr her ambitions and hatreds, was moderate and tentative in h reforms. Until his death in 1765 the Emperor Francis Stephe ruled in conjunction with his imperial consort; this was fo lowed by an uneasy partnership between mother and son, th Emperor Joseph II, who increasingly resented his mother moderation and restraint. In this family dualism Chancello Kaunitz acted as mediator, siding sometimes with one, som times with the other; after 1753 Kaunitz played some pa in internal affairs, in succession to the Silesian-born Hau witz, but his fame rests mainly on his diplomatic achievement With increasing years Maria Theresa regretted the part whic she had played in the Partition of Poland, and she resented th ignominy heaped on the empire by the failure of Joseph an Kaunitz in the Bavarian Succession War.

Mother and son were deeply conscious of the need fo agrarian reform in their dominions. This was acute i Bohemia in the winter of 1770-1, when about 16,000 peasant are said to have died of famine. Joseph, who wished to supe vise relief measures, was forbidden to do so by his mothe Nevertheless, a series of attempted reforms attested Mari Theresa's concern at agrarian discontent. Beginning in 176 she enacted an *Urbarium* for Hungary which defined th minimum limit of peasant property and the maximum labou dues that the lord could enforce; in the succeeding year similar measures were enacted for other parts of the empir This policy was as much fiscal as humanitarian, for it wa designed to bring the peasants within the scope of taxation. But these edicts were obstructed by the landowners, a fact which helps to account for Joseph's bitter hatred of the caste system.

With the death of his mother in 1780 Joseph was, at long last, able to put his ideas into practice. Of all the eighteenth-century rulers he was the most complicated, because he was at once militarist, absolutist, liberal and humanitarian. A pious Catholic, he was uncompromising in his opposition to papal control. Educated in secluded and strictly controlled surroundings, he became introspective, resentful and impetuous. His two marriages were unfortunate—that with a duchess of the House of Parma was happy but ended prematurely with her death, followed by the death of her son; the second marriage —that with Josepha of Bavaria was a diplomatic arrangement and ended in separation. Joseph had shocked his mother and Kaunitz by his expressed opinion that the whole caste system should be abolished, and that the sons of peasants should be eligible for university education and for admission to the civil service; in this direction he at least made a beginning for, in 1781, he abolished serfdom on his hereditary lands. Other measures proved his zeal for radical reform. Clerical control of the Press censorship was abolished; many monasteries were dissolved, and the proceeds applied to educational purposes. In order to secure more freedom of action he reduced the membership of his Council of State from seven to four and rarely summoned it. A large measure of toleration was granted to all the sects; the education of the clergy was reformed; even Pope Pius VI, who went in person to Vienna in 1782, could not move the emperor from a policy which threatened to destroy the power of the papacy in Austria altogether. As well as this, the financial administration was re-cast; strict economy was enforced and even the meagre pension paid to Mozart was reduced. With years Joseph became even more drastic. His subjects in Milan were alienated by his use of spies and informers; in 1787 his attempt to re-model the whole administrative system in Belgium led to open rebellion. Believing that time was running against Austria and in favour of Prussia, he attempted to create as quickly as possible a treasure and an army for the recovery of Silesia. His failure to secure that object was only one of the many failures of his life. Few of his reforms survived for long after his death, an event which occurred in 1790.[1]

II PRUSSIA

The Hohenzollern territories extended in broken fragments from Cleves and East Friesland in the west to East Prussia on the east, having the Ems and the Niemen as the only natural frontiers, with Brandenburg as its core and Berlin as the capital. The addition of part of western Pomerania with the port of Stettin (1721), together with the capture of Silesia, gave to the Hohenzollerns control over the whole course of the Oder; the acquisition of West Prussia by the first Partition of Poland brought with it dominion over the lower reaches of the Vistula. Emden, Stralsund, Stettin, Kolberg and Königsberg were the chief ports; there was also easy access to the Elbe and Hamburg.

Already in the previous century the Great Elector (1640–88) had laid the foundations of an administration[2] which at least created an appearance of unity. This was developed by King Frederick William (1713-40), an apoplectic martinet, whose love for tall grenadiers and negro janissaries (equipped with trumpets and cymbals) was matched only by his contempt for learning and his zeal for order and uniformity. A hint of his character can be gleaned from his amusements. He indulged in painting, his canvases bearing the unconventional inscription: *in tormentis pinxit F.W.*; some of these were

[1] For a good biography see F. Fejtö, *Un Habsbourg Révolutionnaire Joseph II* (1954).
[2] See also above, pp. 57-8.

bought by Berlin merchants. In the evenings he entertained
a small number of his generals and ministers to a *Tabagie,*
when long pipes were smoked and tankards of beer consumed; at these conclaves a favourite amusement was to introduce a pedant in the capacity of buffoon; for which purpose
the historiographer royal provided suitable material. In the
conversation Frederick would suggest a subject for debate in
the academic manner, a favourite topic being " that all savants
are humbugs and frauds ".[1] His son, afterwards Frederick the
Great, inherited this capacity for raillery; but he regarded his
father with fear and dislike.

The depopulation of the Brandenburg lands, mainly in consequence of the Thirty Years War, had been remedied to some
extent by the admission of many thousands of Huguenots, a
policy followed by Frederick William when he admitted about
15,000 Protestant refugees who had been expelled by the
Archbishop of Salzburg. What he wanted was more population—a hard working population—and an army of at least
80,000 men. As the inhabitants of his territories numbered
little more than two millions, the creation and maintenance of
such a comparatively large force necessitated an unusually
large revenue, which could be raised only by an efficient
system of taxation. Now, one of the great lessons of seventeenth-century fiscal experiment had been a demonstration of
the value of the excise as a source of national revenue, provided that it was properly administered. This was because it
fell on so many articles of consumption, including salt and
beer; it was paid indirectly and so, unlike the poll taxes, it was
not regarded as a penal infliction; moreover, as it fell on
necessities, not on luxuries, it was not subject to changes of
fashion. Progressive nations such as the English and Dutch
had made it one of their main sources of revenue; Prussia did
the same. Equally productive were the royal lands which,
efficiently managed, produced a large part of the revenue.

[1] These details are derived from A. Waddington, *Histoire de
Prusse* (1920), II, pp. 364 ff.

Added to this was a régime of strict economy, in striking contrast to that prevailing in France. These measures, together with a meticulous control of imports and well-directed encouragement of industry, help to explain why, in the eighteenth century, Prussia was the most nearly solvent of the European states.

Frederick William was succeeded in 1740 by his son Frederick II, afterwards styled the Great, one of the most remarkable and controversial of figures. He does not fit into any of the conventional patterns of hereditary monarch; indeed he dispensed with all the customary trappings of kingship. An agnostic, convinced that all religions contain elements of good and bad, he condemned the atheism of such *philosophes* as D'Holbach, believing, as did Napoleon after him, that religion serves a social and political purpose since it creates an element of solidarity and obedience among the governed. But it is not necessary in the ruler, since it might create scruples of conscience. His ancestors, he candidly confessed, had become Lutherans in order to acquire church property; later, they had changed over to Calvinism in order to maintain better relations with the Dutch and so facilitate the acquisition of Cleves. He himself professed indifference, if only to ensure the tranquillity of his subjects, a policy which he pursued with consistency, for he was the most tolerant of eighteenth-century rulers, extending his protection to all religions and sects including even the Jesuits, but excepting the Jews, whose addiction to usury he condemned. Frederick's policy had considerable results, since it led to the admission of refugees from France, Poland, Mecklenburg and Thuringia with the result that, by the end of his reign, many thousands of the inhabitants of Prussia consisted of immigrants. As well as this colonists were brought in and new subjects were acquired by the first Partition of Poland, so it is not surprising that the population more than doubled.

Frederick's professed indifference in religious matters was matched by his keen interest in the intellectual movement going on around him, particularly in France. In 1748 he gave asylum to La Mettrie and in 1764 to Toussaint, both of whom had been threatened with the Bastille; and, as early as 1740, he lodged Voltaire with him as his guest, afterwards appointing him a court chamberlain, with a considerable pension. Unlimited capacity for sarcasm and irony must have inspired much good conversation, but it also provoked many quarrels. Of German language and literature he had a very poor opinion, but he was devoted to German music, and played the lute in his own orchestra. For his voluminous writings he used French, a language which he handled with mastery.

These facts alone are sufficient to attest the unusual and complicated character of Frederick the Great. It is possible that the brutal treatment experienced at the hands of his father brought to the surface a sensitive and even idealist element in his character, illustrated in his *Anti Machiavel* (1740), the publication of which he afterwards regretted. This juvenile manifesto was an eloquent plea for morality in international matters. The contrast between the elements of good and bad are so clearly distinguished in Frederick's character as to warrant the application to him of the analogy of Jekyll and Hyde. The Hyde was shown in the cynical perfidy of his foreign policy and the brutality with which he forced foreigners and soldiers of conquered territories into his armies; the Jekyll was revealed in his heroism in defeat and in his solicitude for the well-being of his subjects. To the fullest extent he carried out his own maxim that the ruler is the servant of the state. In the administration which he inherited he made few changes of importance except to ensure more personal supervision on his part, and to give the nobility a monopoly of the higher posts in the army and civil service. The law was codified, but the code was not promulgated until 1784. This code embodied the king's views on the structure of society, and was illiberal in the sense that it favoured the immobility of social classes—the bourgeoisie must not acquire noble lands; the peasant must remain on the estate; the privileges of the nobility must be preserved inviolate. In war time a limited number of bourgeois might be appointed officers, but they were to be dismissed on the conclusion of hostilities, or relegated to garrison duties. But Frederick' practice was better than his precept for, in 1763 the serfs on the royal domains were emancipated, not altogether for humanitarian reasons, but in order that their numbers might increase and so provide a larger number of common soldiers

In his first *Testament Politique* (1752) Frederick surveyed the economic conditions of his realm and the improvement that were being effected. He claimed that the textile industries, conducted in nearly every town and village, brought him more wealth than the mines of Peru brought to the King of Spain. Much land had been reclaimed from the marshes particularly along the Oder and around Stettin, with the result that about 4,000 persons were settled in these areas. Three canals had been built in order to connect the Oder, Havel and Spree; from these the trade of Berlin and Magdeburg greatly benefited. Western Pomerania he had found only half cultivated, owing to the predominance of marshes; his aim was to drain them and establish 100,000 cultivators. He noted that the industries in which there was a marked deficiency were cutlery, paper, cotton goods, gloves and printing presses. Among the royal projects was one for the foundation of a home for widows of officers and another for the building of orphanages in every considerable town, with the object of diminishing the crime of infanticide which, at that time, was common in his dominions. In Silesia, which was under a separate administration, he distinguished between the upper and lower regions; the former, composed mainly of Catholics was cultivated by serfs; while the latter, where the level of agriculture was higher, consisted mainly of Protestants, who were more amenable to Prussian discipline. Silesia, he noted was full of Jesuits, all of them pro-Austrian and anti-Prussian. In order to counteract this he brought in French Jesuits, so that their quarrels would render them harmless.

After 1763 Frederick had to repair the ravages of the Seven Years War which had caused devastation comparable to that of the Thirty Years War. On his own estimate he had lost 300,000 men in his campaigns, and the civilian population had suffered even more, so that the total population may have been reduced temporarily by nearly a third. All his provinces were paying twice what they had formerly paid in taxes; this was mainly because of high interest charges on loans. In the book written for his nephew[1] Frederick advised him not to start another war; in its place he suggested the unheroic expedient of seeking an English subsidy. Looking back in 1764 on the great war that had just ended, he recognised how near he had been to disaster and how fortune, which had favoured him once, might not smile a second time. So, in his later years, he was pacific in intention, though well-armed for eventualities. But his legacy to Germany has not been pacific. Endowed with much more intelligence than other monarchs, he had used his great armies not only to seize a rich province, but to keep his neighbours in a constant state of trepidation. He was always the first to strike, and it was a cardinal maxim of his policy that he who strikes first is not necessarily the aggressor, since such action may forestall attack. Another element in the evil legacy of Frederick is insistence on the maxim *vae victis*—the imposition of the harshest possible terms on the vanquished. These things became deeply embedded in Prussian mentality.

III GERMANY

In this period the area now designated Germany consisted of nearly as many separate states as there are days in the year, all of them under the very nominal suzerainty of the Holy Roman Empire. Among these states there was a kingdom (Prussia), princely electorates, grand duchies, duchies, imperial

[1] above, p. 128 n. 2.

cities and lands of the imperial knights, all of them parts of a crumbling mosaic, Carolingian in origin, fantastic in design and anachronistic in purpose. Theorists had attempted to justify the existence of this heterogeneous collection of states on the ground that it provided some kind of buffer between Russia and Austria on the east and France on the west. As in Italy the achievement of unity was long delayed by association with the empire, and in both areas there were abundant opportunities for intrigue and aggression by powerful neighbours. But already, in both Germany and Italy, two royal houses, the Hohenzollerns and the kings of Savoy-Sardinia, were laying the foundations of unity and national monarchy.

Of the larger German states Bavaria had lost its pre-eminence of earlier years, nor was this altered by the fact that for three years (1742-5) a Bavarian Wittelsbach, Charles VII, held the office of emperor. Little more than a puppet of France, he was succeeded in Bavaria by Maximilian Joseph, who did much to improve the administration of his duchy and extend opportunities for education; he, in turn, was followed by Karl Theodore of the Palatinate branch of the family, whose attempted transfer of his duchy to the Habsburgs provided a pretext for the Bavarian Succession War.[1] In the eighteenth century Munich, the capital, had some importance as a centre of art and music. Saxony, under Augustus II and Augustus III, was linked with Poland, of which these two prince-electors were in succession kings; in consequence they had to maintain two Courts, one in Dresden, the other in Warsaw. As a capital city Dresden, modelled on Paris, experienced much devastation through its occupation by Prussian troops in the early stages of the Seven Years War; but, throughout the later part of the century, the city became of importance as a cultural centre. Augustus III, who died in 1763, was succeeded by his grandson Frederick Augustus, who restored the finances of the electorate, and introduced such improvement in the administration as to be named The Just.

[1] above, pp. 148-9.

Hanover, to which the duke of Brunswick had succeeded in 1692, was the continental possession of the kings of Great Britain and the favourite place of residence of the first two Georges; it was ruled with considerable tolerance and enlightenment. In 1834 it passed to the brother of King William IV, and was absorbed by Prussia in 1860. Its university of Göttingen, founded by George II, was a serious rival to the Prussian university of Halle. Of the smaller states Württemberg derived some reputation from the consistent opposition maintained by its Estates, consisting of a homogeneous body of burgesses, to the encroachments of Karl Eugen, who committed many arbitrary acts. Among the most backward of the German states were those of Mecklenburg, Hesse-Cassel and Hesse-Darmstadt, whose rulers had no compunction in selling troops to other states, many of whom were used in the war against the American colonists. Saxe-Weimar, on the other hand, was well administered by Karl Augustus (1775-1827), who derived some reputation from the association of Goethe with his government. Serfdom was abolished, the law was reformed, and Saxe-Weimar emerged as one of the most enlightened states in Germany.

The civilisation of Germany in this period was limited to widely-scattered towns, many of them almost medieval in their institutions, particularly in their highly organised and exclusive gilds, all of them close-knit, individual communities, severely limited in their contacts with the outside world. Hamburg was the most cosmopolitan; the Rhenish towns could hardly have escaped the impact of French civilisation; the southern towns had relations with Venice and Italy. But there was no capital to give a lead. Hence a certain disparate and provincial element in German culture, accentuated by the rigid social classes into which people were divided. A strict hierarchy of ranks, which put the nobility at the top, maintained clear differentiation even among the professions, that of the law being accounted highest because recruited from members of noble families, many of them intended for high office. The profession of medicine was a poor second. Bankers and wholesale merchants were high on the scale; the Lutheran clergy ranked beneath the Catholic hierarchy; school teachers were at the bottom.[1]

Not until the later part of the century did German become a literary language; until then Latin and French were the media of learned or polite communication, with the result that German civilisation was for long derivative in character. This is true to some extent even of Leibniz (1646-1716) who, in 1678 had entered the service of the Duke of Brunswick, as Goethe was afterwards to serve the House of Saxe-Weimar, a fact of some significance since it means that these two great men-of-letters came into public notice not in their own right, but as servants of noble families. Leibniz taught an abstruse, optimistic philosophy, known to most of us from the ridicule which Voltaire poured upon it in *Candide*. A brilliant mathematician and physicist, Leibniz dissipated much of his energy on projects such as a history of the House of Brunswick, the union of the Protestant and Catholic churches and the diversion of Louis XIV's bellicose ambitions from Europe to the east. He stood somewhat apart from his fellow countrymen; nor did he direct them to any definite line of intellectual development as Descartes had done for France.

Leibniz represented the older type of erudition in which mathematics played an essential part. In this respect he was contrasted with Immanuel Kant (1724-1804) who, as professor of Philosophy at Königsberg, devoted himself almost entirely to metaphysics. As a philosopher, quite distinct from the French *philosophes*, he wrote not for the ordinary man of intelligence, but for specialists in abstruse thought. Locke[2] had started investigation of what might be called the science of knowing, by ruling out innate ideas, and claiming that sense

[1] For studies of German society and thought in this period, see L. Levy Bruhl, *L'Allemagne depuis Leibniz* (1907) and W. H. Bruford, *Germany in the Eighteenth Century* (1935).

[2] For Locke and his influence, see below, pp. 320-1.

impressions are the only material on which the mind can work. By the time (1781) when Kant produced his *Critique of Pure Reason* there had been much discussion about the processes involved in cognition; Locke's theories had been considerably amplified and modified, and his total rejection of innate ideas was steadily becoming less acceptable. Kant, who made a close study of Locke and his critics, may have been influenced by Rousseau who, in his emotionalism, had restored the heart to the place from which the rationalists had dethroned it. Rejecting the possibility of knowing things in themselves, Kant restricted knowledge of things to what they appeared to be (*phenomena*). The sense data are the material on which the mind works; but he concluded that the mind can act on these materials only because it is already endowed with intuitions of space and time, prior to sense experience.

Here was something like a return to innate ideas, for the reason, according to Kant, is already endowed with " ideas ". This was the main principle of what is called the idealist school, derived originally from Plato and destined to influence the thinking of Coleridge and Hegel. It was in effect a denial of the rationalism which had played such an important part in the Enlightenment, and it pointed directly to the poetry of Wordsworth and the Romanticists. Hume had already cast doubt on the part played by reason on human conduct; Kant went farther, for he assigned a greater rôle to will and action, the control of the " good will " over conduct being the " categorical imperative " of his Ethics. It is only fair to add that several distinguished philosophers have confessed their inability to understand Kant, and one of them has stated that his influence on the development of abstract thought has proved a disaster.

In the later part of the eighteenth century there was a revival of Teutonism, so distinct from and contrary to the ideals of the Enlightenment (which was mainly French) that it may be possible here to treat it as something separate and self-contained. This revival of a national spirit, with its creation of a national literature, may be attributed to a number of causes. There was the Seven Years War which evoked an incipient nationalism directed against the intrusion of foreigners in Germany, a reaction strengthened by the sufferings of the German people and by the brilliant success with which Frederick had snatched victory from apparent disaster. Of this resurgent Germany Lessing was the novelist and Ewald von Kleist the poet. Another cause was the revival of German as the national language. This was fostered by the poet Frederick Klopstock (1724-1803) who, though he wrote a tedious epic, did much to promote the study and use of the vernacular and to discredit the popularity of French drama and literature. A third influence was Kant. In contrast with the Latin races, who have always been distinguished by a strong sense of realism, the Teutonic races are subject to waves of sentiment and emotionalism; in this indeed lies their strength and weakness. Kant's "innateism" and idealism—cloudy and diffuse though they may well appear to many readers—met with an immediate response from those who demanded something more exalted than the dictates of reason. On the one hand this entailed the use of such apocalyptic terms as *zeitgeist, immanence* and *transcendentalism,* terms which may mean a great deal or nothing at all; on the other hand it inspired a literature which has taken its place among the literatures of the world. The leaders in this movement were Gotthold Lessing (1729-81), Johann Herder (1744-1803) and Johann von Goethe (1749-1832).

Lessing, a Saxon, studied at Leipzig, afterwards working as journalist and literary critic in Berlin. He spent five years (1760-5) in Breslau, the capital of Silesia, where he wrote two of his best known works—*Minna von Barnhelm* and *Laocoon.* In 1767 he went to Hamburg as director of the municipal theatre there. His literary criticism, unsparing in its condemnation of pedantry and slavish imitation of foreign models, helped to destroy the foundations of the older German culture. But there was a constructive element even in his onslaughts; this was demonstrated in his criticism of a contemporary classic. In 1764 Winckelmann published his great book[1] on ancient art, a manifesto from which can be dated the emergence of a neo-classical school in art and literature. In his emphasis on the importance of proportion and restraint Winckelmann had cited as a model the group of statuary known as the Laocoon (now in the Vatican) which depicts the well-known tragedy of father and sons described by Virgil in the second book of the *Aeneid*. Lessing's reply to Winckelmann's thesis was his *Laocoon* (1766), in which he contended that passion and sentiment, not repose and harmony, are the true inspirations of poetry. In this, the first clear challenge to a cherished ideal, was the new evangel of the *Sturm und Drang* period which eventually led to the Romantic Revival. There was the same revolutionary element in his interpretation of drama. His *Minna von Barnhelm,* with its intimate analysis of human emotion, was the only literary product of the Seven Years War. During his stay in Hamburg, where he worked as a dramatic critic, Lessing succeeded in diminishing the number of French plays put on the stage, substituting German compositions; moreover his criticism helped to create the standards of a new, national drama. It was he who made Saxon the language of his compatriots; like Sainte Beuve after him he showed how constructive criticism can be. His subject matter was German, but his influence was European.

His friend Herder came from East Prussia, where he had studied at the university of Königsberg and had been greatly influenced by the teaching of Kant. A Lutheran minister, he was a philologist of some repute and one of the earliest exponents of Hebrew literature. After 1776 he served as court preacher at Weimar, where he formed a warm friendship with Goethe. It was an age when there was developing a new cult of the primitive, evidenced in England by Macpherson's *Fingal* (1762), Chatterton's *Rowley Poems* (1765) and Percy's

---

[1] J. J. Winckelmann, *Geschichte der Kunst des Alterthums.* See also below, p. 293.

Reliques of Ancient Poetry (1765); what was being done in England for a remote and semi-apocryphal past was done by Herder for medieval German lyrics and folk songs. The Germany of the middle ages was revived with nationalist accretions, and even Shakespeare was dragged in as an example of Teutonic genius. These things provided a preliminary to Herder's studies in the philosophy of history, the results of which he published in the years 1784-91. While Locke and his followers had insisted on the essential similarities of human nature, modified mainly by environment, Herder attributed to each nation distinctive moral and intellectual qualities, all derived from remote ancestry, all permeating its literature, law and religion. These, he held, were imperishable and ineradicable qualities. All this shows that Germany was at last becoming conscious of herself; of her achievements in a semi-historical past and of a destiny that would lead to still greater achievements in the future. The old cosmopolitanism was gone; the Teutonic virtues were contrasted with the Gallic vices, and a great nation was achieving self-expression by rejection of all things French.

Goethe was born at Frankfort-on-the-Main and studied law at Leipzig. His education was continued further at Strasburg, and he specialised in botany, anatomy and alchemy, indeed in all the sciences except mathematics. Of handsome appearance and passionate nature he had a number of love affairs from which he took refuge in flight; a Frenchman would have settled down comfortably with at least one of his lady loves. But Goethe, in his extreme sensitivity and restlessness, was the embodiment of a new, turbulent age, to which he gave a lead in his *Götz von Berlichingen* (1773), the *Sorrows of Werther* (1774) and *Faust* (1775). These productions have meant more for Germany than for Europe. The first is an account of the career of a robber baron of the sixteenth century, whose one redeeming feature appears to be his love of liberty; it was translated by Scott in 1798. The second, partly autobiographical, is a depressing record of one whose hopeless love affairs ended in suicide; the third elaborates the antithesis between the limitless and futile aspirations of the soul and the permanence of ordinary human affection. In all these three compositions, however impressive they may be, there is a suggestion of intellectual disorder or at least discontent, a striving after something neither defined nor attainable; it is a literature of revolt, but against what? Unconsciously Goethe was giving expression to the innermost recesses of German mentality, providing inspiration for the Romantic Revival, which was to destroy the ideals of the *Ancien Régime*.

Chapter IX

PORTUGAL, SPAIN AND ITALY

I PORTUGAL AND SPAIN

Between 1580 and 1640 Portugal was under Spanish rule; her independence, under the House of Braganza, was won by force of arms. Preservation of this independence can be attributed partly to geographical factors, for the country is protected by mountain ranges on the north and east; and her three great rivers, Tagus, Douro and Guadiana, provide no easy access from Spain because they are navigable only after their descent from mountain gorges. A southern latitude and proximity to the sea account for an agreeable climate and luxuriance of vegetation; no country is richer in edible fruits. But Portugal, which had a population of about three millions at the end of the century, is poorly endowed in natural resources. In the valley of the Douro is centred the country's most profitable industry—wine which, after the Methuen treaty of 1703, was sent to England (with bullion) in exchange for textiles and manufactured goods. Poverty and illiteracy were normal among the peasants, employed in conditions of semi-serfdom on the *latifundia* of the nobles. The high proportion of Negro and Moorish elements in the population attested the former importance of Portugal as a maritime and colonial power.

In such conditions and in the absence of an educated middle class, it was natural that a traditional type of divine-right monarchy should survive. John V, who ruled from 1706 to 1750 was noted for piety and profligacy; a priest king, authorised by the pope to celebrate mass, and entitled to the epithet of The Faithful. His pleasures lay in the exercise of sacerdotal functions; "for buildings he had convents; for armies, monks; for mistresses, nuns".[1] One of his sons by an abbess became Inquisitor General. Otherwise John's reign was notable mainly for its architectural monuments, of which the greatest was the Mafro Convent, about 20 miles from Lisbon, built at great cost as a thanksgiving for the birth in 1715 of his legitimate son Joseph. Towards the end of the reign the decline of Portugal was evidenced in the increasing poverty of the countryside and in the ports, as well as by a revival of anti-Jewish sentiment.

The rule of his successor Joseph I (1750-77) was made notable by the revolutionary but short-lived reforms of Sebastian Carvalho e Melho Marquis of Pombal, one of the most remarkable but injudicious of eighteenth-century reformers. Before coming to power as a minister in 1751, Pombal had spent some years in England where, like Montesquieu and Voltaire, he may have been impressed by English institutions; as well as this, his study of history led him to admire the constructive work of Colbert in France, and impressed on him a belief in dictatorial legislation as the only means of building up the economy of a nation. His earliest administrative task was to restore Lisbon after the earthquake of 1755; thereafter, until the king's death, he was, in effect, the ruler of the state. From the outset he was inspired by two hatreds—of the Jesuits and of the nobility. As regards the Jesuits, he resented their control over not only the education, but to some extent the economic life of Portugal and Brazil; as for the noble class, of which he was himself a member, he knew that it was an incubus on the country. But, before we applaud his attitude to the first of these, it should be recalled that in Brazil the Jesuits often protected the Indians against enslavement, a protection resented by the settlers, anxious to have as many slaves as possible, whether Indian or Negro. In this matter Pombal had the support of the colonists, with the result that the Jesuits

---

[1] Frederick the Great, *Histoire de Mon Temps*, in *Oeuvres Historiques de Frederick II* (Berlin, 1846), vol. II, p. 14.

were expelled from Portugal and Brazil in 1757 on the pretext that they were engaged in a conspiracy against the monarchy. This proved to be the signal for their expulsion from other Catholic states.

Pombal's main object was to stop the outflow of specie to foreign countries and to end Portugal's dependence on imports from England and, to a less extent, from France. In place of this dependence he proposed to build up native industries, especially in textiles, even at the expense of agriculture and the wine industry. Generally, his administrative changes were carried out on the standardised pattern of eighteenth-century reforms. He established free trade within the limits of Portugal and with Brazil; he bought back alienated crown lands; factories were established with hosts of regulations and inspectors; the finances were reformed, and schools of instruction in the arts and crafts were set up. Foreign artisans were settled in the towns and the higher administrative posts were opened to commoners. The clergy were alienated by his limitation of mortmain and his grant of civil rights to Jews; after the expulsion of the Jesuits the schools were secularised. For one of the most backward countries in Europe this was an ambitious programme. Pombal, who was as impetuous as the Emperor Joseph II and more violent, employed a secret police system to ferret out his opponents, and the prisons were filled with his enemies and critics, most of them nobles. With the death of King Joseph in 1777 there came the inevitable reaction, and the minister was exiled to his country estate. The new ruler Maria I, daughter of Joseph, married her uncle, who was seventeen years her senior; under the rule of this pious pair the power of clergy and nobility was restored, and Portugal relapsed into her old mode of life.

Climatic and geographical conditions imposed on Spain distinctions and differences which no attempt at unification could wholly remove. Bounded by the Pyrenees, the Cantabrian mountains, the Portuguese border and the sierras of the south and east, Spain is one of the most mountainous and inaccessible countries in Europe. Of the greater rivers two—Tagus and Tormes (Douro in Portugal)—have their exits on the Portuguese coast; the Ebro in this period was navigable for only a part of its course, but the Guadalquivir was navigable from Seville to the sea. All the main roads converged on the capital; elsewhere tracks had to serve for communication. In fine, nature seems to have conspired to keep Spain hermetically sealed from the rest of Europe and to perpetuate ancient antagonisms within its bounds.

The union of Castile and Aragon by the marriage of Ferdinand and Isabella in 1469 did not create a united Spain. Castile, the dominant partner, remained the nucleus of an absolutist monarchy, intolerant of local privileges and particularism, while Aragon, Navarre and the Basque provinces retained many of their ancient *fueros* or privileges. These provinces, intolerant of uniformity, were intent on preserving some measure of autonomy. This dualism between Castile and the other provinces was accentuated by differences of dialect and, according to some authorities, of race. Between Castile and Catalonia this dualism had amounted to a fierce antagonism in the War of the Spanish Succession; it was an irreconcilable contest between a backward, territorial monarchy and a progressive, maritime and industrial state, a contest made more bitter by official prohibition of the Catalan language. But, in the eighteenth century, some measure of unity was achieved by the cautious rule of Charles III (1759-88), assisted by such skilful administrators as Aranda, Campomanes and Florida Blanca. In contrast with Portugal under Pombal and Austria under Joseph II reform in the peninsula proceeded gradually, but even that was not enough to safeguard Spain from the revolutionary movements of the early nineteenth century.

Madrid, situated in the geographic centre, had been the capital only since the reign of Philip II; other cities, such as Seville, Barcelona, Saragossa and Valencia might, because of their better situation, have served as capitals. Apart from Madrid, with its population of about 100,000, few Spanish cities had more than 25,000 inhabitants. The increase of population from about 7 millions at the beginning of the century to 10 millions at the end was very uneven, and appears to have been confined almost entirely to the coastal districts. Of the Castilian towns only Guadalajara, situated about 35 miles east of Madrid, could be described as industrial; it was a cloth-making centre, dependent on the labour of thousands of domestic workers in the surrounding countryside. Of the ports, Seville was being displaced by Cadiz; in the north, Bilbao provided an outlet for the iron work of the Biscainers; in Catalonia Barcelona became the busiest port of Spain and one of the greatest in the Mediterranean.

Second in importance only to the monarchy, the church derived its great wealth from rents, tithe and gifts. Of the clergy, who numbered about 160,000, the seculars accounted for about 70,000, the regulars for 60,000 and the nuns for 30,000. In contrast with France and even with England the higher ecclesiastics were not recruited solely from the aristocracy; so too the parish priests, as in Ireland, came from the peasant class and were popular with their parishioners. In 1753, by a Concordat with the Vatican, the powers of the papacy were greatly reduced, particularly in nominations to episcopal vacancies, and church lands were made liable to royal taxation. Until their expulsion in 1767 the Jesuits dominated higher education, and their *Colegios Majores,* founded originally for the sons of the poor, were now filled with sons of the nobility, intended for higher posts in the administration. The 24 universities were among the most backward in Europe, their curricula being based on the *trivium* of medieval times; it was their boast that they had not changed since their foundation. Aristotle and Aquinas still held sway; Copernicus and Newton might never have existed. In these conditions it is not surprising that the practice of religion was often little different from the fetichism prevailing to-day in many parts of

Latin America. Nuns dressed up dolls, with perruques and canes, to represent Christ and the Saints.[1]

Until 1808 the Inquisition was powerful in Spain; like the church it was endowed with vast wealth. This tribunal, which did not limit itself to heresy as we understand the term, dealt also with medical and religious quacks, in which respect it may have performed a good service for the community. But it treated with great severity those Jews who, in spite of their professed Christianity, were secretly practising Jewish rites, or rather were suspected of so doing. It is customary nowadays in some quarters to depict the Inquisition as an eminently just institution which, so far from soiling its hands with blood, merely handed over convicted and relapsed heretics to the state for exemplary punishment. But the facts do not warrant this view, because the Holy Office often acted on no more than suspicion or hearsay, which it usually accepted as conclusive evidence; moreover much of the information on which it proceeded came from spies and informers or from accusers anxious to have revenge on a personal enemy. This tribunal was responsible for the infliction of barbarous punishment on thousands of men and women whose only offence was either the race to which they belonged, or some slight " deviationism " from the orthodox opinion prevailing at the time; moreover, it was applied even to temporary residents in Spain. Its burnings provided public spectacles. In the reign of Philip V (1700-46) there were more than 700 *autos-da-fe,* some of them attended personally by the king, but his successors disapproved of such severities, as they disliked bull fights, and so did all in their power to limit the activities of this sanguinary tribunal. The result was that, in the reigns of Ferdinand VI (1746-59) and Charles III (1759-88) the number of burnings at the stake greatly diminished. Bearing in mind the public demand for these spectacles, Ferdinand and Charles went only so far as they could go.

There exists no complete guide to the heraldry of Spain, for

[1] G. Desdevises du Dezert, *L'Espagne de l'Ancien Régime,* I, ch. 2.

the good reason that such a large proportion of the population claimed the right to emblazon their arms that a library would be needed to depict all their coats of arms. Elsewhere the nobility usually had some kind of basis for their status, whether in land, money or office; but this was not so in Spain, where a beggar might have his crest and call his hovel a palace. At the other end of the scale the higher nobility were among the most exclusive in Europe. They were headed by the 119 Grandees of Spain, most of them of ancient lineage and vast territorial possessions. Most numerous in this very miscellaneous aristocracy were the *hidalgos,* numbering about half a million, many of them indistinguishable from commoners. Poor as he might be, the *hidalgo* had a number of privileges— he could not be imprisoned for debt; soldiers could not be billeted on him; if he went to prison he could demand a room for himself. In effect, therefore, the population consisted mainly of agricultural workers, priests, hidalgos, beggars, gipsies and vagabonds, with a minority of merchants and artisans.

But neither the paucity of the middle class nor the incubus of the Inquisition prevented altogether the infiltration of more modern ideas into Spain. Spaniards themselves prepared the way. In 1713 the Spanish Academy was founded, an institution which produced a dictionary of Castilian. There was evidence that men of letters were anxious to break down the barriers by which they were surrounded. Of this an example was Geronimo Feyjoo,[1] a professor of theology at the university of Oviedo. A keen student of foreign literature, he began in 1726 the publication of his series of essays entitled *Teatro Critico Universal,* in which he impugned the authority of Aristotle in Spanish education, advocating in its place the adoption of Bacon's inductive method. A critic of the conduct of the medical profession, he insisted on the need for research and recommended, as a model, the medical faculty at Leyden.

[1] For a good account of Feyjoo see R. Herr, *The Revolution in Eighteenth-Century Spain,* ch. 3.

He attempted also to discredit the superstition which led to the persecution of witches. These opinions met with a favourable response and the Essays proved a literary success. There is also evidence that the educated classes were by no means indifferent to the Enlightenment; for, in spite of the examination of books at the ports by officials of the Inquisition, copies of *The Spectator,* the *Encyclopédie* and Buffon's *Histoire Naturelle* were smuggled into the country. The plays of Voltaire could be performed in public, provided the name of the author was not mentioned.

Reference has already been made[1] to the improved administration brought to Spain by the Bourbons. The death of Philip V in 1746 was followed by the accession of Ferdinand VI, his son by his first wife. Ferdinand was pious and under the influence of the Jesuits, but he showed singular tolerance, and his Concordat of 1753 with Benedict XIV served to establish in Spain an almost independent church on the model of that in France. As well as effecting some reforms in the judicial and financial administration, Ferdinand inaugurated an economic revival by building roads and bridges and setting up new manufactures. In this he was aided by two ministers Bernard Carvajal and the Marquis de la Ensenada. It was mainly by the activities of the latter that naval arsenals were brought up to date, the Customs were re-organised, and a serious attempt was made to re-create the maritime power of Spain.

But there were serious obstacles confronting this revival. Of these the most important was the continued imbalance between the imports of precious metals and the return in goods of native manufacture; moreover, the needs of the Spanish empire were still supplied mainly by foreigners.[2] Then there was public finance. The clergy and nobility were not, it is true, exempt from taxation, and some revenue was raised from a purchase tax, but, whether from inefficient administration or from the general poverty of the populace, the yield

[1] above, pp. 56-7.   [2] above, p. 91.

from the numerous excise taxes was disappointing. Taxes were too numerous and the resources of the taxpayers were too slight.

Ferdinand was succeeded in 1759 by his half-brother Charles who, as Don Carlos, had been the subject of such dangerous solicitude on the part of his mother Elizabeth Farnese. Ruler of the Two Sicilies since 1735, Charles III came to Madrid after years of experience in Naples where, with the help of Bernard Tanucci, he had striven to introduce solvency and order into one of the most poverty-stricken states in Europe. As king of Spain Charles entered into the Family Compact of 1761 with Louis XV and went to war with England in 1762 and 1777 : in neither instance did he succeed in his main object—the recovery of Gibraltar. Otherwise, his rule proved to be one of the most enlightened in the annals of the monarchy. Its tangible results were to be seen mainly in Madrid, which became a capital city in the best traditions of the eighteenth century. Museums, picture galleries, observatories and botanic garden were set up and the city became an attractive place of residence. In the countryside roads were built or improved; canals were excavated, and the problem of mendicity was tackled by the establishment of workhouses and vocational schools. After the expulsion of the Jesuits the schools were partly secularised. In 1782 the Bank of St. Charles was instituted.

In all this Charles was assisted by a number of unusually competent ministers. Of these, the Count of Aranda (1719-99) after service as ambassador in Poland, became President of the Council of Castile in 1766. Already, when in France in 1750, he had met Voltaire and Diderot from whom he derived a sympathy with the ideas of the Enlightenment; accordingly, as Charles's chief minister, one of his first steps was to order the expulsion of the Jesuits. This policy of limiting clerical influence, which the king had brought with him from Naples, was advocated also by Pedro de Campomanes (1710-1800) who succeeded Aranda in the presidency of the Council of

Castile. In that capacity he strove, mainly by propaganda, to discourage the pious from leaving land to the church. A voluminous writer, specially interested in the economic revival of his country, Campomanes recommended that the articles in the *Encyclopédie* on the arts and crafts should be translated and circulated throughout Spain. Convinced that technology was the key to progress, he compiled memoirs for the training of the young in industry; in this he was assisted by the Count of Florida Blanca (1729-1808) who became President of the Council of Castile in 1777. These two, united in their campaign against mendicity, hoped that vocational training would solve what was regarded as Spain's most serious social problem. But in these matters human nature proved to be the determining factor; for, although many Spaniards became industrious artisans, there remained a large fringe who lived by begging. So Spain remained the only European country where respectability was not yet a virtue nor poverty a sin.

II ITALY

In the earlier decades of the century Italy provided a battle ground in which France, England and the emperor were engaged in resisting the attempts of Spain to upset the Utrecht settlement and restore Spanish rule in the peninsula. This period was ended in 1748, by which time the following general results had been achieved: the Duke of Savoy was in possession of Sardinia, with a portion of the western Milanese and the title of king; the Spanish Bourbons were established in the Two Sicilies and in Parma and Piacenza; the emperor, secure in his part of the Milanese, had added Tuscany to his Italian possessions. By the treaty of Aranjuez, signed in 1752, Austria and Sardinia guaranteed their possessions in Italy which thereafter enjoyed peace until the Revolution. This distribution of powers compared favourably with that of the previous century in this respect that, with the exception of the

Milanese, all the states were governed by resident rulers, whereas formerly a great part of the peninsula had been subject to remote control from Madrid.

In this patchwork of kingdoms, principalities and republics[1] very diverse polities prevailed. Of the kingdoms Sardinia was modelled on the Prussian system, a great part of the revenue being devoted to the upkeep of an army, a state of things necessitated by the fact that the territory of Savoy was wedged in between powerful neighbours. Turin was becoming a capital of the modern type, having a population of about 70,000, the headquarters in succession of Charles Emanuel (1730-73) and Victor Amadeus (1773-1796). Their Court was modelled on that of Versailles. In spite of frequent involvement in war, the kingdom was increasingly prosperous; but independence of thought was suppressed, and the fiery poet Alfieri had to flee from his vacuous surroundings.

Very different conditions prevailed in the Two Sicilies. In Naples the Bourbon King Charles made strenuous efforts to diminish and even to eliminate the feudalism and clericalism which exercised such a stranglehold over southern Italy and Sicily. For a time, with the help of his minister Tanucci, he succeeded. The number of priests and monasteries was limited; tribute was no longer paid to the Pope, and the Jesuits were expelled. An attempt was made to improve economic conditions, but little could be done to alleviate the poverty, disease and lawlessness that had for so long been endemic in the Two Sicilies. Nevertheless there was some intellectual activity. In the earlier part of the century the university of Naples had provided a professorship for the philosopher and historian G. B. Vico;[2] later in the century Antonio Genovesi (1712-69), by his books and lectures, popularised the study of political economy, while Gaetan Filangieri (1752-88) devoted himself to the study of legislation in a manner that recalls Montesquieu. His volumes on the science of legislation, pub-

[1] For the Italian republic see pp. 68-9.
[2] below, pp. 331-2.

lished in 1780 and 1788 were, for long, standard works. In 1759, when Charles left Naples for Madrid, he was succeeded by his infant son Ferdinand I. The regency was entrusted to Tanucci. On reaching maturity the weak Ferdinand married Maria Carolina, a daughter of Maria Theresa who, with her favourite minister Acton, displaced both the king and Tanucci, with the result that the state was reduced to that condition of obscurantism and squalor from which it had nearly emerged.

Similar conditions prevailed in the Papal States or Patrimony of St. Peter, which had come into papal possession by gift from the Empress Matilda in the twelfth century. Apart from Rome and Bologna, the Patrimony did not include any great cities; moreover the peasantry were so enfeebled by the chronic malaria of the marshes that many areas were uncultivated and depopulated. Frequent lotteries and debasement of the coinage provided no alleviation of the poverty everywhere prevalent. Rome, an agreeable place of residence, became increasingly popular with visitors especially after the tentative beginnings of excavation at Pompeii and Herculaneum, enterprises encouraged by King Charles of Naples, and enhanced by the publication in 1764 of Winckelmann's famous book on ancient art. But much greater importance can be attributed to Rome as the headquarters of the papacy, which somehow managed to outlive the eighteenth century as it had already survived the sixteenth. The Vicar of Christ, originally only Bishop of Rome, had for long exercised a dual prerogative of great dimensions. As spiritual head of western Christendom he summoned councils, appointed cardinals, instituted bishops, established or abolished religious orders, approved or censured dogmas by means of Bulls and Encyclicals. He imposed or took off excommunication; he could grant dispensations and indulgences. In his temporal capacity he wielded absolute authority over Rome and the Patrimony. His spiritual prerogative and his two temporal powers were represented by the three tiers of his triple tiara. He was represented at foreign courts by legates or nuncios, and agents of Catholic states were accredited to him at the Vatican. Since the sixteenth century only Italians had been elected to the papal throne, and these were generally of such mature years that they were likely to combine experience with an aversion to radical changes. The Vatican was no place for youth movements.

The Age of the Enlightenment was not favourable to such vast claims, but the papacy was a proved expert in the delicate art of survival. In the eighteenth century its resilience was tested not by heretics but by orthodox Catholics who, in some cases, were not merely limiting or withdrawing their traditional allegiance, but were attempting to destroy the one Order devoted to the maintenance and strengthening of the papal claims, namely, the Society of Jesus. Why this Catholic dislike of the Jesuits? There were several causes. In their foreign missions, particularly in China, the Jesuits had proceeded circumspectly, winning the confidence of prospective converts by professing sympathy with the teaching of Confucius. From the orthodox point of view this was one of the worst of crimes, for it amounted to compromise with heresy; indeed, in the opinion of many accredited theologians, the Jesuits were heretics, for they believed in salvation for all men, in contrast to the teaching of St. Augustine and the Dominicans, who limited salvation to the Elect. The Jesuits had nearly as many enemies among their commercial rivals for, particularly in South America and the French West Indies, they were engaged in vast business enterprises, at least one of which ended in bankruptcy.

At first it was thought that some compromise might be effected. Benedict XIV (1740-58), acting on the suggestion of Pombal, appointed a commission to investigate the commercial activities of the Society in Portugal. This commission reported unfavourably and recommended that the crown should confiscate its merchandise. Benedict might have succeeded in reforming the Society but unfortunately he died, and his successor, Clement XIII (1758-69), who was devoted to the Jesuits, refused even to discuss their reform. Meanwhile, with the expulsion of the Jesuits from Portugal, France and Spain, the Holy See was placed in a difficult position especially when, in 1769, envoys from France, Spain and Naples appeared at the Vatican in order to demand the extinction of the Society. From this dilemma the pope was mercifully saved by his death. His successor Clement XIV (1769-74) was very different from his predecessor; indeed, he was so critical of the Jesuits as to be suspected of Jansenism. Accordingly, in July 1773, by the Bull *Dominus ac Redemptor*, he pronounced the dissolution of the Society. His successor Pius VI (1775-99) experienced an even greater humiliation. In the hope that he might induce the Emperor Joseph II to moderate his policy of drastic dissolution of religious houses, he took the unusual step of going to Vienna in 1782 in order to present his plea in person. The emperor refused to make any concession. It was Canossa in reverse.

Such were the conditions in the middle and southern portions of the peninsula. In the north the Milanese was probably the most prosperous of all the Italian states. A system of intensive farming, recalling that of the Netherlands, prevailed in the countryside, and the city of Milan became an active business centre, dominated by merchants who displaced the old feudal magnates and civic oligarchs. A new race of native-born administrators grew up under the tutelage of Vienna. As Belgium derived great advantage from the benevolent vice-gerency of Prince Charles of Lorraine, so Lombardy was won over to Austrian rule by the intelligent administration of Count Firmian, who acted as Governor from 1759 to 1782. Farming of taxes was abolished; restraints on trade were removed in favour of a free economy based on physiocratic principles.[1] The privileges of the church were restrained. A new survey of lands made possible the introduction of a more modern system of taxation. As well as this, there was much intellectual activity. The university of Pavia

[1] For these see above, pp. 96-7.

acquired fame from the researches of Alessandro Volta (1745-1827) the discoverer of the Voltaic pile. A group of intellectuals contributed its liberal and reforming views to a journal *Il Caffé,* modelled on *The Spectator,* which appeared between 1764 and 1766. But, after 1780, when Joseph II became sole ruler of the Austrian dominions, the Milanese suffered from the excessive zeal of that monarch, and a secret police interfered with the liberty of the subject.

Of those who contributed to *Il Caffé* the most notable was Cesare Beccaria (1738-94), a native of Milan, whose treatise " Of Crimes and Punishments ", first published in 1764 when the author was only 26, proved to be one of the most revolutionary books of the century. A keen student of the *philosophes,* he applied the ideas of the Enlightenment to the science of penology, or rather he created that science. Briefly, his views may be thus summarised. He insisted on the credibility of witnesses and denounced secret accusations; for the abuse of oaths, so prevalent among his contemporaries, he had nothing but condemnation; he recommended the abolition of both the death penalty and torture—in his opinion the use of torture often led to the acquittal of " robust villains " and the condemnation of physically weak but innocent men. Endurance of torture, he claimed, was a matter of temperament. Equally, severity of punishment frequently defeated its object since men, having already made themselves liable to savage retribution, had no hesitation in committing other crimes. Promptness and certainty of punishment were, he maintained, far better deterrents. Punishment he measured not by its severity but by its duration; consequently, life imprisonment was a more serious penalty than hanging. These views, which now seem trite, were revolutionary when first propounded, and Europe was ripe for their reception, if we except the Dominicans, who disapproved of the abolition of torture. Recognition came swiftly to Beccaria. In 1768 Kaunitz and Firmian appointed him professor of political economy at the Palatine School in Milan, and it is a notable fact that, in the later decades of the century, torture was abolished in many European states. It was in England, however, in the earlier part of the nineteenth century, that the full influence of Beccaria was exercised, as evidenced by the reforms of Bentham, Peel and Romilly, as well as by the great reduction in the number of capital offences.

These considerations suggest that Habsburg rule in Milan was comparatively tolerant and enlightened; the same applies to their régime in Tuscany. There the ruler from 1765 to 1790 was Leopold, younger son of the Emperor Francis Stephen and younger brother of Joseph II. Leopold proved to be the ideal " benevolent despot " of the century. A Council of Regency had prepared the way for him by removing many abuses. As in Lombardy, the power of the church was restricted; the control exercised by the Inquisition was restrained; the number of Saints' Days was reduced; tithe was abolished; rights of sanctuary and the prerogatives of the spiritual courts were limited. Under Leopold's administration the farming of taxes was ended and the state debt was funded. In his Council the Grand Duke provided for the representation of tax payers; as well as this he introduced more uniformity into the many communes of which Tuscany was composed. With the help of his minister Pomponio Neri, thoroughgoing reforms, mainly on physiocratic lines, were introduced. Mortmain and entails were made illegal; numerous gilds were sequestrated; free circulation of grain was established. Subsidies were paid to enterprising Agriculturalists, and an *Accademia dei Georgofili* (Academy of Agriculturalists) was established to give practical guidance to farmers. Leopold expressed his belief that all government is contractual, and that the contract should define and limit the powers of the ruler. But obviously many of his reforms were too far reaching to last; moreover, their enforcement was backed by a system of secret police, a clear example of the association of benevolent intention with extreme autocracy. Nevertheless, he re-created much of the old prosperity of Tuscany, mainly in agriculture and silk weaving, and his reforms at least provided a programme of what an enterprising prince might try to accomplish.

Such were the rulers of the more important states. In general, it may be said that in no other country were the effects of foreign intervention so deeply resented as in Italy, where geography and language, if not race, appeared to point the way to unity and independence. Among the factors that had long impeded the achievement of such unity was the association with empire and papacy, both of them international institutions; but, after the peace of Aix-la-Chapelle (1748) which ended for a time the foreign invasions, intelligent Italians, able to take stock of the situation, may have recalled Machiavelli's plea for an Italy " freed from foreigners ". Long before the *Risorgimento* some of the bases of unification had at least been explored. One of these was derived from language and literature. As early as 1612 the Florentine *Accademia della Crusca* had published a dictionary which helped to make Tuscan the literary language of Italy: in 1690 the Academy of the Arcadians was founded in Rome for the promotion of Italian literature. In the same year an institute was established in Bologna for the study of arts and sciences. The first large-scale history of Italian literature was published at Modena in the years 1772-81 by G. Tiraboschi, librarian to the Este family. Accordingly, in language and literature at least, some sense of nationalism was taking shape. A similar process was evidenced in historiography. Of this the most notable example was provided by L. A. Muratori (1672-1750), a native of Modenese territory who, after service in the Ambrosian Library at Milan, became Archivist to the Duke of Este. Continuing the great traditions of the Benedictines, Muratori edited and published many medieval sources in his series *Rerum Italicarum Scriptores,* 29 volumes of which were produced in the years 1723-51. Between 1744 and 1749 he published in Italian the 12 volumes of his " Annals of Italy ", extending from the early middle ages to his own day. Muratori's work was of importance not only for its scholarship, but for its elucidation of the element of continuity in the history of the peninsula.

Even more important for this nascent nationalism was the cult of Etruria and the Etruscans as the sources of Italian civilisation. This was strong in Florence, where an Etruscan Academy was founded in 1726. Already Vico had drawn attention to this pre-Roman civilisation, but his description did not warrant the conclusions afterwards drawn by enthusiasts about the superiority of the Etruscans over other primitive peoples. Now, in the development of nationalism, origins, or rather a theory of origins, may exercise a decisive influence because, for the nation as for the individual, reputable ancestors provide the best starting point. Frenchmen traced the achievements of their race to the Frankish conquerors of Gaul; the Irishman perpetuates the legends of Celtic kings and saints; the German insists on the valour, the freedom and the racial purity of his Teutonic forebears; to some northern enthusiasts the half-legendary Picts were the original architects of Scottish achievement. Only the Englishman—exceptional in this as in so many other respects—appears indifferent to any sentiment of origins, for he accepts the assurance that his Anglo-Saxon ancestors were half-barbarous and that his own civilisation dates from his defeat by the Normans. In the eighteenth century many Italians had at last found their original progenitors in the Etruscans. After all, a good family tree is a sure basis of self-esteem, and self-esteem is the inspiration of nationalism.

Chapter X

FRANCE

Even as late as the eighteenth century France[1] was by no means a homogeneous state. Cities such as Marseilles, Bayonne and Dunkirk preserved a certain element of independence; Alsace retained her Customs barrier on the French side; Lorraine and Corsica, after their incorporation into France, were almost foreign provinces. Even to-day, the use of Breton and Provençal is common in Brittany and Provence. As well as this, there were certain enclaves, such as Avignon and the Comtat Venaissin. This separatism added to the difficulties of administration; still more, it impeded the transport of cereals from one area to another in times of shortage, for many Frenchmen, thinking in terms not of the nation, but of the *pays,* or *généralité* or even the parish, were convinced that any benefit to another area must be at the expense of their own. Hence a certain provincial psychology. " He is not in my parish " was one way of expressing complete indifference to the affairs of other men.

I THE MAIN CLASSES OF SOCIETY. TAXATION.

At the basis of the social system there were about 40,000 villages, each having limited rights of arranging its own affairs. At their meetings they elected the *syndic* (trustee), the tax collector, the herdsman, the school teacher and the postman. They also appointed the dates of the harvest and apportioned the common lands; they arranged for carrying out the royal *corvée* of road and bridge building. Collectively they

[1] For the French constitution see above, pp. 64-8.

ook their complaints to the *intendant*. As there was much
verlapping of royal and seigneurial jurisdiction disputes were
requent; village meetings were tumultuous, and were often
ollowed by litigation. In the *Pays d'Elections*, where the
aille was a personal tax, the office of collector was one to be
voided as much as possible, since it might mean ruin to the
erson elected—usually by hostile neighbours—for he had to
ake good deficiencies in the collection. On failure to do so,
e often took refuge in flight. Thereupon the *élus*—royal
fficials responsible for the *taille* of an *élection*—applied the
rinciple known in French finance as *solidarité* which meant
hat, as the total sum due from the village had not been paid,
he deficiency must be made good by a levy on the more sub-
tantial inhabitants. Nor was this all. As the assessment on
village was a fixed amount, no account was taken of a de-
rease in the number of tax payers, a decrease usually ac-
ounted for by acquisition of one of the many small offices
onferring immunity from the *taille*. Here again the deficiency
ad to be made up. In the *Pays d'Etats*, where the local
states arranged with the Controller General for a lump sum
rom the province, the *taille* was more equitable, as it was
evied mainly on owners of real estate.

There were great inequalities in the administration of the
owns. In the *Pays de Droit Ecrit*, that is, in the south and
outh-west, the municipalities were governed by *Consulats*, of
whom a small number acted in the name of the whole body;
n the north and north-east, they were controlled by the *mairie*,
onsisting of mayor and aldermen. All these civic authorities
ad extensive judicial powers, for they enforced their decrees
y fine and imprisonment, and they issued *lettres de cachet*
whereby a townsman might be taken into custody without
ause shown. Their judicial activities came into European pro-
inence in the notorious cases of Calas, Sirven and De La
Barre.[1] As well as this they enforced sumptuary legislation.
General control of industry in the towns was shared by the

[1] below, p. 342.

municipality, the lieutenants of police, the *intendants* and a host of inspectors who, in conjunction with the gild patriarchates, usually exercised a policy of rigid conservatism and opposition to new inventions. Combinations among the journeymen were illegal, but they existed nevertheless. There were also conflicts between the gilds[1] and merchants controlling the supply of raw material, such as silk; this led to a serious revolt at Lyons in 1744.

The rapid expansion of French industry and commerce in this period enhanced the importance of the merchants, for the great profits of the slave and sugar trades brought into existence a new mercantile patriciate—the *noblesse des iles*. Many rich merchants applied their profits to banking transactions, as did Joseph Pâris-Duverney who, in conjunction with his brothers, conducted the *Visa* operations which led to a reduction of the national debt at the accession of Louis XV. In the régime of the Duc de Bourbon and Madame de Prie (1723-6) he acted almost as a minister, especially in the higher ecclesiastical appointments; later, as an associate of Madame de Pompadour, he exercised considerable influence in the choice of generals and even on the direction of strategy. A more creditable representative of this banker-merchant class was Samuel Bernard (1651-1739) who lent large sums to Louis XV and devoted much of his fortune to works of charity. There were also the *fermiers généraux* who, with their profits from the farming of the taxes and their thousands of employees, formed almost a separate estate of the realm. Many of them married into noble families or acquired titles for themselves, with the result that the pre-revolutionary aristocracy of France was nearly as much financial as territorial.

The status of nobleman in France was not so clearly defined as in England, partly because all the children of a French nobleman were deemed noble. In 1777 it was estimated that there were about 16,000 nobles or about 80,000 persons en-

[1] For the gilds see above, pp. 22-4.

itled to the privileges of nobility;[1] this means a proportion of
bout one aristocrat to three hundred *roturiers* or commoners.
're-eminent among them were those whose claims were based
n ancient lineage—the *noblesse de race* or *d'épée*, having at
east four quarterings of nobility. They were followed by
hose of more recent creation, by letters patent; there were
lso titles derived from the holding of certain noble fiefs. In
756 there was created a military aristocracy by which every
eneral officer was ennobled, and in 1781 all military commissions were confined to those who could prove at least four
quarterings of nobility. This was intended to prevent the pur-
hase of commissions by wealthy bourgeois families. Tenure
f high municipal office accounted for the *noblesse de cloche*;
nother category was created when a noblewoman married a
ommoner, as the children were accounted *nobles de ventre*.
There was also a large class of persons holding the nominal
itle of king's secretary, and there were the *maîtres des re-
uètes*; purchase of one of these offices brought with it a title
f nobility. As well as this, there was the vast *noblesse de
obe*, consisting of the thousands who officiated in the thirteen
arlements; at first, these were despised by the nobility but, by
ntermarriage and community of interests, they became more
losely connected with the older aristocracy. Generally, there-
ore, the only characteristic of the eighteenth-century aristo-
racy was the absence of homogeneity. Everyone wanted an
ffice or title, if only to escape the *taille*.

The nobility could engage in wholesale but not in retail
rade. In 1721 much scandal was caused by the Duc de la
'orce who used his profits from investment in Law's[2] schemes
o set up a business in soap and perfumery. He was repri-
manded by the Paris *Parlement* and the tradesmen associated
vith him were fined. As the century advanced a greater
umber of the aristocracy engaged in industry, either in their

[1] H. Carré, *La Noblesse en France et l'Opinion Publique au
XVIIIème Siècle* (1920), p. 14.
[2] below, pp. 253-5.

own names or in those of nominees. The example set by the royal porcelain factory at Sèvres was followed by many of the nobility in the exploitation of mines and chemical works. Even in the army, the traditional sphere of occupation of the upper classes, there was an opportunity for profit because, until the reforms effected by Choiseul at the end of the Seven Years War, the colonels, who were chosen almost invariably from noble families, could expect to make profit from the clothing and equipment supplied to their men, whom they regarded almost as their property. More and more the nobility were becoming mercenary; they were even losing the one prerogative on which their privileged position depended—their inherited valour. Some of them showed cowardice, as at the battle of Dettingen in 1743, and in the Seven Years War their incompetence and arrogance were notorious. Public opinion gradually turned against the noble class, which the Marquis d'Argenson compared to the mildew on overripe fruit; and long before the Revolution they had come to be regarded as a serious incubus on French society.

The clergy of France included 131 archbishops and bishops, with about 1,500 commendatory abbés and priors and 2,700 vicars and canons; the parish clergy numbered about 60,000 *curés*. The contrast between the wealth and status of the upper clergy on the one hand and that of the lower clergy on the other was even more striking than in England. In the course of the century all the archbishoprics and bishoprics became confined to the aristocracy; as many of them were absentees they administered their dioceses by deputies. The higher clergy, many of them ultramontane in sympathy, were usually out of touch with popular opinion, nor were they often men of piety or learning; indeed, they regarded their great emoluments as the obligation of society to their rank. In all this there was little to distinguish them from their secular brothers and cousins. By contrast, the lower clergy included many who, on a wretched pittance, devoted themselves to pastoral work; a number of them were of Jansenist opinions and they became increasingly resentful of the social system which condemned them to penury and obscurity. Here indeed was a potentially revolutionary element in French society.

Abbots had long been classified as regular or commendatory; the first, who were usually resident, presided over the spiritual and secular life of a monastery while the second, who drew a large part of the revenues, left the management of the monastery to a deputy. Many of these commendatory abbés were in minor orders and celibate, but the religious element in their lives was tenuous in the extreme, and in this respect they bore some resemblance to the old life fellows of Oxford and Cambridge colleges, who combined celibacy with leisure and a modest competence, conditions which favour either idleness or devotion to some branch of science or literature. Indeed, a worth-while book might be written about the contribution to learning made by men who, in these special circumstances, were relieved from family cares and from the need to earn a living. This is true of the abbés of eighteenth-century France, as attested by such names as that of the Abbé de Saint-Pierre who devoted his numerous writings and discussions in salons to the causes of humanity and *bienfaisance*; the Abbé Condillac, who based a theory of knowledge on the phenomena of sense experience; the Abbé Prévost, who popularised the novels of Richardson in France and wrote one of the most sentimental novels of all time—*Manon Lescaut*; the Abbé Lacaille, one of the greatest mathematicians and astronomers of the century. But not all of these men were orthodox in their religious or social opinions; some were inflammatory. The Abbé de Prades wrote contributions to the *Encyclopédie* of a strongly materialist character; in 1770 the Abbé Raynal published a violent attack[1] on the exploitation of natives by Europeans, usually on the pretext of religion. Among the abbés were to be found some of the most consistent opponents of contemporary institutions.

[1] *Histoire Philosophique des Etablissements et du Commerce des Européens dans les Deux Indes.*

Such, in brief, were the main divisions of French society. They were governed not by a uniform jurisprudence but by many overlapping and interlocking systems, whether of customary law, or of church courts, or of seigneurial jurisdiction, or administrative departments endowed with judicial functions, many of them survivals from remote times. These jurisdictions had mostly parted company with their original justification; but in pre-Marxist society, as in nature herself, there was a force of inertia which resisted change. There were innumerable officials but no co-ordinated civil service such as was taking shape in England, Prussia and Austria. In the provinces the work of administration was exercised by 30 *intendants*, each controlling a considerable area known as a *généralité*, and assisted by *subdelegués*. There were scarcely any limits to the duties of the *intendants*. By regular correspondence with the Controller General they kept the government informed about local conditions; they made arrangements for the billeting of troops, for the setting up of new industries, for the circulation of foodstuffs, for improvements in agriculture, for repair of highways. They supervised parochial and municipal finance, they acted as tax collectors and sanitary inspectors, in all of which activities they had to face the opposition or obstruction of the local *Parlements* and their subordinate tribunals. Considering the multiplicity of their duties, the wonder is that the system worked at all. The *intendants,* chosen from the *maîtres des requêtes,* were usually men of good family and ample fortune; moreover, some of the greatest administrators of the century had served their apprenticeship in this capacity, notably Turgot, who acted as *intendant* of the Limousin[1] between 1761 and 1774. On the whole, the *intendants* appear to have acted with justice and mercy, and many of them were popular with the poor; at times indeed they acted as a check on the executive by disobeying or ignoring a government order.

An illustration of the absence of efficient control at the

[1] below, pp. 270-1.

centre is provided by taxation, usually the most sensitive index of administrative competence. Some taxes, such as the *taille* were *en régie,* that is, directly administered by the state; though, as has already been noted, the harsh duty of actually collecting the tax was enforced on the villagers themselves. But most of the taxes were *en ferme*—farmed out to syndicates of financiers who bought their *ferme* at an auction—usually a mock auction, as things had been arranged beforehand. The *fermiers* advanced a capital sum and agreed to pay an annual rent, recouping themselves from the taxes which they were authorised to collect. In the time of Colbert the various *fermes* had been consolidated into the *fermes générales,* in which were included the *gabelle,* the *traites* (customs), the *aides* (subsidies) and the tax on tobacco. By the eighteenth century the grant of the *fermes générales* was for a period of six years to a syndicate of sixty persons. The contract was made on behalf of the government by the Controller General who, on completion of the arrangements, received a *pot de vin,* or bribe. Substantial *croupes* or " rake offs " were paid by the farmers to courtiers, even to the king himself, and many pensions were assigned on this source. Between 1726 and the Revolution there were eleven such grants, each designated by the name of one of the servants of the *fermiers,* a device which helped to secure anonymity. But the *fermiers généraux* were by no means all men of bad reputation for, among their number were Helvétius the philosopher and Lavoisier the chemist. For the collection of these assigned taxes about 20,000 persons were employed.

From a modern point of view the most extraordinary of these taxes was the *gabelle,* or salt tax. This was heavy in some provinces, light in others; a few provinces were exempt. There were provinces called the *Pays Rédimés* which, having paid an extra *taille* in lieu of the *gabelle,* were supposed to be free from the tax; they were sometimes disillusioned. This must have been one of the most irritating of all the taxes because salt was a government monopoly, and people might have to travel a long way in order to fetch the minimum amount that they were required to take; moreover, as the salt was of inferior quality, a better variety was often made in the maritime provinces by the (illicit) evaporation of brine. There was also much smuggling from provinces where the commodity was cheap into provinces where it was dear. The penalty for these irregularities was death.

There were many other sources of revenue. Creation and sale of new offices became an increasingly important source of royal revenue in this period. Finance ministers imposed or tried to impose taxes on income, such as a tenth or a fiftieth, levies usually resisted by the privileged, including the clergy who, however, might obtain exemption by payment of a *don gratuit*. Capital might also be raised by lotteries, of which the management was often suspect; or by the sale of life annuities with a chance that, in times of stringency, the interest might be reduced, or the arrears cancelled altogether. French finance was not a gamble; it was a certainty—that the financiers and courtiers would gain and that the public, especially the poorer members of the public, would lose. It was archaic and unjust even on contemporary standards, for other nations had already adopted a more equitable system of public finance. In England, by the system of funding, large loans could be obtained from the public with the assurance that the interest would be paid regularly from the proceeds of specified taxes; as well as this, by the consolidation of funds, the lender had the guarantee that a deficiency in one source would be made up from another. In this way confidence was created in the integrity and stability of the national finances—qualities entirely absent in France. The result was that enterprising finance ministers were often reduced to two expedients—obtaining better terms from the farmers on the renewal of a *ferme* or repudiating national obligations. Of these the first gave disappointing results; the second led to bankruptcy.

II THE REGENCY 1715-26.
JOHN LAW.

By his will Louis XIV had appointed as Regent his nephew Philip, Duke of Orleans with restricted powers; but this was revoked by the Paris *Parlement,* so Orleans succeeded with an unrestricted prerogative. This was one side of a bargain with the *Parlement,* the other side being the restoration to the *Parlement* of the right of remonstrance. Philip, a man of some ability and good will, an ancestor of that line which was one day to give France a king in Louis Philippe, might well have been popular, particularly as he headed a reaction against the restraints and austerity of the preceding régime. From his mentors Fénelon and Saint Simon he adopted the view that the bourgeois administrators on whom Louis XIV had relied should be swept away and their places taken by the nobility. Accordingly, he began his rule with the help of seven councils, each composed of ten persons, mostly nobles, for finance, foreign affairs, war, navy, home affairs, commerce and " conscience ", that is, religious matters, a scheme similar to that propounded shortly afterwards by the abbé de Saint-Pierre in his *Polysynodie.* Had Philip been possessed of sufficient energy and determination he might have effected considerable reforms, because he was known to be in favour of the restoration of the Huguenots and suppression of the Jesuits; he was also credited with the idea of summoning the States General. But he was pleasure-loving and debauched; moreover, he soon had to face the enmity of the nobility, the financiers and of the *Parlement* which had endowed him with such powers.

These enmities were aroused by the financial activities in which the Regent was involved with John Law, an enterprising Scot who, like his compatriot William Paterson of a generation earlier, had grasped the basic principles of credit and was anxious to apply them to public finance. In 1716 Orleans, on the instigation of Law, created by charter a *Banque Générale,* modelled on that of Amsterdam, with power to issue notes, an institution which at first proved successful; in the following year he was authorised to launch his trading company, the *Compagnie d'Occident,* intended to exploit the products of Louisiana, a colony still almost entirely undeveloped. To this Company was added a monopoly of the China and East India trades, together with the fur trade of Canada. At the same time, with the help of the Pâris banking family,[1] a strict investigation or *Visa* was made of all outstanding claims on the government arising from the war recently concluded; repudiation of many of these claims aroused the resentment of the financiers, intensified by the erection of a tribunal for the trial of war contractors accused of malpractices. This was accompanied by extensive devaluation of the currency, but none of these measures had the desired results. Meanwhile, these schemes were fiercely attacked by the Paris *Parlement,* which attempted to take over control of finance; this the Regent forbade and, in a *lit de justice,* he required it to accept the prohibition. More and more Philip was coming to be dependent on Law. Late in 1718 he dissolved the seven councils, reverting to the traditional system of single ministers and the four secretaries of state. In face of increasing opposition the *Parlement* was exiled in April 1720 and Law was appointed Controller General of the Finances.

The success of Law's schemes was bound up with the profitable colonisation of Louisiana, but comparatively few Frenchmen were willing to emigrate, and the new Controller was authorised to use force in the shipment of boat loads of unfortunates across the Atlantic. Meanwhile, there was much speculation in the shares of the Company, which were first issued in 1719, and could be bought on the instalment system. As with the almost exactly contemporary South Seas Company in England, Law and his associates then took over part of the French National Debt by inducing holders of government

[1] There were three brothers, headed by Joseph Pâris-Duverney.

rentes (i.e., annuities) to exchange them for shares in the Company. The next step was for Law's bank, now the *Banque Royale,* to make a large issue of notes in order to finance a trading company which had practically no resources. As the nominal value of shares in the Company rose, there was a fever of speculation and many fortunes were made by those who sold out at inflated prices; as many were lost by those who held on until the bubble burst. By December 1720 Law's schemes, or the System as they were called, had crashed to the ground and their promoter fled into exile. This disaster, which had created no diminution in the amount of national wealth but only a change in its distribution, had momentous consequences. It confirmed French dislike of banks, paper money and government securities. A Bourse, it is true, was set up in Paris in 1724 and in 1776 a *Caisse d'Escompte* was erected which issued notes to bearer; but nevertheless France failed to create the national institutions for the maintenance of public credit.

On the other hand, the collapse of the " System " was not all pure loss. Law's Company—afterwards named the *Compagnie des Indes*—included Louisiana, Quebec, Senegal, Mauritius and Madagascar in its province; within a few years it was in a state of prosperity. Still more, it gave a lead to French overseas enterprise which, by 1730, provided employment for about 5,000 ships and over 40,000 seamen. Between 1716 and 1743 the value of French overseas commerce increased by four times.[1] The Company enjoyed its greatest period of prosperity under Fleury; from its headquarters at Lorient it exported wine and brandy in exchange for coffee, cocoa, sugar, indigo and camphor. It is even arguable that this maritime expansion, together with the profitable sugar trade with the Antilles, may have staved off bankruptcy and revolution.

The Regency of Orleans, which was ended by his death in 1723, proved to be little more than an interlude in which attempted changes, such as restoration of the nobility to a

[1] E. Lavisse (ed.), *Histoire de France,* VIII, pt. 2, pp. 38-9.

prominent place in public affairs, had ended in failure. It was
fortunate that these were years of peace—indeed Orleans's
associate and chief minister Cardinal Dubois had done much
to form the alliance with England, on which the peace of
Europe depended until 1733. The Regency was also a period
of reaction following on cessation of the tension of Louis
XIV's rule, a reaction stimulated by publication of Memoirs
compiled by some of the leaders in the Fronde (1648-52), a
half-serious, mock-heroic revolutionary movement. There was
much talk of " republicanism " and of *bienfaisance,* but nothing happened, possibly because people were engrossed in
Law's schemes. After 1723 the lead in the direction of the
state was taken by Louis-Henri, Duc de Bourbon, a descendant of the great Condé who, having few opinions of his own
except on field sports, was content to entrust his prerogative
to his mistress Madame de Prie and the Pâris banking family.
Meanwhile, in the background was an astute ecclesiastic—
Louis XV's tutor André Hercule de Fleury, Bishop of Fréjus
(1653-1743) who, partly by favour of his royal pupil and
partly because of the unpopularity of Bourbon, succeeded as
chief of state in 1726. He had advised the king, now sixteen
years of age, to be his own first minister, so he did not usurp
that title. Fleury, who became a cardinal in 1726, was anxious
to ensure peace for himself and his country, objects in which,
to a great extent, he was successful.

III THE ADMINISTRATION OF FLEURY, 1726-43.

Fleury was ably assisted by subordinates. For ten years after
1727 he was aided by Louis de Chauvelin, Keeper of the Seals
and Secretary for Foreign Affairs, who at first favoured a peace
policy recalling that of his contemporary Walpole. But
Chauvelin, who was ambitious, may have had designs on
Fleury's place, so he was dismissed and exiled. In the Chan-

cellor D'Aguesseau Fleury had a more dependable subordinate who, confining himself to his legal duties, did much to remedy abuses in civil and criminal procedure and to introduce order into the laws of succession and entail. The key post of Controller General was held for the unusually long period of 15 years (1730-45) by Philibert Orry, a ruthless but efficient administrator who took Colbert as his model. After the devaluations of the Regency period, the currency was at last stabilised, and a tax on revenue, the *Dixième,* was levied in the years 1733-6 when France was paying for her part in the Polish Succession War. Economies were effected by repudiating arrears in the payment of government *rentes;* a strict protectionist policy was imposed which discouraged imports by high duties and, on the Colbertian model new, privileged industries were established. Most notable of Orry's reforms was the institution of a well-planned scheme for road and bridge construction. Already, there existed a school for the training of engineers in road making; and Orry, who planned on a national scale, erected workshops on all the main highways, staffed with inspectors who were given disciplinary powers over the peasants, on whose compulsory and unpaid labour the success of the scheme depended. This was a new *corvée,* the *corvée royale,* and its merciless enforcement increased the unpopularity of the minister.

Fleury's administration, which thus coincided with a period of great commercial prosperity, might well be regarded as a convalescence, well suited to the advancing years of the Cardinal, who showed singular astuteness in disposing of actual or potential rivals. Nominally, in these years, Louis XV was his own first minister, but the royal dislike of business and his continual moving about from one château to another gave Fleury a free hand. After an abortive arrangement for a Spanish marriage, the king in 1725 married Marie Lesczinska, daughter of Stanislas Lesczinski who, for a short period, had been King of Poland. The prospect of restoring Stanislas to the Polish throne provided one of the motives for Louis's intervention in the Polish Succession War.[1] By his marriage Louis had eleven children, of whom seven survived—the Dauphin and his six sisters. The Dauphin died in 1765.

Like all the Bourbons Louis was devout, but he was not bigoted. The same cannot be said of all his bishops, many of whom became more anti-Protestant in proportion as they became more ultramontane. Nominally, all the subjects of the French crown were Catholics, but there were strong communities of Huguenots in Languedoc, Dauphiné and Burgundy who continued to practise their cult under increasing difficulties; it was in the hope of extirpating these heretics that, in 1724, the higher clergy had procured an edict which was savage, even on the standards of the time. This edict imposed life imprisonment on all who attended conventicles; baptism into the Roman Catholic faith was made compulsory within 24 hours of birth; marriages of Huguenots were declared illegal, and Protestant preachers were to suffer death by hanging. This code was applied, with varying degrees of severity, throughout Protestant France, and gave some point to the attacks of the *philosophes* on the hierarchy. Soon there was added another occasion for intolerance, this time within the bosom of the church. This arose from the old Jansenist controversy, a legacy from the previous century. The Jansenists, bitter enemies of Jesuits and Ultramontanes, had a theology which savoured as much of Calvinism as of Catholicism, but, as they insisted on their orthodoxy and refused to leave the church, they were accounted schismatics rather than heretics. They were strongly entrenched among the upper bourgeoisie of Paris, especially in the members of the *Parlement*; and, as Gallicans, they favoured the supremacy of the crown against the pope in ecclesiastical matters.

All this had created a serious problem for Louis XIV in his later years, but increasing zeal for orthodoxy and the influence of his Jesuit confessor had induced him, in spite of

[1] above, pp. 134-6.

his own Gallican policy, to accept the Bull *Unigenitus* (1713) which condemned 101 propositions extracted from a commentary on the New Testament published by the Jansenist Quesnel in 1678. *Parlement* had been obliged to register the Bull, but had refused to accept it, an attitude which had the sympathy of the Regent Orleans and Cardinal Noailles, Archbishop of Paris; but, with their deaths, the old controversy was revived, and now assumed a more political form, because it was bound up with the recalcitrant and aggressive attitude of the *Parlement*. For long France was divided between those who accepted the Bull, or " Constitution " as it was called, and those who did not. A clue to the situation is provided by number 91 of the propositions condemned by the Bull. This was the proposition that fear of an unjust excommunication should not deter one from doing one's duty. Here was the Ultramontane position in a nutshell—the anathema of the church must override the secular duties of the excommunicated layman, even if he was in the right.

Most of the bishops were for the Bull; many of the lower clergy were against it. It was the layman who had to bear the brunt of this squabble, because many bishops insisted that, before the rites of the church could be performed, the layman must produce a " *billet de confession* " certifying that he had made his confession to an orthodox priest, that is, one who had accepted the " Constitution ". Otherwise the layman might be refused Christian burial; if he had already been buried, his remains might be disinterred and thrown over the wall of the churchyard. The dispute was kept alive by the production, first in manuscript and then in print, of the *Nouvelles Ecclésiastiques,* which stimulated opposition to those priests who refused absolution or burial to laymen who had not made their confession to the " constitutional " clergy. To make matters worse, the non-conforming or Jansenist clergy soon had a saint. This was the deacon Paris, whose burial in the cemetery of St. Médard (in the Latin quarter of Paris) was followed by violent convulsions and miraculous cures among the many who flocked to his tomb. Soon the miracles were the talk of Paris. Now, miracles are all very well, provided there are not too many of them, and provided each is authenticated by the certificate of a bishop. Fleury, greatly perturbed, awaited with trepidation the latest bulletins from the cemetery, and the Archbishop of Paris (Charles de Vintimille, nicknamed Ventremille from his capacious appetite), with a surprising burst of modernism, proclaimed that either the " cures " were due to medical measures, or the certificates attesting them were bogus. So in January 1732 the cemetery of St. Médard was closed to the public and the history of this corybantic Lourdes came to an end.

This controversy was not lessened until 1756 when Pope Benedict XIV issued an encyclical in which, although reaffirming the Bull *Unigenitus,* he forbade the *billets de confession.* Even this wise concession did not conciliate the intransigent Paris *Parlement,* which refused to accept the encyclical on the frivolous ground that it had been printed in France without permission. The other *Parlements* joined in this unreasonable opposition. This Jesuit-Jansenist controversy kept intruding itself into matters with which it had no real connection. Thus, in 1757, on the occasion of the attempt on the life of the king by the madman Damiens, it was recalled that Damiens had, for a time, been a servant of Jesuits, so the attempted assassination was a Jesuit plot, until it was discovered that Damiens had also had Jansenist employers. All this showed a deep fund of emotionalism beneath the apparent rationalism of the French people. As so often happened in French history matters were conjoined which had no relation to each other, and mob hysteria was the result.

It is possible that, had Fleury had his way, France would not have joined in the War of the Austrian Succession, and the same is true to some extent of Walpole. But in both countries there was a strong war party, that in France being led by Belle Isle, a descendant of the notorious Fouquet, Louis XIV's finance minister, who had been convicted of malversation; his descendant was anxious to redeem the family honour by successful military enterprise. This is an instance of an absurd pretext for dragging a nation into war; another example of its kind was Louis's intervention in the Polish Succession War in order to secure a crown for his father-in-law and so enhance the status of his consort. But the retirement of Walpole early in 1742, followed by the death of Fleury in the following year removed the only impediments to full-scale participation of both countries in the continental campaigns of the Austrian Succession War. In these campaigns Louis played a distinguished part, conducting himself with considerable courage at the French victory of Fontenoy in 1745, on which account his admiring subjects accorded to him the title of *Bien Aimé*. This was the one point in his reign when the king was popular. But the peace of 1748 was a grievous disappointment and was linked, in popular estimation, with other " plagues ", namely, the " System " (Law's schemes), the " Constitution " (the Bull *Unigenitus*) and the convulsionaries of St. Médard. French opinion, always intent on linking cause with effect, insisted on associating these unrelated events.

IV MADAME DE POMPADOUR. CHOISEUL. EXPULSION OF THE
JESUITS. 1743-70.

The rule of Fleury was succeeded in 1743 by that of Madame de Pompadour (1722-64). Daughter of a Paris butcher, Mademoiselle Poisson married the nephew of one of the *fermiers généraux*, whom she left in order to become mistress-in-chief. For over 20 years she exercised considerable influence, for it was often by her favour that ministers, ambassadors and generals were appointed, and by her disfavour were dismissed; in conjunction with Pâris-Duverney she even exercised some influence on the conduct of the Seven Years War. Her political importance, it is true, has sometimes been exaggerated, but it is certain that she set the fashion in everything, including dress, furniture and perfumery. Her sympathies were with the *Parlement* against the Jesuits; as the friend and patroness of the *philosophes* she received warm tributes from Voltaire. European rulers, including the conventional Maria Theresa, addressed her as one of themselves. Tolerant of other mistresses, she showed tact in her relations with the complacent queen, who found solace in the pleasures of the dining table. There were occasions however when the king surrendered his prerogative in favour of the mistress.

Of this one example may be cited. In 1750 Machault d'Arnouville, the Controller General, proposed to impose a new *vingtième* on all classes in order to help pay for the expense of the war recently ended. Because *Parlement* and clergy put up a vigorous resistance, Louis yielded, and this, together with the influence of Madame de Pompadour, resulted in the dismissal and disgrace of the minister. Here was one of the occasions on which the king failed to insist on supporting his minister and maintaining the royal prerogative; he had yielded to opposition from clergy and magistracy. But this unusual alliance proved to be short lived. In 1753, when there was a renewal of the Jansenist trouble, *Parlement* issued a Grand Remonstrance, accusing the clergy of maintaining an existence independent of and hostile to the state. As several of the remonstrants were exiled, *Parlement* went on strike; and, as they were joined by a number of provincial *Parlements*, the administration of justice was held up for nearly a year.

Parlement was soon to win what must have appeared its most notable victory. Its members may have heard or read of Pombal's[1] expulsion of the Jesuits from Portugal in 1757; there now occurred an opportunity for emulating this example. The head of the Jesuits in the French West Indies—Père Lavalette—was engaged in extensive commercial transactions which were ruined by England's destruction of French colonial trade, with the result that he went bankrupt. After an adverse

[1] above, pp. 227-8 and 238-9.

decision in a Marseilles court, he unwisely appealed to the Paris *Parlement* which ordered an investigation into the constitution and proceedings of the Society. The investigators pronounced that the Jesuit doctrines were pernicious and un-Christian, and that their activities were inconsistent with their allegiance to the crown. So in August 1762, by a decree of *Parlement*, the Society was abolished in France and its dependencies; its property was also confiscated. Thus ended for a time a bitter controversy which had divided French opinion since the seventeenth century, and the triumph of the *Parlement* appeared to be complete. But in the long run the layman is seldom a match for the priest. In 1790 the *Parlement* was abolished for all time; in 1814 Pope Pius VII re-established the Society, and its members were soon back in France.

The expulsion of the Jesuits by no means ended the disputes of which they had been the centre, for many of them remained under the name of *Pères de la Croix*; moreover, they had the warm support of the *dévots*. Still more, they acquired additional prestige from the increasing opposition to the *Parlement*; and this alignment of forces, pro- or anti-*Parlement*, had considerable influence on French politics during the later years of the *Ancien Régime*. Sustained opposition to the taxation necessitated by the Seven Years War served almost to place the *Parlement* in the position of an anti-national party; nor was this remedied by a rapid succession of finance ministers who strained every effort in the almost hopeless attempt to raise the necessary supplies. Of these Controllers General the Marquis de Silhouette is notable if only because his unsuccessful struggles with war taxation served eventually to add one more word to the English language. Beginning with the usual expedient, that of trying to obtain better terms from the tax farmers, he aroused public indignation by exposure of the enormous profits which the *fermiers généraux* were making; he then proceeded to increase old taxes and add new ones—on domestic servants, carriage horses, children who took the vows before attaining their majority. The minister, as he held office for only eight months (in 1759), appeared to have crossed the stage only in profile, so that the public never had more than a side view; accordingly, the profile portraits then coming into vogue were called *silhouettes*.

Financial embarrassments were by no means the only impediments to French achievement in the Seven Years War. There were too many French officers, many of whom lived in luxury even when on campaign; nor were they even supplied with good maps. Some of the generals indulged in pillage, an example followed by their troops. To make matters worse Louis intervened with another " secret ", this time the *secret de guerre,* by which subordinate officers were encouraged to make complaints to the Court about the conduct of their superiors. The result was constant jealousy and resentment among the leaders. As well as this, the use of artillery was ineffective, mainly because this branch was under separate control, officered by civilians or *roturiers,* for whom the generals had nothing but contempt. Class prejudice and unwillingness of the privileged to pay taxation provided two of the reasons why France, so much more populous and wealthy than England, suffered such defeats in the Seven Years War.

To her credit, however, it must be said that Madame de Pompadour made one good appointment, though it came too late. Early in the War she had advanced the interests of a young dilettante, the Abbé de Bernis who, in his capacity of Secretary for Foreign Affairs, signed the treaty with Austria[1] in 1756. But Bernis was so disquieted by events in the first two years of war that he recommended the opening up of peace negotiations with England. For this loss of nerve Madame threw him over and transferred her favour to another protégé of very different calibre—Etienne François de Choiseul, Comte de Stainville, and later Duc de Choiseul (1719-85), who had already served as ambassador in Rome and in Vienna. In 1761 he became Secretary for War and two years later Secretary for Marine; he was therefore the

[1] above, pp. 141-2.

statesman who directed France through the closing scenes of the Seven Years War. A man of energy and ability, he could not save his country from defeat, but at least he perceived the defects of her military and naval organisation, defects which he did much to remedy. Numerous reforms were effected. The prerogatives of the colonels were greatly diminished; recruiting was taken from their hands and placed on a national basis. A beginning was made in the technical education of military and naval officers; with the help of Gribeauval the artillery was integrated with the army, and was no longer designed solely for siege warfare. Reforms in the navy were as spectacular. Losses of ships were made good, and an ambitious programme of building eventually gave France over 60 ships of the line, or enough to engage in combat with England on fairly equal terms. Choiseul's activities extended to France's colonial empire, in the future of which he had a firm belief. So the monopoly of the old *Compagnie des Indes* was ended, and the government took over direct administration of the colonies.

Even before the end of the Seven Years War Choiseul had aimed at concentrating his forces against England and limiting the help given to Maria Theresa. Believing that Spain would provide a more useful ally than Austria, he arranged the Family Compact with the former country in 1761, and devoted himself to the substitution of a French for a British interest in Holland and Portugal. He was really thinking in terms of the next war; for this reason it was mainly by his reforms that France proved such a formidable adversary in the War of the American Revolution.[1] If he had had his way France might have gone to war with England in 1770 over the Falkland Islands, ownership of which was in dispute between England and Spain; wisely perhaps, the king refrained from hostilities, knowing from experience that the *Parlement* would place every obstruction in the way of raising war taxation. A situation had indeed been reached when Louis must choose between

[1] below, pp. 274-7.

Prerogative and *Parlement,* for opposition by the magistracy was impeding full exercise of the royal powers. So the king had to sacrifice Choiseul, whose departure was hastened by the influence of the new mistress-in-chief Madame du Barry. In December 1770 the Duke retired to his estate at Chanteloup, where he devoted himself with great success to the cultivation of melons, and the war of revenge against England had to be postponed.

V THE REFORMS OF MAUPEOU, 1770-74.

Among the favourites of Madame Du Barry was René Nicolas de Maupeou (1714-92), son of a former President of the *Parlement,* who had been appointed Chancellor in 1768. Maupeou had the intelligence to perceive that only by ending the obstructive tactics of the *Parlements* would effective rule by the king be made possible. This view may well have commended him to Madame Du Barry who was the enemy of the *Parlements* as Choiseul was their friend. As well as this the Chancellor had concrete ideas of judicial reform. Venality of office, bribes to judges, the application of torture—these were among the things which he wished to abolish; he would also have eliminated the whole system of seigneurial justice. He proposed to codify the customary law; he had a scheme for providing counsel on behalf of accused persons, and he even advocated discontinuance of the practice whereby not only were the goods of a felon confiscated, but his family was subjected to ostracism.[1] These were among his proposals in a memoir presented to the king in 1771. Meanwhile, matters were precipitated by events in Brittany where the Duc d'Aiguillon was acting as Governor. Suspected of sympathy with the Jesuits, d'Aiguillon was soon at cross purposes with both the local Estates and the *Parlement* at Rennes. In spite of his equitable administration of the province, he was accused by

[1] F. Pietri, *La Réforme de l'Etat au XVIIIème Siècle*, pp. 162 ff.

his enemies among the magistracy of abusing his powers, and a trial was demanded, a demand led by the Procurator General La Chalotais, who had acquired renown for his part in the expulsion of the Jesuits. The trial was held in the Paris *Parlement* which upheld the case against the Duke, who had to resign his governorship. Here was one more humiliation for the king at the hands of the magistracy. At the same time the *Parlements* were corresponding with each other in order to form some kind of confederacy. Louis and Maupeou agreed that the *Parlements* would have to go.

Meanwhile d'Aiguillon had been appointed Secretary for Foreign Affairs and the Abbé Terray Controller General; these two, with Chancellor Maupeou, formed the Triumvirate which, under the auspices of Madame Du Barry, ruled France in the last four years of Louis's reign. With the backing of this ministry the king, in January 1771, performed one of the few authoritarian acts of his reign. The *Parlement* of Paris and the *Cour des Aides* were suppressed; the same treatment was accorded to two local *Parlements*—those of Rouen and Douai—and the other *Parlements* were reformed, though a considerable number of the old magistrates were retained in the new. Ancient abuses such as venality of offices and acceptance of bribes were abolished, and an attempt was made to limit the new magistrates to their judicial functions by grouping them into a hierarchy of councils, headed by a central court of justice in Paris. Many deplored this abrogation of the old *Parlements,* and Maupeou was attacked in a number of diatribes, some of which accused him of Jesuit designs. No political issue was straightforward at this time; the expelled Jesuits and the melon-growing Choiseul were dragged in as the secret instigators of public events.

But even these things were obscured by the measures of Terray, the new Controller General. These related to bread and taxes. Progressive ministers had always favoured free circulation of grain within the country so that a shortage in one area might be made up from another; moreover, the government had erected large granaries for storage of corn. But the intense provincialism of France made it difficult for the state and even for the *intendants* to promote free internal movement; and the peasant, always suspicious, was easily led to believe that the granaries were part of a design for holding up supplies in time of scarcity, so that fortunes might be made. Hence the legend[1] of the *pacte de famine,* of which more was to be heard before the Revolution. Terray, who was opposed to free trade in corn, made purchases of wheat on a large scale; and, in spite of protests by the *intendants,* he obtained a decree in December 1770 which abolished internal and external freedom of trade. Instead of conciliating provincial prejudice this measure aroused suspicion that the Controller and Madame Du Barry were creating a monopoly and deriving vast profits from enforcement of that monopoly. In finance Terray's policy was equally disquieting. He suspended payment of interest on government bonds and wiped off several millions of debt by drastic reduction of arrears due to the holders of the bonds; as well as this he postponed re-payment of capital when the re-payments fell due. At the same time he increased a number of taxes and extended the claims of the *fermiers généraux* by bogus law suits in which a decision was always given in their favour.[2] In such ways were the demands of the Court and of Madame Du Barry supplied. But discontent was increasing, and there were several bread riots in Paris.

VI LOUIS XVI. TURGOT. THE WAR OF AMERICAN INDEPENDENCE. 1774-83

Louis XV died from smallpox on May 10 1774 and was succeeded by his twenty-year-old grandson Louis XVI, son of the Dauphin and Maria Josepha of Saxony. He had married

---

[1] Now discredited.
[2] D. Dakin, *Turgot and the Ancien Régime* (1939), p. 161.

Marie Antoinette, daughter of Maria Theresa, in 1770, by whom he had three children. In appearance and temperament the new king resembled his Saxon mother more than his Bourbon father, for he was sluggish, vacillating and anxious to please, having little of the inflexibility and pride in personal pre-eminence so characteristic of his royal ancestors. As a ruler, he was devout and well-intentioned, passionately devoted to the chase, but easily swayed by men of stronger fibre. He was distinguished from other monarchs by the fact that he had a hobby—the making of locks and keys; from the outset he was overshadowed by the stronger personality of his consort who, as a foreigner, was the victim of many malicious intrigues. Her task was an impossible one—to win the loyalty of the French people and obey the insistent behests first of her mother and, after 1780, of her brother the Emperor Joseph. Inevitably, the spinelessness of her husband obliged her to influence ministerial appointments, or rather ministerial dismissals, in which her judgement was bad. Frivolous and pleasure-loving, she encouraged her Court in extravagance remarkable even in the eighteenth century.

The king's aunts Adelaide and Louise were of the *dévot* party, and it was mainly on their advice that Louis decided to pass over Choiseul for a ministerial appointment. The Duke had never been forgiven for his opposition to the Jesuits, but he had a number of supporters at Versailles. The royal choice of chief minister fell on Maurepas, now 73 years old; he had served Louis XV well as Minister for Marine, but had been dismissed in 1749 because of a malicious epigram on Madame de Pompadour. His status was that of chief adviser and he was given no ministerial appointment; in character he was astute, always with an eye on the main chance and an unfailing aptitude for the *bon mot*. One of his wise acts was to secure the appointment of Anne-Robert Turgot (1727-81) as Controller General in place of Terray; Maupeou was displaced as Keeper of the Seals by De Miromesnil, but retained the Chancellorship which was a life appointment. D'Aiguillon's office of Secretary for Foreign Affairs was conferred on the Comte de Vergennes (1717-87), and the charge of home affairs was given to Chrétien Guillaume de Malesherbes, one of the most enlightened of French ministers in this period, who was born in 1721 and perished on the scaffold in 1794. Louis had begun well, but in August 1774, possibly in a conciliatory mood, he committed an unwise act by reversing the Maupeou revolution and recalling the *Parlements,* with the result that from the beginning of his reign he was obstructed by the most reactionary element in French society.

Of the new ministers Malesherbes, Turgot and Vergennes were good representatives of the best traditions of the *noblesse de robe,* all of them endowed with an almost hereditary instinct for prudent administration. Temperamentally, however, they were alien to Louis XVI and Marie Antoinette; moreover, they belonged to a different generation, for they were at least 20 years older than the royal couple. Vergennes, who had distinguished himself in several foreign missions, had played a prominent part in the Swedish revolution of 1772;[1] it was he who, in spite of the king's very justifiable misgivings, negotiated the treaty with the American colonists in 1778. Malesherbes, one of the famous Lamoignon family which had so distinguished itself in *Parlement* and in ministerial office, had served as *Directeur de la Librarie* between 1750 and 1763, the years in which the greater part of the *Encyclopédie*[2] had been allowed to appear in print. A humanitarian, he succeeded, while in office, in mitigating the harsh conditions prevailing in French prisons and, if he had had his way, he would have granted civil rights to the Huguenots. His friend Turgot, after serving as a *maître des requêtes,* had acted as *intendant* of the Limousin from 1761 to 1774. There his ingenuity and patience had been fully tested; for the Limousin, a hilly and infertile district of mid-western France, was cultivated by a peasantry possessed of small holdings, of 5 to 10 acres in extent, averse to improvements and reduced to the

[1] above, p. 188.   [2] below, pp. 324-5.

poverty line because it was not easy to find a market for their timber, peaches, flax and hemp. Turgot had set himself the difficult task of raising the economic level of this backward province. He abolished inequality of taxation among the parishes; he reformed the arrangements for enforcing the *corvées* and raising the militia; by draining of marshes he brought more land under cultivation. He applied an edict of 1764 which permitted internal circulation of corn. Better strains of seed were distributed and the potato was introduced as a domestic crop. Closely connected with Quesnay and other leaders of the Physiocratic school, Turgot demonstrated how successfully the new theories could be applied in even the most backward areas. His two main objects were increase of production and removal of obstacles to distribution; successful application of these principles may account for his appointment as Controller General in 1774.[1]

As minister Turgot found himself in a hotbed of intrigue. In the background was Choiseul, anxious to return to power with the support of a pro-Austrian faction among the nobility and a Jansenist element among the magistracy. Opposed to the appointment of Choiseul were the *dévots,* led by the king's aunts; this party had been against the recall of the *Parlements,* and scented danger to the church in every proposal for reform. Even more powerful were the *parlementaires* and the financiers, both sensitive to everything that appeared to threaten their interests. It was unfortunate that Turgot, who had no sense of finesse, decided to act quickly. He began with the old stand-by of financial reformers—obtaining better terms from the tax farmers; *pots de vin* were discontinued, and the " rake offs " to courtiers greatly diminished. In September 1774 he restored free internal circulation of corn and was even prepared to allow the import from abroad of the grain which France so badly needed. In spite of these measures there were bread riots which, with characteristic obliquity,

---

[1] For a good account of Turgot's administration of the Limousin see D. Dakin, *op. cit.,* ch. 3.

were attributed to the machinations of the nobility, the clergy, the queen, Maupeou and even Turgot himself. A cattle plague added to the agrarian discontent.

The atmosphere was therefore unfavourable to thorough-going changes, but Turgot went ahead. In 1775 he introduced a number of reforms including the abolition of many gilds and of the royal *corvée* of road-making by the peasants. Several monopolies and sinecures were terminated. In these activities he was ably assisted by Malesherbes who, however, was convinced that radical reform could come only from the king, with the co-operation of the States General. At the same time both ministers tried to induce the clergy to adopt a more conciliatory attitude to the Protestants by the grant of civil rights and validation of their marriages, an attempt which had no success until 1787. Turgot also outlined an ambitious scheme for reforming the administrative system of the country. His plan envisaged a complete decentralisation of authority and its devolution on a hierarchy of local municipalities and councils, based on towns and villages, and endowed with extensive powers in the assessment and raising of taxation. The whole was to be surmounted by a national council of municipalities sitting in Paris. In this scheme the king was to retain his legislative power but was to act with the advice of the supreme municipal body. There is reason to believe that Louis was completely opposed to this proposal.[1] He was credited with the opinion that the hierarchy of councils would prove a chimera unless backed by the support of the nobility; and, as for control of taxation by a popularly elected body, it had been proved by the experience of the Abbé Terray that one could never be sure of a tax unless it was imposed by the orders of those who would not have to pay it. This sounds too cynical for Louis XVI, but it sums up one of the financial principles of the time.

The climax was reached in March 1776 when Turgot added to his edicts abolishing the *corvée royale* and the gilds' four

[1] *Œuvres de Louis XVI* (1864), II, pp. 33-4.

other edicts intended to remove ancient abuses in the provisioning of Paris, including the *Caisse de Poissy,* a notorious butchers' gild. These were the famous Six Edicts. They proved a signal for union among all the forces opposed to Turgot and reform. Maurepas deserted his colleague; the king resented the abrupt and hortatory manner of his Controller General; nobility, clergy and magistracy were naturally opposed to one who would diminish their privileges. In May Malesherbes resigned; within a few days Turgot was dismissed. Like the Emperor Joseph II and Pombal he had tried to do too much in too short a time. Instead of tinkering with the superstructure he had made a beginning with the removal of rotten foundations; this was fatal. Only Maurepas and Vergennes were left as the responsible ministers of Louis XVI.

The first of the abuses to be restored were the *corvées* and the gilds, followed by suppression of free trade in corn. In October 1776 Turgot's duties were entrusted to Jacques Necker (1732-1804) a Genevese banker who, having come to Paris in early manhood, had established himself in his profession. A Protestant, he could not hold the office of Controller General, but he performed its offices. Having introduced some improvements in the fiscal system, he recommended, in a memoir presented to the king in 1781, that the *Parlements* should be restricted to their judicial functions. In the same year he adopted the unusual device of taking the nation into his confidence by publishing a *Compte Rendu,* or balance sheet, in which he claimed that his economies effected since 1776 had created a balance of ten million livres[1] of surplus over expenditure. This was a most dangerous piece of information to make public since it encouraged Marie Antoinette and the Court to indulge in fresh extravagances and lulled the nation into a false sense of security. Still worse, his figures were wrong, for actually there was a large deficit, attributable mainly

---

[1] The *livre* in eighteenth-century France was reckoned to have the value of one shilling and eight pence in English currency of the same period.

to his policy of financing the American war by extensive borrowing. It was this policy of piling up debt that made reform impossible, and eventually led to the Revolution. But meanwhile his economies had alienated the governing classes, led by the *Parlement*; and so, in face of concerted opposition, he resigned in May 1781, to be recalled in 1788. Necker had done no more than stave off bankruptcy. But bankruptcy became inevitable in the financial administration of Charles Calonne, whose failure to replenish the treasury, together with the reckless extravagance of the Court, resulted in 1788 in a confession of inability to pay even the interest on national loans. It was this fact that led to the summoning of the Assembly of Notables, the first step in the Revolution.

These difficulties had meanwhile been intensified by France's engagement in a war of revenge against England—the War of the American Revolution. Trouble in the thirteen colonies on the eastern seaboard of North America had long been brewing. There was an attitude of separatism in the New England colonies where a rigid Calvinism was allied to a reverence for English common law principles which, it was assumed, provided guarantees for liberty of the subject; to this extent the colonists were insisting on principle, however misguided they may have been in the application of principle. But this was not appreciated by either George III[1] or Lord North who assumed that the insurgents were hooligans, likely to be dispersed by the first volley from regular troops. As in all revolutions there was much self interest and mob oratory, but most of the New Englanders were convinced of the justice of their cause, however much they may have been indebted to English creditors and however much they may have persisted in violating the laws of trade. In the years following the conclusion of the Seven Years War Grenville had tried to stop violations of the Navigation Acts mainly by the use of vice-admiralty courts, and the Stamp Act of 1765 had aimed at little more than inducing the Americans to pay a fraction of

[1] above, pp. 63-4.

he cost incurred by the home country in defending them
gainst the French. This raised the cry of No Taxation with-
ut Representation. There were other causes of disagreement.
'or long there had been friction between royally-appointed
overnors and their colonial legislatures; there was some
esentment at the Privy Council's exercise of the right to veto
olonial legislation—a right which had been exercised with
ingular moderation. More important may have been the argu-
nent adduced by Tom Paine in his *Common Sense* (1776)
hat the colonies were necessarily involved, to their disadvan-
age, in the wars of the mother country.

At first only a minority of the thirteen colonies was in favour
f independence, and there was a large group of American
oyalists which suffered much loss from its insistence on the
raditional allegiance. A crisis was reached by the affair of the
3oston "tea party" in 1773. In April 1774 the colonists
inited for the first time in a continental congress; a year later
he first skirmish between their militia and British regular
roops took place at Lexington. On July 4, 1776, a congress,
neeting in Philadelphia, issued the famous Declaration of
ndependence. This document, which attributed all the
olonial grievances to the personal initiative of George III,
enounced allegiance to the British crown. The War of
ndependence had begun.

General Burgoyne's surrender at Saratoga in October 1777
onvinced Vergennes that the time for public intervention had
urrived, and accordingly a Franco-American treaty of Febru-
ry 1778 pledged France to support the cause of American
ndependence. In order to clear the decks the French minister
efused tempting offers from Austria of territory in the
Netherlands in return for intervention in the Bavarian Succes-
ion War,[1] and this in spite of strong pressure exerted on
ehalf of her relatives by Marie Antoinette. At the same
ime he rejected Spanish offers of substantial advantages in

[1] S. F. Bemis, *The Diplomacy of the American Revolution* (1957),
hapters v and vi.

Brazil in return for helping Spain to destroy Portuguese independence. The war of revenge against England must come first. In April 1779, by a convention with Charles III, it was agreed that Gibraltar was to be restored, with which object Spain declared war on England in June 1779, followed by a French declaration of war on the same country. The siege of Gibraltar was at once begun, and lasted until 1782. As England was now at war with both France and Spain she turned to the Dutch, with a request that they would carry out the treaty of 1678 whereby both nations had agreed to support the other if attacked. But the Dutch, determined to maintain their neutrality, refused, on the ground that the treaty related only to events in European waters. As they had long been supplying stores and ammunition to the Americans, Britain replied by declaring war on the Dutch in December 1780. By that time the situation of England seemed almost desperate. In the west she had a great rebellion on her hands; in Europe she was at war with France, Spain and the United Provinces, whose combined naval forces were superior in numbers to the British fleet. In these circumstances she turned for help to a most unexpected quarter—Catherine of Russia. But the empress, aggrieved by attacks on Russian ships in the North Sea and Mediterranean, devoted herself to the formation of the Armed Neutrality of the North in order to preserve freedom of navigation for neutrals.[1] Fortunately, this semi-academic association did not seriously interfere with the British right of search at sea, though it destroyed the hopes of an Anglo-Russian agreement. Britain was fortunate also in this that although, for a time, French and Spanish fleets dominated the Channel, their crews were decimated by scurvy.

The best of the French admirals was Suffren, of the English Rodney. In alliance with Haider Ali, Suffren defeated Admiral Hughes before Madras, a naval victory which was followed by a number of indecisive actions. The Dutch settlement of Negapatam was captured by the English fleet

[1] above, p. 94.

But the situation in India was relieved in the summer of 1781 when, backed by Warren Hastings, Sir Eyre Coote defeated Haider Ali at Porto Novo and restored British supremacy in the Carnatic. In the West Indies French naval activity was more effective. Although Rodney succeeded in capturing St. Eustatius from the Dutch, he could not contest the supremacy maintained by De Grasse, with the result that Tobago was captured and enemy troops were landed on the mainland. There the Spaniards captured Florida and in the Mediterranean they took Minorca, but they failed to make any headway with Gibraltar. The uninterrupted landing of French reinforcements on the Chesapeake under the protection of De Grasse's fleet made inevitable the surrender of Cornwallis at Yorktown in October 1781; nor was the situation relieved by Rodney's brilliant victory at The Saints (off Dominica) in April 1782, for this success came too late. At the same time the fall of Lord North's ministry left only the king anxious to continue hostilities. In France and Spain there was war weariness, and Vergennes may have been disillusioned by his American confederates.

Rodney's victory at The Saints and the heroic resistance of Gibraltar made the peace negotiations easier for Lord Shelburne, who had succeeded Rockingham as Prime Minister in July 1782. After prolonged deliberations involving England, the Colonists, France, Spain and Holland the treaty of Versailles was signed in September 1783. Its most important clause was the recognition of a new and independent power—the United States of America. England ceded to France a number of West Indian acquisitions including St. Lucia and Tobago as well as Senegal and Goree on the West African coast. In India Surat, Pondicherry and Calicut were restored to France and, in return, England recovered Grenada, Dominica, St. Vincent and Montserrat. Spain obtained Florida and Minorca. Conquests made from the Dutch were restored, with the exception of Negapatam.

But these clauses convey little of the profound effects of the war in Europe. These effects were felt least in Spain, where the government at last resigned itself to the loss of Gibraltar. In the south-east of Europe Catherine, free from interference by the west, was busily engaged in the infiltration of Russian influence into the Turkish empire; in Austria, the death of Maria Theresa in 1780 enabled Joseph to go ahead with his reforms. Elsewhere the effects were more disquieting. In the United Dutch Provinces the weakness of William IV's rule had been clearly revealed, with a consequent strengthening of the opposition or " patriot " party; in England there was a demand for radical reform of the constitution, an attitude summed up by the younger Pitt in May 1783 when, on introducing a motion for parliamentary reform, he referred to " the melancholy series of events in America by which the people have been disgusted and obliged to turn their eyes inwards on themselves ".[1] His motion was lost. Six years earlier, when a similar motion had met with the same fate, Wilkes had declared that the American War was one of the strongest arguments for regulation of the franchise. " America ", he declared with prophetic insight " will be the leading figure of this age ".[2] But these warnings fell on deaf ears, and the demand for parliamentary reform was again postponed by the Jacobin scare of 1793 and the outbreak of the Terror.

In France the atmosphere was very different. The war of revenge had been won; after years of humiliation France was again resurgent and triumphant. Never had Parisian society been so brilliant as at this time. The national finances, it is true, were in greater disorder than ever, but many people had money to spend and, following the example of the Court, they spent freely, or speculated or gambled. America was *à la mode,* and societies were founded in order to commemorate association with the new republic, notably the Order of Cincinnatus (approved by the king). Some, it is true, had reserves about negro slavery in the southern states but that, it was

[1] W. Cobbett, *Parliamentary History,* XXIII, 827 ff.
[2] ibid, XVIII, 1286 ff.

thought, would disappear in time. The imaginative writers Crèvecoeur and Chastellux depicted North America as inhabited by Nature's originals, living in conditions of pastoral simplicity and rectitude, conditions similar to those which had inspired Rousseau. All this was accompanied by a revival of the spirit of *bienfaisance,* such as had followed the death of Louis XIV; in the one case, relaxation of tension, in the other, pride in achievement led to greater sympathy for human unfortunates. More interest was taken in the hospitals and their improvement, and in 1786 the *Société Philanthropique* was founded in order to give assistance to the old and blind. A clerk in the Foreign Office designed a form of braille by means of which the blind were enabled to read.

But there were other, less idealist elements in French society at this time. On the Paris stage the most popular comedy was Beaumarchais's *Le Mariage de Figaro,* with its unconcealed sarcasm at the expense of social distinction. Among the upper classes there was a craze for new or revived cults. Freemasonry was making many converts, particularly the revolutionary sect of the *Illuminés,* founded by the Bavarian Weishaupt; from Berlin came the Rosicrucians. The mystical doctrines of Swedenborg were in vogue; somnambulism made its appearance in some parts of France. In 1778 the Viennese doctor Mesmer came to Paris, where he purported to effect cures by release of animal magnetism; two years later he was joined by the Sicilian Cagliostro, whose magical potions and elixirs were popular with fashionable women. More important was the great increase in the number of journals, magazines and newspapers after the conclusion of the American War; among the literate a great reading public was in process of formation, inevitably a politically-minded public, deeply conscious of what had been achieved, partly by French aid, in the recent Revolution; how a new republic, vaster than any known to the old world, had successfully vindicated the principles of liberty and independence against an effete and tyrannical monarchy. A new era of human rights appeared to be on the horizon; it seemed that, after all, the dreams of the *philosophes* about human perfectibility might be realised. But, deeper down in French society, there were portents ominous for the future. Throughout the 1800 cafés of Paris catchwords such as: *guerre aux châteaux, paix aux chaumières* (" war on the châteaux, peace for the cottages ") were freely quoted; even more serious were the numerous personal resentments, steadily gathering in force—resentment of the bourgeoisie against the arrogance of the aristocracy; of the peasantry against the increasing demands of the seigneurs; of the workers against the constantly rising price of food. Numerous bread riots attested the eruptive forces coming to the boil beneath the thin crust covering French society. Within a few years that crust was to be blown off.

Chapter XI

SCIENCE. THE VISUAL ARTS. MUSIC

I SCIENCE

In the field of Science the eighteenth century was the legatee of the seventeenth. The achievement of Newton was so vast that time was needed for its assimilation, a process hastened by popularisers such as Voltaire, with the result that, by about 1730, the Newtonian principles were widely known and accepted, though there still lingered a fairly strong body of opinion in favour of the Cartesian doctrines. Some of the Newtonian hypotheses were established by investigation; for example, his theory of attraction was confirmed by experiments with the pendulum; and, in 1736-7 when Maupertuis and Clairvault went to the head of the Gulf of Bothnia in order to measure the length of a degree of latitude in that area, their results substantiated Newton's conjecture that the globe is flattened at the polar regions. To some extent, therefore, scientists were absorbing and applying discoveries or hypotheses of the preceding century. In this they were aided not so much by the universities as by the scientific academies to be found in nearly every capital city of Europe.

Nevertheless, the eighteenth century shows a remarkable record of scientific achievement. This was made possible by two things—the very high standard of workmanship in wood and metal and by inventions or improvements in the instruments necessary for research. Thus, the grinding and polishing of lenses for optical work had long been an active industry in several Dutch cities, notably Amsterdam; in this category the most notable achievements were those of Antony Leeuwenhoek (1632-1723) who devised microscopes with which he conducted important investigations in physiology. He is credited with having isolated a number of germs. In other spheres, there were advances of comparable importance. In the earlier years of the century three researchers—the Swede Celsius, the French physician Réaumur and the Danzig physician Fahrenheit were engaged in the production of accurate thermometers. The telescope was greatly improved by the Englishman John Dollond (1706-61), one of those to whom the invention of the achromatic lens has been attributed; later in the century the Hanoverian-born William Herschel (1736-1822), working at Slough with the help of his sister, devised a reflector telescope having a focal length of forty feet, with the aid of which he discovered the planet Uranus in 1781. Chemical experiments were facilitated by the practice of collecting gases in tubes inverted over water; for water-soluble gases Priestley used mercury. More sensitive balances for measuring weight proved of enormous importance in the advance of chemistry, and it was by accurate quantitative analysis that the misleading hypothesis of Phlogiston[1] was eventually discredited. There were other achievements, some of them spectacular. Towards the end of the century steam carriages were tried on roads and steam vessels on rivers, but these were not a success. The Montgolfier brothers startled the inhabitants of Paris by their balloon ascents, and in 1794 the French victory over the Austrians at Fleurus was said to have been aided by observations of enemy movements from a Montgolfier balloon.

It is possible here to mention only some of the main achievements. In mathematical investigations trigonometry and the calculus were greatly advanced. The calculus of variations was established by the Swiss Conrad Euler (1707-82) who also inaugurated spherical trigonometry. Invited to Potsdam by Frederick the Great, he was for many years a leading

[1] below, pp. 184-5.

figure in the Prussian Academy of Science. He was rivalled by a compatriot John Bernouilli (1667-1748) who made many applications of the differential and integral calculus to his scientific work. In 1766 the Frenchman Joseph Lagrange (1736-1813) succeeded Euler as Director of the Prussian Academy. Lagrange had begun at the age of 19 as professor of mathematics in the school of artillery at Turin; by his researches in mathematics and astronomy he proved himself one of the ablest continuators of Newton in the eighteenth century. Among his many discoveries was that of the periodic variations in the major axes of the solar system. He survived the Revolution, to be rewarded by Napoleon with a seat in the Senate.

In physics the main discoveries were made in the theory of heat and the beginnings of the science of calorimetry. These subjects engaged the attention of Joseph Black (1728-99), a physician who was professor at Glasgow in the middle decades of the century, where he was closely associated with James Watt. Black's theory of latent heat was deduced from the fact that application of heat to ice does not result in immediate liquefaction, for a large portion of the heat is absorbed at latent heat, without rise in temperature; so too, the application of heat to boiling water does not result in immediate evaporation. With some degree of accuracy Black was able to measure this latent heat, which enables a body to resist change of state.[1] From observation he also deduced that different amounts of heat are needed in order to raise different substances through the same number of degrees; for comparison, he took water as his standard, and so was able to compile tables of specific heat. All this proved important not only in abstract science, but in the development of the steam engine. Black, who rarely followed up his discoveries, was one of those to whom the dis-

---

[1] It is now known that this latent heat is potential energy, produced by changes in the arrangement and movements of the molecules.

covery of carbonic acid gas has been attributed. It is evidence of the virtuosity prevailing in this period that his academic chair was of chemistry and anatomy.

Many of the phenomena of static electricity were already well known to observers. Early in the century Stephen Gray, a pensioner of the Charterhouse who died in 1736, experimented in the conduction of electricity by different materials and formulated the distinction between conductors and insulators. Copper he found to be a good conductor; glass and resin good insulators. Soon the experimenters were intent on making devices for storing electricity, which was thought to be a form of matter, and the credit for the invention of the Leyden Jar appears to be due to the Dutch physician Peter Musschenbroek (1692-1761), who devised his Leyden Jar in 1746. This was followed up by Benjamin Franklin (1706-90), so distinguished in other spheres of activity, who experimented with a kite in order to draw electricity from thunder clouds. He concluded that clouds may be positively or negatively charged. Henry Cavendish (1731-1810), one of the most brilliant researchers of the centuryy, deduced the law of inverse squares of electrical repulsion from his observations of an electrical charge on the surface of a conductor. Later in the century Galvani of Bologna showed the contraction of muscles resulting from electric shock, and Volta of Pavia produced an electric charge from plates of copper and zinc in an electrolyte. This was the Voltaic Pile. But in this period electricity, still little more than a curiosity for its devotees, was usually limited to static electricity produced by friction, or to that contained in a Leyden Jar. Not yet was there any possibility of its practical application.

Chemistry had ancient antecedents; for long, indeed, it had been indistinguishable from alchemy. Its progress in the eighteenth century was delayed by acceptance of the theory of Phlogiston, first enunciated by the Prussian chemist G. E. Stahl (1660-1734). On this theory Phlogiston was a substance to be found in all combustible bodies and was liberated by

Chemistry and Biology

burning or calcination. Not until about 1765, when Cavendish and others had made a systematic study of gases, did Phlogiston lose its hold. Meanwhile the chemists were isolating gases in their test tubes but, in the absence of an accepted scientific terminology, there was much confusion and overlapping. Thus, Black isolated carbonic acid gas which he named " fixed air "; Daniel Rutherford (1749-1819), an Edinburgh physician and botanist, stumbled across nitrogen, which he termed " noxious air "; for long hydrogen was known as " inflammable air ". The discovery of oxygen is usually attributed to Joseph Priestley (1733-1804). Much material evidence was therefore being collected for A. L. Lavoisier (1743-94) when he set out to establish a revised nomenclature, on which chemistry is now based. " Noxious Air " became nitrogen; " Inflammable Air " hydrogen. Compounds with oxygen he described as oxides; with sulphur sulphides. Those substances which could not be broken down by analysis he called elements. This new nomenclature was outlined in a treatise published in 1789.

In biology scientific nomenclature may be said to date from 1735 when the Swedish botanist Karl Linné or Linnaeus published his *Systema Naturae*. From much material collected by his predecessors he classified plants according to their stamens or male organs, subdividing each class according to the number of styles or female organs. He believed until late in life that the number of species was fixed. This idea of immutability of species was first contested by the French naturalist G. L. Buffon (1707-88), whose *Histoire Naturelle,* which had occupied him and his collaborators for many years, was published in the years 1749-88 in 36 volumes. This colossal work was concerned mainly with the earth's crust and its evolution, but contained many observations on birds and quadrupeds. Buffon, who substituted Nature for God, claimed that the earth was much older than his contemporaries supposed; this he deduced from the study of fossils, the distribution of which proved that vast changes of climate had occurred in the course of millenia; as well as this he succeeded in differentiating the sciences of anthropology, geology and archaeology. He was the founder of modern geology and a precursor of the theory of evolution. In 1744 his *Théorie de la Terre* shocked the orthodox by its rejection of the biblical account of the creation, with the result that he was obliged by the Sorbonne to retract his views.

Generally, Buffon rejected the idea of fixity of species, claiming that nature is in a continual state of flux. Hence he found a common origin for many groups of animals usually regarded as distinct. These views were shared by the most wayward genius of the century, Denis Diderot (1713-84), who reasoned that the earth had progressed through an infinite series of transformations in the course of which many monsters or "sports" had failed to survive. According to his "transformistic" theory all existing forms of life have developed from the living molecules of primitive chaos; every animal is more or less man, every mineral is more or less plant and every plant is more or less animal. On this view man ceased to be a privileged exception in the order of nature, for he was no more than a clever or lucky survivor.[1] It was fortunate for Diderot that so many of his writings were not published until after his death. Another contributor to these anticipations of the theory of evolution came from an unexpected quarter—from Goethe,[2] whose interest in the function and transformation of bodies led him to coin the word "morphology". His anatomical studies induced him to conclude man's essential relationship with the animal kingdom, a heresy so devastating that it probably passed unnoticed. This partially explains why there was no antagonism between science and religion in the eighteenth century as there was in the nineteenth. In the foreground were the Deists and Atheists, giving cause for scandal or disquiet; in the background were the prophets of a

---

[1] R. L. Cru, *Diderot as a Disciple of English Thought* (1913) ch. IV
[2] In his *Versuch die Metamorphose des Pflanzen zu Erklären* (1790).

theory of evolution in which the supernatural had no place.

The scientific achievements of the period, though characterised more by ingenuity than genius, were nevertheless considerable and served to maintain that continuity of experiment and conjecture on which all great discoveries are ultimately based. It will have been noticed that the small states—Switzerland, Scotland, Sweden and Holland—were making contributions to science out of all proportion to their population, and that the physicians ranked high among the contributors. On the other hand, with the exceptions of the Dutch Hermann Boerhaave (1668-1738) a pioneer in clinical medicine, and the Hunter brothers, William and John, who did so much for the advancement of surgery, the doctors appear to have made few contributions of importance to their own art. The progress of medicine lagged behind that of the other sciences. Various reasons might be suggested for this. While anatomy and physiology were comparatively well advanced, chemistry was not systematised until the end of the century, and the microscope had not yet revealed the germs save perhaps to Leeuwenhoek. Except for herbal remedies, drugs were usually powerful and even dangerous salts of minerals, and organic chemistry was unknown. Still more, medicine was for long an academic subject in which formal debate on academic themes was of more importance that research; nor was it until the later part of the century that the physician made personal contact with his patients in hospital. Until then the apothecary was the general practitioner. Men had to wait until aseptic surgery and anaesthetics revolutionised medicine.

II THE VISUAL ARTS

About such a vast subject as the visual arts in the eighteenth century only a few generalisations can here be attempted, and these very tentatively. One's most obvious impression is that of a new sense of spaciousness, exemplified not only in great mansions and expansive parks but in the town planning which, by sweeping away congested slums, has given us the magnificent squares to be found in every great European city. The square displaced church, bridge and cathedral as the centre of urban life. In the interiors tapestry and wall paper had for some time superseded panelling, a change which gave employment to the decorative artists; paintings tended to become smaller, as they were wanted for the decoration of private houses as much as for the walls of royal and public galleries. As for the artist himself, although his status was approximating to that of the professional man, nevertheless he remained essentially a craftsman, often marrying into the families of other craftsmen. Hence the dynasties of artists—in France, the three Lemoynes, father and two sons, all of them sculptors; the architects Mansart and his brother-in-law Robert de Cotte; the Coypels and Vernets, both of them families of artists. This inter-relationship may have favoured the maintenance of continuity and avoidance of innovation; it may also have promoted excellence of technique.

One factor in the stimulation of interest in art was the popularity of reproductions in line engraving, aquatint and mezzotint, with the result that the masterpieces of painting and architecture were brought to the knowledge of men of moderate means. Sumptuous volumes of such reproductions were often real achievements in themselves, greatly prized by the collector; and one publisher, Alderman Boydell of London, made this almost a minor industry, to be continued in the early nineteenth century by the German refugee Ackermann. Exhibitions, as in the London Royal Academy and the Paris Salon, helped still further to diffuse a knowledge and appreciation of art. There were also great patrons, not all of them intelligent patrons—the royal mistresses and financiers in France, the petty princes of Germany, the Habsburgs in Vienna, Catherine of Russia, wealthy connoisseurs in England, led by Lord Burlington and Horace Walpole. The taste of the patron often helped to shape the performance of the artist, but in western Europe public taste was becoming better informed, if not by reproductions then by discussion of aesthetic matters in the numerous popular journals. Art was also an element in the education of the wealthy, particularly of the young Englishman of fortune who was encouraged by the Grand Tour to acquire a knowledge of foreign architecture and picture galleries, especially in Italy.

Artistic activity also helped to emphasise the social character of this period. It was an age of great portrait painters, as witness the names of Reynolds, Gainsborough and Raeburn in England, of Nattier and Madame Vigée Le Brun in France, of Goya in Spain. The coloured and highly ornamental dress of the men—so contrasted with the uniformity of to-day—gave more scope to the artist, since he had to depict the texture and colour of materials; as well as this, he usually excelled in the grouping of his subjects, thus combining a distinctive ensemble with the delineation of individual characteristics. Sometimes a hint of personality can be deduced merely from the place assigned to members of the group, as in Goya's well-known painting of the family of Charles IV of Spain, where the masterful queen dominates the scene from her place in the centre foreground, while the submissive king is almost effaced by his position at the side. In no other age were the lineaments of prominent personalities, men and women, so brilliantly depicted as in the eighteenth century.

One outcome of this socialisation of art was the beginning of art criticism as a definite literary *métier*. Many eminent men including Montesquieu, Burke, Goethe and Lessing attempted to analyse, from a philosophic point of view, the appeal made by the beautiful. In this way some cloudy theories of aesthetics were evolved. Montesquieu at least was clear, and he was probably voicing the general opinion prevailing in the earlier part of the century when, in contrasting Gothic and Greek architecture, he declared that whereas the former, by its variety of ornaments, confuses the eye and so presents us with

an enigma; the latter, by contrast, is uniform and, having no
divisions, does not distract one's attention from its essential
simplicity and grace. The soul needs variety, he declared, but
also symmetry; " symmetry spares pain in the observer ".[1]
This dictum may be applied to much that was best in the art
and music of the eighteenth century. A very different view
was presented, during the Romantic Revival by Goethe,[2] who
claimed to find the " daemonic " in the highest forms of poetry
and music. This he regarded as an elemental force, neither
good nor evil, driving men to glory or destruction. He experienced it in the music of Beethoven and was afraid of it.
The imaginative life of the eighteenth century lies between the
poles represented by these two opinions.

Diderot was the first of the professed art critics. Art salons
had been held in Paris since 1667, and in the eighteenth century they were of frequent recurrence, each one lasting for
about 20 days. Between 1759 and 1781 Diderot wrote as an
art critic in the *Correspondance Littéraire,* basing his observations on visits to the salons and on his personal acquaintance
with such artists as Chardin, Pigalle, Boucher and Vernet. In
this way he acquired some knowledge of the technicalities of
painting and devised a new literary approach for their exposition, in which he related art to its social background and
expressed himself in the intimate, almost conversational form
known as the *causerie,* which Sainte Beuve afterwards brought
to perfection. He applauded the moralising art of Greuze, an
artist who, like many of the Victorians, believed that every
picture should be edifying; he disliked the insipidity of
Boucher, and he lived long enough to welcome the grandiose
solemnity of David. His discourses were made easily intelligible by avoidance of abstract terms.

This virtue has not always been characteristic of art critic-

[1] Montesquieu, " Essai sur le Gout " (undated); afterwards printed
in the *Encyclopédie.*
[2] For this see L. A. Willoughby, " Goethe the Natural Philosopher "
in *Goethe after Two Centuries,* ed. C. Hammer (1952).

ism. For long the subject has been bedevilled by two popular words—baroque and rococo—which have been applied to so many forms of artistic expression that it is often difficult to see what meaning they can have. Even about the derivation of these words there is the greatest difference of opinion. In the eighteenth century the word " baroque " was a jewellers' term for an imperfect or badly-shaped pearl; but there are several other suggested derivations. Rococo is of equally obscure genesis, its origin being commonly attributed to the French *rocaille,* meaning rock work or grotto work, and hence by implication rocky or stony. It is from the application of these obscure terms that difficulties arise. One writer assures us that the secular, " absolutist " architecture of Vienna is baroque; another tells us that Bavarian rococo must be considered in relation to snowy mountains and wooden chalets. We can be sure however that baroque means flamboyant, over-decorated art, of which rococo is a later form, so exaggerated as to be almost grotesque. It appears that, between the Renaissance and the advent of neo-classicism in the 1770's there was, particularly in Austria, Bavaria, Spain and southern Italy, a period in which the over-ornate was fashionable, notably in architecture and internal decoration. These were areas where the classical influence had never deeply penetrated; moreover, in Spain and southern Italy oriental influences still survived. Twisted pillars, tortured spirals, abundance of cherubs and angels, profusion of blue and gilt, avoidance of straight line and right angle—such are the main characteristics connoted by these two terms. But unfortunately the words have been applied to spheres other than architecture and internal decoration, with the result that Bach is now classified as a " baroque " composer, although no one has ever said that his music is flamboyant or over-ornate.

The trouble may have arisen from the attempt to bring every form of imaginative expression under one general heading, such as is implied in the term the " baroque period "; moreover there is a mystic virtue in words of which we do not quite know the meaning. So far as architecture and decoration are concerned, it may help if reference is made to two names of which the derivation and meaning are indisputable. These are the terms Palladian and Churrigueresque, of which the first is derived from the name of the Italian architect Andrea Palladio (1518-80) and the second from the Spanish architect José Churriguerra (1650-1723). Their styles, diametrically opposed, represent the extremes between which the architectural and even the artistic taste of the eighteenth century can be disposed. Palladio, a keen student of the great monuments of antiquity and of their Roman expositor Vitruvius, popularised an architecture distinguished by the qualities of dignity, repose and restraint in contrast with Churriguerra who, especially in his ecclesiastical design and ornamentation, made fashionable a style, ornate to the point of distortion, a closely-congested medley of highly-coloured bric-à-brac which, to many observers, appears more suited to the fair ground than the church. Specimens of the latter school can be seen in Spain and Latin America; elsewhere, as in Austria and Bavaria, there are examples which made some approach to this extreme. Another consideration may be adduced. It is possible that the type now known as rococo may owe something to Chinese influence, which acquired some popularity in this period. Importation of oriental porcelain and lacquer work, together with the painting of wall paper, helped to spread an appreciation of the characteristics of Chinese art—its delicate brush work, its minute rendering of colour and texture in fabrics, its depiction of scenes where the foreground shows pagoda, river and bridge against a highly improbable background of mountains and precipices.

With this example before them some artists of the west substituted ingenuity and fancy for that patient study of nature in all its moods on which true art depends. Critics have found an affinity between Chinese landscape and that of Watteau; there is even more obvious affinity in such *chinoiseries* as Frederick the Great's Dragon Cottage at Potsdam and the

Japanese pavilion at Sans Souci. Men were experimenting in various styles derived from every corner of the earth, as witness the extravagances of William Beckford at Fonthill and Horace Walpole at Strawberry Hill. Even these, however, were outdone by a prince of Montbéliard whose park contained a Swiss farm, an anabaptist chapel, a Gothic-Moorish gateway, a Tyrolean mill, a grotto surmounted by a Turkish parasol and flanked by Doric pillars.[1] But, by the 1770's, the taste for exotic art was going out of fashion, and its place was taken by such diverse and even contrary cults as the revived Classicism of Winckelmann, the taste for picturesque ruins and that resort to mountains which heralded the advent of the Romantic movement. Thereupon one more term—Romanticism—was added to the vocabulary of the expert.

This section concludes with a reference to some of the achievements of the visual artists in the eighteenth century. After his death in 1708 Mansart, the architect of Versailles and of the Place Vendôme, continued to exercise great influence through his pupils and his brother-in-law Robert de Cotte. It was De Cotte who designed many of the new *hôtels* in the fashionable districts of Paris; the chapel at Versailles was also his work. Another disciple of Mansart, Germain Boffrand (1667-1754) built châteaux in Lorraine and was one of those French architects who reconstructed a great part of Nancy, mainly in the Palladian style. Still another pupil of Mansart, J. A. Gabriel (1698-1782) built the Petit Trianon at Versailles and made the first designs for the Place Louis Quinze, afterwards enlarged into the Place de la Concorde, perhaps the most magnificent square in Europe. In the later part of the century when taste became more severe and classical, the leading French architect was Jacques Soufflot (1708-80) who designed the *Panthéon,* modelled on the Pantheon in Rome. This, one of the most impressive of buildings constructed in the Palladian style, became, after the Revolu-

[1] D. Mornet, *Le Romanticisme en France au XVIIIème Siècle* (1912), p. 63.

tion, the burial place of France's famous men. It was built in the years 1769-90.

French painting in the early eighteenth century was marked by reaction against Italian influence and against the formal magnificence of Le Brun. Pictorial art became more free and colourful, more Flemish than Italian, better suited to the apartments of private houses than to great galleries. Of this decorative school Antoine Coypel (1661-1722) and the Walloon Antoine Watteau (1684-1721) are examples, the latter excelling in the depiction of *fêtes galantes* and military scenes. His "Embarquement pour Cythère" (in the Louvre) is his best-known painting, and admirers of his work have found in it a spiritual elegance which provided a substitute for the poetry so lacking in this period. This tradition was maintained by François Boucher (1705-70), the favourite painter of Madame de Pompadour; his voluptuous art, depicted on tapestry and canvas, was so erotic and sometimes inane as to incur the condemnation of Diderot. There was more variety in the work of Honoré Fragonard (1752-1806), a Provençal, whose portraits and pastoral scenes were keenly appreciated by Madame Du Barry and the *fermiers généraux*. His near contemporary J. B. Greuze (1725-1805), who showed some Dutch influence, won great popularity by his enigmatic pictures, depicting domestic scenes in humble life. The Avignonese Joseph Vernet (1714-89) founded a dynasty of painters whose achievements served as a link between Claude and Corot; indeed, this school showed a real appreciation of nature, particularly in seascapes and delineation of ports and harbours. The later decades of the century witnessed a revival, mainly under government auspices, of historical paintings on the grand scale, a movement culminating in the work of Louis David (1748-1825), whose zeal for the republics of antiquity qualified him to be the artist of the French Revolution. Thus, the pictorial art of eighteenth-century France provides a clue to the social revolution—from the sensuous pastorals and mythological scenes of Watteau, Boucher and Fragonard, so

gratifying to the jaded taste of an effete, over-sophisticated
society, to the grandiose canvases of David, depicting the
triumphs of republican virtue and self-sacrifice.

Eighteenth-century Venice provided the setting for a group
of artists headed by Antonio Canaletto (1697-1768) and
Francesco Guardi (1712-93), whose topographical paintings
enable one to visualise the city of the lagoons more vividly
than is possible with any other city of the period. As a background for the artist Venice recalls Amsterdam of the previous
century. In both, there was the bustling, cosmopolitan life
brought by the sea; the two cities abounded in patrician
merchants intent on the internal decoration of their homes
and palaces, and in both cities there were long streets and
canals, broken here and there by bridges, all providing intricate
problems of shadow, reflection and perspective. But, ever
since the days of Titian and Tintoretto, Venice had been the
home not of line but of colour, and Canaletto was the foremost
of a school which thought primarily in terms of colour. The
bright Adriatic sky served to enhance the delicate shadings,
often cool grey and green, predominating in the decaying
masonry of the city, contrasted with the strong blue of the
lagoons, all of it richly diversified by the rigging of small craft
and the sombre lines of the gondolas. While Canaletto
showed Venice by day, Guardi showed it by night, in scenes
where the faces of revellers are lit up vividly by torch-light.
Of other Italian artists of this period reference may be made
to G. B. Piranesi (1707-78), an engraver, whose numerous
depictions of the antiquities of Rome were produced in the
middle decades of the century. These had great influence on
architects and designers, as they were works of faithful and
accurate record. But there was another and unusual side to
Piranesi's character. In his series of engravings *I Carceri* (The
Prisons) he appears to have drawn on a fevered imagination
for the depiction of vast, lofty interiors, having galleries that
led nowhere and long ladders that suddenly stopped short,
interspersed with elaborate instruments, apparently for the

infliction of torture and death, all of them suggestive of delirium rather than design. These engravings provide the greatest indirect indictment of the penal system of the *Ancien Régime*; any one of them might well have served as a frontispiece to Beccaria's " Treatise of Pains and Penalties ".[1]

A similar element of terror can be found in some of the work of Francisco Goya y Lucientes (1746-1828), the greatest visual artist of the century and one of the finest portrait painters of all time. His deafness, which cut him off from social intercourse, may have confirmed him in his determination to avoid merely giving pleasure to people; certainly his choice of subjects, such as " Saturn eating one of his Sons ", " The Mad House ", " The Plague Hospital " were not calculated to provide aesthetic enjoyment. One of the most disturbing of all artists Goya was an almost brutal satirist of the Spain that he knew. This satire is to be found mainly in the series *Los Caprichos* in which, like Piranesi, he allowed his imagination to run riot. He was fond of emphasising the resemblance between the physiognomy of human beings and that of monkeys; in one of his *Caprichos,* for instance, he shows a fop looking into a mirror, where he sees an ape. A similar purpose was sometimes served by the donkey. For slavish submission to authority, so characteristic of the academic world in Spain, he selected the parrot—witness his depiction of an assembly of learned men, their faces all showing sub-normal intelligence, listening with rapture to a parrot perched above them. Goya, who fits into no school, proves the impossibility of generalising about eighteenth-century art.

III MUSIC

It was in music that the eighteenth century achieved its highest imaginative expression. Within the limits of certain widely-accepted conceptions of harmony and counterpoint, most of

[1] above, p. 240.

he possible types of composition were embodied in innumerable musical scores, leaving to later ages the task of achieving fulfilment in less disciplined and sometimes extravagant modes of expression. Hence a certain element of completeness and even finality in the music of the period extending from Handel to Mozart and Beethoven.

Various reasons may be suggested for this. The polyphonic style of the sixteenth century was at first superseded by the more direct harmonic style of the "new music" at the beginning of the seventeenth century, when the Italians developed, for secular purposes, many instrumental and vocal forms of expression. This change of outlook had many important results: it enabled composers to develop harmonic thinking; it provided a medium in which pure instrumental music could exercise its individual characteristics and, as it made a more direct appeal to the hearer, it enlarged the impact of music. Later in the seventeenth century when the revolution had done its work and a firm basis of harmony and instrumental idiom had been established, composers could again turn to contrapuntal methods in the form of harmonically-based instrumental polyphony, which reached its peak in the work of J. S. Bach. Here was a medium capable of expressing all the composer's thoughts, capable also of infinite development in styles as widely different as the close-knit fugal structures of Bach, or the "galant" serenades of Mozart, or the vast symphonic structures of Beethoven. In other words, the musical achievements of the eighteenth century rested on a basis provided by the advance of vocal and instrumental music in Italy and of organ music in north Germany. Of the former Arcangelo Corelli (1653-1713) is an example; in regard to the latter, it should be recalled that the Lutherans retained much of their old church music and that, ever since the time of Luther himself, they had infused into their chorales an intensity of devotion such as can be found in no other form of musical expression. They proved conclusively that the Devil does not always have the best tunes. This religious element may account for a certain dualism. In the later eighteenth century Bach was unknown in Vienna; equally Gluck and Haydn were scarcely known in Hamburg or Berlin.

Other factors help to account for the pre-eminence of music in the eighteenth century. There were numerous and intelligent patrons, many of them capable performers. The Habsburgs were musical. Charles VI played on the harpsichord at musical recitals, his daughter Maria Theresa sang in private operatic performances. In England the three Georges were ardent admirers of the music of Handel. Frederick the Great, himself no mean performer on the flute, wore out his royal orchestra with his interminable flute concertos. Few German princes were without their orchestra and *Hofkomponist*; in most German towns there was a municipal band, and in cathedrals and churches there were choir schools where music was taught and publicly performed. In London there were pleasure gardens such as Ranelagh and Vauxhall where the songs of Purcell and Arne could be heard. Under the direction of Telemann Hamburg, in the earlier part of the century, became a centre for concerts of instrumental music; later, the maritime city was displaced by such centres as Mannheim, Vienna and Salzburg. Most European capitals had an opera house, and in Italy they were to be found even in small towns, especially in the poverty-stricken Papal States. Keen rivalry between adherents of different composers served to stimulate public interest in their art. In France there was the contest between Gluckists and Piccinists; England was divided between the Handel and Bononcini factions. Public controversy is often the best form of advertisement.

An innovation at this time was the publication of comment on musical matters—an entirely new type of reading matter, similar to that which Diderot was producing for the visual arts. Of the musicologists the best known was Charles Burney (1726-1814), son of a distinguished family, an organist and music teacher who acquired such fame in Johnson's England as to be elected a member of the Literary Club. This shows

he comparatively high social position accorded to musicians
n the eighteenth century as contrasted with their low status in
he nineteenth. In 1770 and 1772 Burney made prolonged
ours of continental countries, visiting many musicians and
ttending many concerts, afterwards recording his impres-
ions in singularly readable accounts. The four volumes of his
History of Music appeared between 1776 and 1789.

Bach and Handel, the two greatest composers of the century,
vere exact contemporaries, both having been born in 1685,
he one at Eisenach in Thuringia, the other at Halle in
Prussia. They were alike in their strength of character, their
ardent Lutheranism and their great skill as organists. Other-
vise they present an interesting contrast. In early manhood
Handel served as an organist and studied law at Halle; in
703 he joined an opera orchestra in Hamburg; in 1709 he
isited Italy, where he became a friend of Corelli and the
lder Scarlatti. After two visits he settled in England in 1715,
ecoming Director of Music at Canons, near Edgware, the
great house of the Duke of Chandos; in 1726, when he was
naturalised, he was appointed Composer to the Court and
utor in music to the daughters of the Prince of Wales. Mean-
vhile, working with prodigious energy, he produced over 40
operas in the Italian manner which were performed at the
Haymarket and other London theatres. Church music, such
as the Chandos Anthems, triumphal Te Deums as for the
Peace of Utrecht in 1713 and the victory of Dettingen in 1743,
many suites and concertos for keyboard and orchestra—all
hese were overshadowed by his Oratorios. In 1742 the
Messiah was performed for the first time in Dublin; since then
t has become a national institution. In 1784 the first com-
memoration of his music took place in Westminster Abbey.

Handel's well-deserved success was thus achieved in his own
ife time. He made good use of what was best among his
predecessors, notably Purcell, Lulli and Scarlatti but, on the
other hand, he showed little development in his own style, nor
lid he advance his art considerably in any one direction. His

music has always made a strong appeal to lovers of straightforward, uncomplicated melody, easily appreciated at the first hearing, though it often has real depth of feeling and dramatic intensity.

By contrast Bach achieved little reputation in his lifetime except as an organist. Orphaned at the age of ten, he was brought up by an elder brother. He never left his native country and his life was passed in conditions of happy though obscure domesticity. Beginning as organist at Arnstadt, he served for a time as Kapellmeister in the Court of Duke William at Weimar, his compositions there consisting mainly of organ works and church cantatas. This post was exchanged for that of Kapellmeister at Cöthen, in the employment of Prince William of Anhalt Cöthen; there, by 1720, he was producing much secular work mainly for instrumental combinations. In 1723 he went to Leipzig where he acted as choir master and teacher of Latin in the choir school attached to St. Thomas Church, a post which brought him many vexations and humiliations, for the charity boys of the school were unruly, and the church authorities were un-cooperative and even obstructive. Public audiences showed little appreciation of his compositions. But it was there that his masterpieces were produced—the Magnificat in D, the St. John and the St. Matthew Passions and the component parts of the Mass in B minor, which was not performed as a whole until Mendelssohn conducted it in Berlin in 1829. As well as this, a great many church cantatas were composed at this time. Almost the last event of his life was a visit to Berlin where he improvised on a theme set by Frederick. Bach lost his sight through an unskilful operation to his eyes, and in 1750 he died in poverty, leaving in published form only a few minor compositions.

It was fortunate that one of his sons, C. P. E. Bach, preserved the scores of his Passion music; only by lucky chance have so many of his other works been preserved. No one courted popular acclaim less than did Bach. This partly accounts for a certain intimacy and integrity in practically all that he composed, much of it performed not before a fashionable audience, but in the seclusion of the home, where he was assisted by members of his large family, two of whom, J. C. and C. P. E. Bach, achieved real eminence and recognition in their art. It was in such conditions, where the level of critical appreciation must have been very high, that Bach completed a consistent development, dictated by his spiritual promptings and never deflected by demands of fashion or changes of taste. This phenomenon is probably unique in musical history. His genius reached its supreme expression in the St. Matthew Passion where the music, though intensely devotional, shows nothing of "religiosity", where the drama is one of supreme sacrifice not so much by the Son of God as by the Son of Man. But it was not until the early years of the nineteenth century that a dedicated minority made known to the world the magnitude of his achievement, and even thus another century had to elapse before his music could in any sense be described as popular. This again must be attributed to the sustained enthusiasm of a few devoted men.

In recent years there has also been created an interest in the music of Antonio Vivaldi (1678-1741) who, not so long ago, was known only from Bach's transcriptions of several of his violin concertos. This new interest is accounted for mainly by recent discoveries of Vivaldi scores in Dresden and Vienna. Like Bach, Vivaldi made little figure in his own day save as a virtuoso violinist. Becoming a priest in 1703, he was employed for nearly forty years as musical director of an orphanage in Venice, one of the many *Pietàs* of Italy which became famous for a high standard of vocal and instrumental performance. In contrast with Bach, however, he was appreciated by his employers, who enabled him to visit many musical centres, including Vienna, where he died. A prolific composer of church and operatic music, Vivaldi is best known for over 400 concertos scored for a variety of instruments, mainly strings, in which he showed great originality and ingenuity of orchestration. In these he combined counterpoint with the "accompanying melody", where a single instrument, usually the violin, is dominant, the other instruments playing a supporting rôle. The drawback to Vivaldi's scheme of composition is an almost inevitable similarity of theme; the wonder is that so many of his concertos have an individuality of their own, particularly in the middle or andante movements, which are things of great beauty in themselves.

In France musical taste was for long dominated by J. B. Lulli (1623-87), the most popular operatic composer at Versailles, whose work was somewhat lacking in character and distinctiveness. A break through in the Lulli tradition was made by two French-born composers François Couperin (1668-1733) and J. P. Rameau (1683-1764), both of whom began as church organists, though neither of them achieved great success in devotional music. Couperin is best known to-day for his delightful harpsichord compositions, many of them inspired by young women of his acquaintance, though his *Passacaille* strikes a deeper note; what was most gracious in the Versailles of Louis XIV and Louis XV is commemorated in these short but memorable pieces. Bach admired his work and corresponded with him, but the correspondence has not survived. Rameau's achievement was on a broader scale. His treatises on harmony caused some controversy; on the other hand several of his operas such as *Hippolite et Aricie* (1733) and *Castor et Pollux* (1737) have survived the test of time. In the earlier half of the eighteenth century French opera was distinguishable from Italian by its closer adaptation of music to words and gesture, as well as by its greater variety of ballet, chorus and overture.

To omit opera[1] from a study of eighteenth-century Europe is like omitting the stage from an account of Elizabethan England. Both were characteristic expressions not only of imaginative but of social life. One of the oldest forms of dramatic

[1] For a good account see D. J. Grout, *A Short History of Opera* (1961).

representation, opera assumed something of its modern shape early in the seventeenth century, when its mingling of scenery, acting, vocal and instrumental music became popular throughout Italy. It was the Neapolitan Alessandro Scarlatti (1659-1725) who still further extended its popularity, mainly by developing the vocal and instrumental parts. The opera houses soon rivalled the cafés in popularity with all classes of society; in Venice they were thronged with gondoliers, in Naples with artisans; during the recitatives, members of the audience might play a game of cards or have a meal, to be brushed aside as soon as a favourite singer appeared on the stage. Some of the singers became public personages, notably the Neapolitan Carlo Farinelli (1705-82), who amassed a fortune, and was summoned to Madrid in order to assuage the melancholy of Philip V by his voice. In the reign of Philip's successor Farinelli was appointed Chancellor of the Order of Calatrava and played a beneficent part in Spanish public affairs. Opera-goers became keen connoisseurs in the merits of singers, whether male or female; these held a place in public esteem comparable to that of the pianist in the nineteenth century and the conductor in the twentieth. Opposing factions vaunted the merits of their favourites. But these differences were as nothing compared with the rivalries of temperamental prima donnas; indeed Handel himself had been obliged at times to supplement persuasion and entreaty by resort to physical force. Some of these ladies were notorious for arrogance:

> Ra, Ru, Ra Rot-ye,
> My name is Mignotti,
> If you worship me not-ti,
> You can all go to pot-ti.

In England, although Purcell had produced a masterpiece in his *Dido and Aeneas,* no characteristic school of opera had developed, and the Italian form was, for a time, discredited by the great success of John Gay's *Beggars' Opera* (1728) which ridiculed the prevailing taste by putting the trills and arias of grand opera into the mouths of actors representing London's underworld. This set-back to Italian opera had a bad effect on the finances of Handel. But in 1734 Farinelli visited London, where he achieved such success with his singing that the taste for Italian opera was revived, with increasing resort to theatres and opera houses. This revival so alarmed the House of Commons that in 1735 a Bill[1] was introduced to restrain "the number and abuses of playhouses". In the debates much indignation was expressed that the "flattering, fiddling impertinences" of Italian eunuchs and signoras should be foisted on sober-minded Englishmen. Still worse, these "animals" were receiving salaries equal to that of a Lord of the Treasury; with the money so accumulated they would be able, on their return home, to buy estates and set up as landed gentry. The Bill was dropped only because its passage would have involved an extension of the powers of the Lord Chamberlain, who exercised jurisdiction over players and playhouses. It is possible that the debates on this Bill throw some light on the reasons why England failed to develop a distinctive type of opera in the eighteenth century and had to wait so long for Gilbert and Sullivan.

In the later part of the century musical activity shifted from Italy and Naples to Austria and Vienna. The Habsburg capital became the residence of Pietro Metastasio (1698-1782) who served as Court Poet to the emperor from 1729 until his death. His libretti were set to music by composers from Handel to Mozart; it was by his knowledge of music and his instinct for its correlation with blank verse and lyric that he preserved some measure of continuity in the vast operatic output of that long period. But opera, which has usually been a faithful reflection of changes in human mentality, was coming to be influenced by the wave of sentiment represented by the novels of Richardson and the return to nature popularised by Rousseau, with the result that the public demanded greater naturalness, even on the stage. In

[1] W. Cobbett, *Parliamentary History of England*, IX, 944 ff.

1764 Winckelmann published a book[1] which initiated a period of neo-classicism, based on the model set by ancient Greece, with its "noble simplicity and calm greatness". Here was exemplified the "naturalness" which men were now seeking. It was translated into opera by C. W. Gluck (1714-87) with the help of his librettist Raniero Calzabigi (1714-95). After visits to England and France Gluck, who was the son of a Bohemian forester, settled in Vienna in 1756, where he introduced some striking innovations into his art. In revolt against Metastasio, he reduced the libretto almost to the point of austerity; the music was freed from ornamentation, and the old formula of a string of recitatives varied by arias was changed to that of a series of tableaux, each impressive in its statuesque repose. The stilted themes of Roman antiquity were displaced by Greek drama portraying the hopeless struggle of passionate humanity against the decrees of inexorable fate, a theme which had already inspired the genius of Racine; what Racine had achieved in poetry was achieved by Gluck and Calzabighi in opera. The great success of their *Orfeo* and *Alceste* marked the end of Italian domination; and, as Handel had ended one epoch of serious opera, so Gluck ended another. In the preface to his *Alceste* he summed up the essentials of his operatic reform—elimination of capricious singers, music inseparably connected with the poetry, simplification of the drama to essentials and elevation of the overture to an integral part of the composition.

In the later decades of the century the honours of musical composition were almost evenly shared by F. J. Haydn (1732-1809) and W. A. Mozart (1756-91), both of them Austrian-born. Haydn, who began as a choir boy at St. Stephen's Cathedral, was patronised by the Esterhazy family and did much to make Vienna the musical metropolis of Europe. He might be regarded as a continuator of Bach through the intermediaries of J. C. and C. P. E. Bach, to both of whom he acknowledged his indebtedness; but, on the other hand, he

[1] J. J. Winckelmann, *Geschichte der Kunst des Alterthums.*

broke fresh ground, for he made the quartet and symphony standard forms of musical composition, infusing into both characteristic elements derived from his deeply-moulded personality. He was also one of the first to make effective use of folk-song melodies. The great development of the symphony after about 1750, especially by Haydn and Mozart, is of some interest to the student of history. The symphony did not supersede the concerto; but it revealed, in the world of music, a deep-seated, slow-moving change in human relationships, whereby the individual was emerging from the group.[1] A concerto[2] was usually a contest between one or a number of instruments against other instruments—in the nineteenth century it was often piano versus orchestra—with the composer as umpire; whereas the symphony derives its character from unity, a unity enabling the composer to sustain, in ordered sequence, the development of a great or beautiful thought. Moreover, the larger number of instruments required for a symphony adds to the force and variety by means of which the composer can expound that thought. Not until the Romantic period did this comparatively new form of imaginative expression reach its peak in the individuality of Beethoven's symphonies.

It was in Mozart however that the secular music of the eighteenth century attained its full efflorescence. An infant prodigy, his first compositions were published when he was only seven years of age. He found patrons in the Archbishop of Salzburg and the Emperor Joseph, but in neither case was the relationship fortunate, and he was passed over for several appointments that would have made his lot easier, with the result that his short life was spent in a struggle against poverty. Regarding opera as primarily a matter of music rather than of drama, he revived the Italian opera, in which he surpassed his predecessors by his mastery of counterpoint and his start-

[1] above, pp. 36-40.
[2] The word is derived from the Latin *concertare*, to struggle or contend.

ling originality of invention; this he often combined harmoni-
ously with Teutonic fervour. He proved himself a master of
symphony. In *The Marriage of Figaro, Don Giovanni* and
The Magic Flute he produced compositions which have never
been surpassed in this type of opera; as well as this, he
excelled in orchestral and chamber music, enormous in volume
and variety. By far the most popular of all the eighteenth-
century composers his music, often profound, though occasionally trivial, can be appreciated by the widest possible range of
listeners. This is accounted for not only by his never-failing
sources of melody, but by his conception of the individual,
rathen than the type, as the proper subject of opera—the
individual particularly in his love affairs. Here was a touch of
modernity in the irresponsible gaiety of Vienna which marked
the closing years of the *Ancien Régime*; " in Mozart's music
the eighteenth and the nineteenth centuries meet ".[1]

[1] D. J. Grout, *op. cit.,* p. 297.

Chapter XII

THE ENLIGHTENMENT

The term Enlightenment is applied to an intellectual movement, dominant in eighteenth-century France, intended not for the subversion of society, but for its amelioration. As this object was to be achieved mainly by the spread of education, its motto might well have been : " there is no darkness but ignorance ". With such an object in view, the Enlightenment must be numbered among the causes of the French Revolution; but its importance, in comparison with other factors such as the economic and financial, is still a matter of debate, though we can be sure that, among educated men at least, the new ideas helped to undermine many of the assumptions on which eighteenth-century institutions were based. But the movement had far wider implications than those arising from mere criticism. From the scientists and philosophers were derived principles which, applied to the study of human nature, initiated that psychological and sociological approach with which we are so familiar to-day, and these principles also inspired a theory of progress pointing to the ultimate perfectibility of humanity. This coincided with the gradual evolution of a wider conception of personality and individuality, to which reference has been made in the first chapter of this book.

I EDUCATION. THE UNIVERSITIES. THE CENSORSHIP

The church was still the main director of education, and in most towns there were church schools and seminaries where education was provided either free or at low cost. Of the priestly instructors the most successful were the Jesuits, who excelled in Latin scholarship, and provided their pupils with a solid groundwork, qualifying them for the study of other subjects; moreover, by their emphasis on Latin prose and verse composition, they at least obliged their students to think out clearly what they intended to say. On the other hand it is probably unreasonable to attach any particular importance to the fact that such famous sceptics as Descartes and Voltaire were pupils of the Jesuits because, as so many of the best schools and colleges were controlled by the Society, parents able to pay for the education of their sons would be likely to send them to such institutions. After the expulsion of the Jesuits their educational work was taken over either by other religious communities, such as the Oratorians and Benedictines, or by town councils or, in some instances, by the state.

In England there were many endowed grammar schools, mostly founded in late medieval times or in the sixteenth century, in which the curriculum was limited to the classics, or rather the philology of the classics, and boys were prepared for the university and the church. In Scotland, where education had long been valued for its own sake, the parish school was often directed by a dominie who, though he had failed to become a minister, was likely to be qualified in Latin and Greek; in this way there was at least a chance that the humblest of children might receive an education enabling them to train for one of the learned professions. Elsewhere in Europe the children of the poor were lucky if they received enough schooling to save them from illiteracy, though several rulers tried to ensure elementary instruction for all. Frederick the Great made primary education compulsory; in Austria the *General Schulordnung* of 1774 attempted to enforce attendance at elementary schools, for which purpose local resources were to be supplemented by a state grant. In France compulsory education in rural districts was nominally in force. But there was always a wide gap between the legislative enactment and the local resources available for schools and teachers. This was true even in Scotland, where many parishes could not provide the funds; it was still more true of Russia and Spain, where the almost total absence of the necessary facilities made nonsense of high-sounding decrees for education of the masses. For the children of the poor, therefore, instruction was likely to be limited to the three R's, and it was a matter of chance whether that would be obtainable. In the cities, particularly cathedral cities, the educational prospects were usually good, though they might have to be paid for; in towns they varied greatly; in the countryside they were often non-existent. Most agricultural workers were illiterate, but that does not mean that they were unintelligent.

In regard to higher education, there was a demand, in many parts of Europe, for technical instruction and for training in the vernacular and in foreign languages. Latin gradually lost its monopoly as the medium of expression for men of learning, though it continued to be used by some German scholars; French, already the international language of diplomacy, was popular with the upper classes, even in Russia. Dictionaries and grammars of the national languages were published in practically every European state. This widespread demand for " modern " subjects in place of the old classical philology was met by the English Dissenters who, in the later years of the seventeenth century, had set up schools of their own, in which foreign languages, history and mensuration were taught, with the result that pupils from these Dissenting Academies had a better chance of obtaining employment in the rapidly expanding branches of the civil service, particularly in the Customs and Excise; to such an extent indeed that some Anglican parents sent their sons to these schools. On the continent, schools for mineralogy, road making and mining were set up in France; for accountancy and book-keeping in Prussia. But the clearest evidence of this newly-experienced need for vocational knowledge is provided by the many articles in the *Encyclopédie* devoted to arts and crafts.

A similar process can be seen at the universities. At Cambridge the organised teaching of mathematics was fully established at the beginning of the century; in Oxford instruction in natural science followed the establishment of the " Old " Ashmolean in 1683 and spread to some of the colleges. Applied mathematics was taught in the Academy of St. Petersburg and in the university of Moscow (founded in 1755). Even in Portugal, in consequence of Pombal's reforms, " new " subjects were taught at the university of Coimbra. Universities also came to be associated with observatories, as at Upsala and Oxford, or with hospitals and medical schools, as at Leyden, Edinburgh, Paris, Montpellier and Vienna; in these ways there began to emerge a newer and larger conception of the university and its place in national life. But old academic traditions died hard, and it has to be confessed that the universities played a minor rôle in the intellectual movements of the century.

Some characteristics of eighteenth-century universities can be illustrated by reference to Scotland, Spain, England and Germany. In Scotland the four universities of St. Andrews, Glasgow, Aberdeen and Edinburgh provided for the sons of a poor population an education that was non-sectarian, non-residential and inexpensive. Some of the professors were of international repute—Thomas Reid and Dugald Stewart in philosophy, Adam Smith in political economy and moral philosophy, William Cullen in medicine and Joseph Black in science. Only in classical studies were the Scottish universities undistinguished; in philosophy, medicine and science their reputation was very high, and this served to attract many Dissenters from England and northern Ireland. A contrast was presented by the twenty-four universities of Spain; but, in fairness, it should be noted that some of the Spanish universities were little more than " teaching chapters " attached to cathedrals, many of them poorly endowed, and all of them insulated from the intellectual progress made by Europe since the close of the middle ages. So the problem in Spain was not to increase opportunities for higher education, but to diminish them, as was done in 1807 when several universities were abolished. On the other hand the Jesuits had included the teaching of mathematics and physics in their colleges, an example followed by some Spanish institutions after the expulsion of the Society.

In England the two universities of Oxford and Cambridge maintained a system that had no counterpart elsewhere. This was based on the dualism, sometimes antagonism, between the university and the colleges. The university, which was earlier in point of origin, had few endowments; its professorships were limited to a narrow range of subject, and a student might complete his course at Oxford or Cambridge without having once attended a university lecture. In contrast, many of the colleges had been richly provided for by their founders —including medieval kings and bishops—as acts of charity intended for two main objects : to diminish the duration of the donor's stay in Purgatory and to provide for the education and maintenance of the sons of the poor. Both of these laudable purposes were destined to be entirely frustrated. Purgatory was, in effect, abolished by an Act of the Reformation Parliament and, by the eighteenth century, the two universities were becoming the close preserves of the middle classes and the rich, though some of the poor might be admitted by the back-door in the menial capacity of sizars and servitors. All the colleges were residential; oral, individual tuition was supplied by those members of the governing body who were tutors or lecturers. In the performance of their duties the tutors were often idle or remiss, and Gibbon's condemnation of the tutorial system as he experienced it at Magdalen College, Oxford, is well known. At Cambridge, both Newton and the poet Gray held professorships, but neither exercised any influence on college teaching, and the significance of the Newtonian physics was first expounded not at Cambridge, but at Edinburgh. The great Cambridge scientist Henry Cavendish

onducted his researches in London. Apart from a few excep-
ons the two universities, or rather their constituent colleges,
ere little more than annexes to the established church.

A very different ideal was represented by the German and
austrian universities, of which there were more than thirty;
or, in different degrees, these tended to become state institu-
ons, and so their activities might be subordinated to con-
iderations of public policy. Halle, founded in 1694, was
istinguished not only for its association with Pietism, but
vas a centre for the training of Prussian civil servants. The
udy of Latin was displaced by that of German and foreign
anguages. It was rivalled by the Hanoverian university of
Göttingen founded (nominally) by George II in 1737. This
nstitution, a state department as much as a university, was
ntended mainly for young men of good birth. The classics
vere not neglected, but prominence was given to jurisprud-
nce, which included not only the old Germanic law, but the
nore nebulous *Jus Naturale,* as expounded in the works of
Grotius, Pufendorf, Vattel and a host of others. At Göttingen
lso, as at Vienna, instruction was provided in *Kameralwissen-
chaft,* that is, public finance, political economy and admini-
trative law, the subjects qualifying for one of the higher posts
n the civil service. Herein was a contrast with English prac-
ice which excluded such subjects from university curricula,
nd entrusted the work of administration to amateurs. More-
ver, except in science, there was little contact between these
nstitutions and the outside world. Frederick II forbade
tudents to go abroad for their studies on the ground that
here were plenty of universities at home.

It is probably not unreasonable to include the salons
mong the educational institutions of the eighteenth century
f only because they brought together men of intelligence, and
elped in the diffusion of new ideas. The salons were distinc-
ive of French society and of the increasingly important part
layed by women in that society. The women who made a
uccess of their salons were not necessarily distinguished for

beauty or learning; on the contrary, they were mostly middle aged, unendowed with any great fund of knowledge, but in possession of a natural intelligence and realism which enabled them both to stimulate discussion and to "moderate" in the disputes of rival enthusiasts. Still more, eighteenth-century opinion recognised the advantages that a young man of parts might derive from association with a woman of mature years who had lived in good society; for women, more than men, are the repositories of social experience, and can think of men as "great babies". Montesquieu was not far wrong when he declared that France was governed by women; they certainly exercised a profound influence on artists and men-of-letters usually in the direction of toning down what otherwise would have been harsh or excessive. In a salon an author might air his views before publication and benefit from friendly critic- ism which, in other circumstances, would have been conveyed in a hostile review; or he might express opinions too extreme or dangerous for exposition in a printed book; or he might even secure the necessary support for election to the French Academy.

They were not all run by women. During the Regency the *Club de l'Entresol,* composed of about twenty members, met at the lodging of the Abbé Alary in the Place Vendôme; in summer this conclave became peripatetic in the gardens of the Tuileries. Here the leading spirit was the Abbé de Saint-Pierre, who discoursed on a great range of topics; he was assisted by a number of distinguished men, including the Marquis d'Argenson, one of the most acute critics of the social institutions of his day, Lord Bolingbroke, then a refugee from England, Fénelon, the aristocrat who had been alienated by the régime of Louis XIV, and Vauban, the brilliant military engineer who, having done so much to make possible the conquests of that monarch, fell into disgrace because he publicly denounced their futility and waste. This club or salon lasted from 1724 to 1731, when it was closed down by the orders of Fleury, who disliked discussion of fundamentals.

The Salons

Less controversial subjects were handled in the salons of Madame Geoffrin, who gave hospitality to artists on Mondays and to men-of-letters on Wednesdays. Among her guests were Fontenelle, Montesquieu, D'Alembert, Buffon and Grimm. Over this conclave Madame exercised a benevolent despotism, fortified by her wealth rather than by pedigree or education; this lady was distinguished by her quality of sympathy and her ability to end or divert an awkward discussion by her command : " soyez plus sage ". Her husband, an administrator in the glass factory at St. Gobain, sat at the bottom end of the table, where he said nothing. One evening, as his place was vacant, a guest asked who and where was the silent gentleman. " He was my husband " replied Madame Geoffrin, " he is dead ".[1] From this one can conclude that the husband was out of place in his wife's salon. Of other ladies who ran salons, the Marquise du Deffand and Madame de Tencin were noted for their intelligence (the latter included D'Alembert among her natural offspring); Mademoiselle de l'Espinasse was renowned for her beauty; like Madame de la Popelinière she specialised in music. In general, the salons encouraged literary criticism or discussion of foreign literature, and the Duchesse d'Aiguillon must have sorely tried the patience of her guests by reading, in a loud voice, from her translation of Pope.

Later in the century there was a change as the salons concerned themselves more with politics than with literature or philosophy. It is true that the *Club de l'Entresol* had discussed political questions, but the members were influenced by stimulants no stronger than tea and lemonade; it was otherwise, more than a generation later, when the German-born Baron d'Holbach acted as *maître d'hôtel* of his " synagogue " in the rue Royale, from which women were expressly excluded. This salon, at different times, was frequented by Hume, Diderot,

[1] E. Lavisse (ed.) *Histoire de France*, VIII, pt. 2, p. 214. For this subject see M. Glotz and M. Maire, *Les Salons du XVIIIème Siècle* (1944).

Grimm, D'Alembert, Turgot, Buffon and Raynal; Rousseau left it in disgust because of its consistent irreverence. D'Holbach, known to contemporaries as "the personal enemy of the Almighty" appears to have encouraged unrestrained language, especially about the clergy, From this example it may be inferred that a salon, when deprived of the feminine element, became a club; and, without the feminine touch, the eighteenth century would lose much of its charm.

The main advantages of the salons were that opinion was limited to the spoken word and there was no censorship. Expression of opinion in print or by its circulation in manuscript was controlled in most European countries by the censorship, which differed in strictness in various states, and might even vary within the same state. In England the old Licensing Act had lapsed in 1695, and thereafter the penalties imposed even for the expression of blasphemous opinion were moderate. In Prussia Frederick allowed great latitude of opinion and welcomed a number of writers whose writings had been proscribed elsewhere; by contrast, in Spain and in some of the Italian states the Inquisition prevented free circulation of books from abroad. The Papal Index forbade the reading of practically all the notable books published in this period, to such an extent that to be put on the Index was an indirect tribute to an author. A licence to read prohibited books could be obtained by an authorised person for purposes of refutation.

Censorship in France varied greatly throughout this period, mainly because it was in the hands of three separate authorities —the Government, the Sorbonne and the Paris *Parlement*. That the great *Encyclopédie* was published in full was due to the tolerance of the Government, represented by Malesherbes, who was *Directeur de la Librairie*. It is said that this tolerance was aided by the favour of Madame de Pompadour. On the other hand Rousseau's *Emile* was condemned by the *Parlement*, the Sorbonne and the General Assembly of the French Clergy; it was also placed on the Index and was adversely criticised even by Voltaire; it was the most generally condemned book of the century.[1] Voltaire, who suffered imprisonment on two occasions because of his opinions, lived in dread of the censorship and strove to secure his safety by a variety of devices; by anonymity, by writing under a pseudonym, by occasional disavowal and by making his permanent residence at Ferney, within a short distance of the Swiss frontier. In all the states where the censorship was active imprisonment might follow conviction. Because of these restrictions many authors had their books printed abroad, usually in England or Holland, and there was much smuggling and peddling of illicit books— a dangerous occupation, since capture might be followed by imprisonment or a period in the galleys. In some of the German states the censorship was severe and unjust; in Russia and Poland the question scarcely arose, as there was not yet a reading public in these states. The same applies, to a less extent, to the Scandinavian countries.

II THE PRECURSORS

As in science, so in philosophy, the eighteenth century was the legatee of the seventeenth. Descartes, Newton, Bayle and Locke exercised an influence which long survived their deaths, and the Enlightenment may be regarded as the fulfilment of the promise of the previous century. In the *Encyclopédie* Turgot declared that Newton had done no more than describe the land which Descartes had discovered—an opinion eloquent of the high regard in which the French thinker was held even as late as the 1750's. Starting from a belief in innate ideas and rejecting every hypothesis that appeared to be untenable, Descartes had claimed that truth is attainable by logical reasoning, proceeding from one step to another, and that truth is recognisable as such once it has been achieved. Truth is thus a residuum left after all errors have been drained off, and is

[1] For *Emile* see below, pp. 346-7.

the final achievement of a process which begins with doubt. To some, this may seem to beg the question : what is truth? How can one be sure of one's vaunted discovery? These are matters for the metaphysician. On the other hand, Cartesianism was undoubtedly responsible for a higher critical standard in the application of the reasoning faculty to observed facts, and resulted in impatience with all that is legendary, or apocryphal or mystical. By the discredit which it cast on the emotional and intuitive it may have had a bad influence on the imaginative arts; indeed Boileau is said to have remarked that Descartes had cut the throat of poetry. Moreover, for the application of Cartesian methods, one did not have to be a " philosopher " in the modern sense of the term, as integrity of intellect rather than profundity of knowledge was the main requirement. Hence the emergence of the eighteenth-century *philosophe*—the man who, without any special equipment, could apply his intelligence to the elimination of error and the elucidation of truth. The inevitable result in many cases was an element of superficiality.

After about 1730 the influence of Descartes was gradually superseded by that of Newton. Only a trained mind could properly understand or appreciate the scientific discoveries of the great Englishman, but every intelligent person must have been impressed by the clarity and concision to which physical laws were reduced. His economy of words contrasted sharply with the vastness of the phenomena to which he had given definition. This alone had a profound effect; moreover Newton himself had suggested[1] that all the phenomena of nature might, like motion, be expressed in simple, universal principles, based on mutual attraction or repulsion. He even extended this hope beyond natural philosophy to moral philosophy, on the assumption that the principles of human conduct might be embodied in a few incontrovertible laws. This hint

[1] In the preface to his *Principia* and at the conclusion of his *Optics*. For this see B. Willey, *The Eighteenth-Century Background* (1940) p. 138.

was eagerly followed up. Locke and others maintained the curious opinion that only in mathematics and ethics was absolute certainty attainable; on this hypothesis even physics was at a disadvantage, since it is concerned not with abstractions, but with tangible things. Nor was this the only direction in which the influence of Newton was manifest. The English philosopher David Hartley (1705-57), in his elucidation of the theory of association of ideas (in which subject he was a pioneer), attempted to correlate the working of the human mind with the Newtonian vibrations. These vibrations, he held, correspond to the variety of sensations impinging on our minds; one vibration will excite another, and so ideas will come to be associated. Equally the phenomena of memory, judgement and the passions were reduced to physical causes. These views were expounded by Hartley in his *Observations on Man,* published in 1749. The author, who was probably the first to use the word " psychology ", had thus embarked on an entirely new line of enquiry, based on an attempt to apply Newtonian principles to the working of the mind, and in this way a greater prospect for the future of humanity appeared to be opening up. Morality, so far from being something innate or supernatural, becomes an almost physical quality, built up on association of the pleasurable with the good and of pain with the bad; ethics, hitherto an appendage to theology, might in this way become a science, bringing immeasurable benefits to humanity. Hence the optimism so characteristic of much of eighteenth-century thought.

Although on a less exalted plane, the influence of Pierre Bayle (1647-1706) led more directly to the Enlightenment. Obliged to leave the France of Louis XIV because of its intolerance, Bayle settled in Rotterdam where he was a professor of history and philosophy. A sworn enemy of superstition and intolerance, he secured wide circulation for his views in a semi-learned, semi-popular journal—the *Nouvelles de la République de Lettres*—in which scientific and literary subjects were discussed in a manner intelligible to the educated layman.

Deprived of his university chair on the allegation of impiety, he devoted himself to literary work, its most important result being the *Dictionnaire Historique et Critique,* of which the first edition appeared in two volumes in 1697. In this Bayle applied the Cartesian methods of scepticism and impartial analysis to the vast store of legend and hearsay in which the historiography of the past was embedded. The book had many critics, but subsequent editions established its reputation as a dependable guide to the sacred and profane past. The *Encyclopédie* may be regarded as the fulfilment of what the *Dictionnaire* set out to do, and it may be claimed that the *philosophes* began where Bayle had left off.

Almost exactly contemporary was John Locke (1632-1704) who exercised a profound influence by two great books—his *Two Treatises of Government* and his *Essay Concerning Human Understanding,* both published in 1690, though composed several years earlier. Son of a Puritan, Locke had a life-long dislike of dogmatism and pedantry. Having trained at Oxford as a physician he entered the service of the great Lord Shaftesbury and, because of his political opinions, he had to go into exile in the reign of James II. As a practical man of affairs he served on the Board of Trade, which had been established in 1696; hence he maintained a keen interest in questions of trade and finance. So Locke was no recluse; on the contrary he regarded book learning with contempt, as the mere repetition of other men's ideas. Interested in theories only in so far as they would work, he expressed admiration for the achievements of skilled craftsmen, claiming that the men who had invented the watch spring or the balance wheel were as great benefactors of humanity as those who had advanced the science of algebra. His literary style was diffuse and prolix; there was nothing " brilliant " about Locke.

In his *Essay Concerning Human Understanding* Locke was concerned not to propound a new philosophy, but to describe his own conclusions regarding the working of the human mind. Rejecting innate ideas altogether, he maintained that the mind is a *tabula rasa* on which impressions are made by the senses. The correlation and combination of these sense impressions account, on this theory, for what we call ideas. This interpretation was afterwards developed by Condillac in his *Traité des Sensations* (1754), a treatise which directly links human mentality with sense impressions. Locke's theory, though much modified afterwards by such thinkers as Hume and Kant, had a large following throughout the eighteenth century mainly because, by ruling out the innate and the transcendental, it emphasised the natural equality of men, and appeared to explain their divergence from that equality by accidents of education and environment. A Red Indian and an Anglican Archbishop had really started off with the same intellectual and moral endowment—a revolutionary opinion. It may well be objected that Locke ignores all that a man potentially or sub-consciously knows; moreover, knowledge derived from the senses does not necessarily exclude innate ideas. This objection was effectively urged in the early nineteenth century by Coleridge and Blake, who held that the Lockian hypothesis failed to account for inspiration and poetry.

III SOCIAL RELATIVITY. THE ENCYCLOPEDIE

The views of Locke and Hartley paved the way for the study of psychology, since it was now generally assumed that mental processes are determined by sense impressions. What happens if one of the senses, e.g. sight, is absent? In his *Lettre sur les Aveugles* (1749) Diderot addressed himself to this question, and came to the conclusion that one's estimate of moral values may be altered by defects in the senses; thus a blind man may regard theft more seriously than do normal persons because he is so helpless against it. On the other hand the blind man may excel in matters of pure speculation because his intellect is not deflected by material objects. From this starting point Diderot made the daring suggestion that morality itself is relative to sensory equipment; take away or add one sense and the ethical standard is altered. Had science been more advanced in his day, he might have reinforced his argument by alluding to the effects of altitude and barometric pressure on temperament and even on character, for we are all adjusted, as it were, to life at or near sea level.[1] But Diderot did not limit himself to sensory experience, for he claimed that our moral susceptibilities might be influenced by trivial matters, such as distance; thus, we hesitate to kill a man at close quarters, but we have less compunction in shooting at him from long range. Not surprisingly, these views were regarded as dangerous, and their author was imprisoned for a time. Diderot was more cautious with his next psychological study—*La Réligieuse*—written in 1760. This he left in manuscript, and it was not published until after his death. A minute description of the abnormal mentality likely to be engendered by seclusion in a nunnery, this study of female aberration is one of the most remarkable and " modern " of all the imaginative writings of the eighteenth century.

This linking of human character with sensory environment —obviously developed from the Lockian hypothesis—might be described as social relativity. It had a much wider application than that to which Diderot gave expression. In this period western civilisation was beginning to be much more conscious of itself; indeed, the word " civilisation " (of French origin) was coming to be used in its modern meaning. Now, in any scientific enquiry, the first requisite is to establish standards of measurement; for the study of humanity some kind of standard was provided by exploration and accounts of exploration. Descriptions of travel to remote places by Chardin, Tavernier and Bougainville were eagerly read, and from them readers could visualise inhabitants of the globe from China to Tahiti. In this way " natural man " was evolved, his only qualifica-

[1] For this see Sir S. Barcroft, *The Respiratory Function of the Blood*, pt. I, *Lessons from High Altitudes* (Cambridge, 1925).

on being freedom from the over-sophistication of western
urope; against this neutral background or "control" the
ollies and excesses of over-civilised man could be measured
nd condemned. Moreover, the censorship might more easily
e evaded by this oblique method of airing one's views.
Natural Man might be of any colour—he had begun as a black
man in Mrs. Aphra Behn's *Oroonoko* (published in 1698); he
ad an olive tint in the two Persians who figured in Montesquieu's *Lettres Persanes* (1721) and in the Ethiopian Rasselas
of Samuel Johnson (1759); he might even be a European, as
a the Poles and Corsicans whom Rousseau considered "ripe
or the contract". For purposes of comparison the inhabitants
of imaginary lands were dragged in, as in Swift's *Gulliver's
Travels,* or in the account by the Dane Holberg of a journey
o the centre of the globe, or in Voltaire's *Micromégas,* where
interplanetary travel provided material for contrast with civili-
ation as we know it. There was even room for cannibals in
his universal and comparative valuation of humanity. In
725 Voltaire visited a number of savages who had been
rought from the Mississippi to Fontainebleau for propaganda
urposes. With his insatiable thirst for information the philo-
opher asked a lady member of the community if she had ever
aten anyone. She replied in the affirmative, adding that it
vas better to eat deceased enemies than leave them to the
rows; on the other hand, according to this "natural woman",
o eat one's compatriots would be an offence "against the social
irtues". Choice of menu was therefore influenced by pat-
iotic considerations. This set Voltaire thinking. The great
vil, he concluded, is to kill others; but, after one's death, it
oes not matter whether one becomes a roast or a candle, for
n honest man is not ashamed to be of service to humanity
ven after his death.[1]

But this reduction of humanity to a natural and material
asis proved to be no more than preliminary spade work.
The Lockian emphasis on the part played by the senses

[1] Voltaire, *Dictionnaire Philosophique,* sub voce *Anthropophagie.*

together with the suggestion, derived from Newton, that the moral sciences might be reduced to simple laws valid for all time helped to promote an optimistic theory of progress. Now that men were considered equal at birth in moral and intellectual capacity and contrasted, as adults, only in their environment and sense impressions, then (it appeared) much might be done to ensure their greater happiness by education and by elimination of such artificial things as class distinction. Here was the revolutionary idea of the century. It found its highest expression in the Marquis de Condorcet (1743-94), a distinguished mathematician and associate of D'Alembert, Voltaire and Turgot, who afterwards served in the Legislative Assembly and in the Convention. Condorcet believed in the unlimited perfectibility of the human race, a thesis maintained in his *Esquisse des Progrès de l'Esprit Humain,* which was published in 1795. Adoption of the Lockian psychology and the systematic spread of education were the bases of this belief. Pursued by agents of the Terror, Condorcet took his own life in March 1794.

That the *philosophes* were sincere in their high regard for education is shown by the publication, in the years 1751-72 of the *Encyclopédie ou Dictionnaire Raisonnée des Sciences, des Arts et des Métiers,* completed in seventeen large folio volumes. The general editors were Diderot and D'Alembert, of whom the first contributed articles on the arts and crafts. Practically all the *philosophes* took a hand in this gigantic publication; Voltaire wrote on *l'esprit* and on literature; Montesquieu on taste; Buffon on nature; Rousseau on music; Helvetius on religion. There was much plagiarism, inevitable perhaps in a work of this kind; there was also concealment of daring or original ideas under the cloak of sarcasm or irony. During the twenty-two years over which its production was spread there were periods when its publication was suspended altogether. Generally, the *Encyclopédie* advocated a secular morality, having human happiness in this life as its object; that it was not suppressed altogether may be because so many

of the contributors wrote with restraint, and the monarchy
was always treated with respect.

The objects of the *Encyclopédie* were outlined in a preliminary discourse by D'Alembert. One aim was to show
" the order and concatenation in human knowledge ", for
which purpose the volumes included both the liberal and
mechanic arts, and aimed at tracing ideas to their sources.
Emphasis was laid on the desirability of reducing the sciences
to as few principles as possible, because there is more " fecund-
ity " in a small group of axioms. Locke's influence is evident
in the praise accorded to the humble and anonymous craftsmen who, by their patience and ingenuity, have contributed
as much to human happiness as the most renowned philosophers. All this was harmless enough; moreover, in the
seventeen volumes, there was little that could be regarded as
prejudicial to religion; but, throughout this vast work, there
was maintained a clear distinction between immorality and
religious scepticism (usually regarded as identical), and there
was an implication that the cause of humanity would be promoted not by the right theological doctrines, but by the right
secular knowledge. Quietly and efficiently the supernatural
sanctions on which the *Ancien Régime* rested were taken away.

IV REASON AND SENTIMENT

On the assumption that the Newtonian methods might be
applied to social and moral subjects, and in the hope that
results of similar universality would be achieved, the *philosophes* thought of reason not as something pursued in solitude,
but as a mental process directed to study of life around us,
having for its object the betterment of that life. This view was
confirmed by the jurists of the Natural Law school—" reason
is the only means by which men can seek happiness ".[1] Soon

[1] Burlamaqui, *The Principles of Natural Law* (trans. Nugent),
1748, p. 50.

reason was to be tempered by sentiment or sensibility, a sensitiveness to impressions from the outside world which provided an alternative to the dictates of logic. It is in this alternation between reason and sentiment that much of the charm of the eighteenth century is to be found.

Reason in this sense of the elucidation of laws conducing to our well being was thus an eminently social quality; and sociability, in turn, was the source of morality;—

> The science of morals is perhaps the most complete of all the sciences, when we consider the truths of which it is composed. It all rests on one simple and incontrovertible fact—the need which men have for one another, and the reciprocal obligations which that need imposes. All the moral laws follow from this. The interests of the individual and the group are never incompatible.[1]

The three virtues of this new social morality were toleration, *bienfaisance* (the word coined by Saint-Pierre as a substitute for " charity "), and humanity. In France, the vogue of such idealist aspiration is partly accounted for by the reaction, in the years after 1715, against the régime represented by Louis XIV.

On a lower plane this rationalised sociability was identified with good sense and the right conduct to be observed in social life. For the upper classes—and the eighteenth century was the century of the upper classes—the rules of good breeding were codified by Lord Chesterfield in the famous letters which he wrote to his son in the years 1738-50. Good breeding he defined as " the result of much good sense, some good nature and a little self-denial for the sake of others. Good manners are to particular societies as good morals are to society in general—their cement and their security ".[2] In order to

[1] D'Alembert, *Eléments de Philosophie*, quoted in P. Hazard, *European Thought in the Eighteenth Century* (trans. J. Lewis May, 1946), ch. 4.
[2] Lord Chesterfield, *Letters to his Son*, letter cc, Nov. 3, 1749. The succeeding quotations are from the *Letters* in their chrolonogical order.

secure such desirable ends certain rules have to be observed. In writing and speaking old sayings and common proverbs should be avoided, as these are proofs of having kept low or bad company; Courts and camps are the only places to learn the world in, for there " human nature is seen in all its shapes and modes ". Points of history, matters of literature, the customs of particular countries and the several orders of knighthood are better subjects of conversation than the weather, dress or fiddle faddle stories. The company which you must avoid is low company, because " it is low in rank, low in manners and low in merit ". Nothing is more offensive to a company than inattentiveness or distraction; " I prefer the company of a corpse to that of an absent-minded man ". " Veteran women of condition " who have lived in Courts and have had some gallantries may form a young fellow better than all the rules. In Courts you must expect to meet " connexions without friendship, enmities without hatred, honour without virtue, appearances saved and realities sacrificed; good manners and bad morals ". Most characteristic of all was the advice: " smile, but never laugh ".[1]

Chesterfield's *Letters* provide a complete code of conduct for polite society. Now, codification implies that a stage of evolution has been completed, and that it can be systematised for the guidance of posterity. But social conduct was only one of the many activities to which principles might be applied, for rules were adopted and formulated by academies of painting and sculpture. As in ancient Greece Aristotle had promulgated in his *Poetics* the laws of taste and had imposed the Unities on dramatic composition, so in France Boileau in his *Art Poétique* (1674) and in England Pope in his *Essay on Criticism* (1711) prescribed the rules which should govern poetic composition. Inspiration there must be, but inspiration in harness. The harness consisted of good sense, a social virtue implying moderation and restraint, also a respect for the conventions accepted by men of repute, even if this

[1] Letter cxliv, March 9, 1748.

involved a sacrifice of the poet's individuality. Of this poetic evangel the sacred text was the well-known line in Horace's *Ars Poetica*:

Scribendi recte sapere est et principium et fons

Recte sapere, "thinking rightly" was paraphrased as "good sense"; hence, in his milieu of a polite and highly critical society, the poet must avoid all that is tedious, or fatuous or excessive, since these things show bad taste and taste, so far from being a personal quality, is really a consensus of opinion about what is right. As well as this Horace had prescribed the subjects with which a poet might properly concern himself:

Aetatis cujusque notandi sunt tibi mores

With this limitation poetry might be little more than an elegant portrayal, sometimes satirical, of the *mores* of one's contemporaries.

These were really the qualities not of good poetry but of good conversation. Conversation, now a lost art, was at its best in the eighteenth century, when so many of the distractions which trouble us were absent, and a meal was valued not only for the menu, but for the intelligent conversation that might accompany it. Leisure made possible the pursuit of a theme and its summation in a felicitous epigram. There were similar possibilities in letter writing—another of the lost arts. From this point of view the poetry of Pope and his school may be regarded as little more than elegant conversation in verse. The couplet might serve to give it an epigrammatic quality—the equivalent of the *bon mot* in conversation—and in this way many sententious maxims about humanity were compressed into memorable lines. But this moralising about one's fellow men might equally well lead to satire, the most essentially social of all forms of literature, because it castigates all who have offended against the conventions of society.

The question whether socialised verse can be considered

poetry was answered in the negative by Joseph Warton in his *Essay on the Genius and Writings of Pope* (1746). In this famous manifesto Warton declared that a clear head and an acute understanding were not enough to make a poet. " It is a creative and glowing imagination . . . that can stamp a writer with this exalted and very uncommon character [of poet]; the sublime and the pathetic are the two chief nerves of all genuine poetry ". More than half a century later, in his *Biographia Litteraria* (1817) Coleridge said almost exactly the same thing : " the imaginative faculty, allied with creative power, makes the poet ". Not until the Romantic Revival did poetry as we know it come into its own; the eighteenth century, so rich in oratory, in the essay, in satire, was almost entirely denied this supreme gift.

The fact that Warton's protest was voiced so early as 1746 precludes us from accepting the generalisation that the eighteenth century was the age of reason. In any considerable period there are so many cross currents and back washes that the stream of history may appear to change its bed completely and the facile, text-book generalisation usually breaks down. As early as the 1740's Samuel Richardson (1689-1761) was popularising the sentimental novel in his *Pamela* and *Clarissa Harlowe*. Richardson, who was not of the class which at that time was associated with literary production, for he was the son of a joiner and was himself a successful printer, did not begin writing until comparatively late in life; indeed, he was an intrusion from the outside world. At first, his sententious, almost lachrymose analyses of commonplace situations in middle-class life brought on his head some ridicule, but soon it was clear that he had enriched literature with something for which men craved—the unaffected delineation of those emotional disturbances which affect the lives of so many, rich and poor. This helped to create a new and greatly enlarged reading public in England; it spread to France, where the Abbé Prévost popularised Richardson by his translations.

Prévost, an erratic and voluminous writer, was already well known for his *Manon Lescaut* (1733) an account of low life in Paris, one of the "psychological" studies of the century. The age of sentiment had dawned; it was to prove the solvent of much that was conventional and artificial.

"Sentiment" is often a convenient term to describe movements having little in common with each other save a revolt against a highly socialised conception of life and society. One of these movements was a new attitude to nature. Until about 1760 nature meant cultivated, humanised nature, as seen at its best in Gray's *Elegy*; but (so intractable are these things for purposes of generalisation) Gray himself, after a visit to the Alps in 1739, was one of the first to experience and express an appreciation of mountain scenery. Formerly, mountains and great solitary spaces had been regarded with horror; why this change of attitude should have taken place is one of the many unanswerable questions. Equally difficult of explanation is the new obsession with night, death and graveyards, the obvious antitheses of the warm, candle-lit society of the time. Another form taken by the wave of sentiment was the revival of the primitive, as seen in the publication of Bishop Percy's *Reliques of Ancient Poetry* (1765) which at once aroused interest in the ballad literature of England and Scotland; or James Macpherson's *Fingal* (1762) and *Temora* (1763), alleged translations from a Celtic poet Ossian, which caused many readers to revel in the mists and desolate shores of the western Highlands; or the revival of old German folk lore by Herder[1] and the Grimm brothers. The years immediately after 1760 were good years for those whose "sensibility" did not stop short of tears, for they included the publication of Rousseau's *Julie ou la Nouvelle Héloise* (1760), Henry Mackenzie's *Man of Feeling* (1771), both of them easily outdistanced by Goethe's *Sorrows of Werther* (1774). These books depicted the sufferings and even tragedies experienced by over-sensitive souls brought into contact with the harsh

[1] above, pp. 223-4.

realities of life. Long before the end of the century the revolt against reason was complete. In 1748 Chesterfield had counselled his son never to laugh; a generation later he might have advised him never to weep.

V   VICO AND MONTESQUIEU

Giambattista Vico (1668-1744), the son of a bookseller in Naples, was for many years a poorly-paid professor of rhetoric in the University of Naples and became historiographer royal of the kingdom of the Two Sicilies. A profound, though solitary, student of classical antiquity, philology and jurisprudence, he was out of sympathy with the fashionable Cartesianism of his time, which seemed to him responsible for much shallowness of thought; on the other hand he had an intense interest in what was then a comparatively new subject —the evolution of civilisation. Could that evolution be reduced to definite principles? His attempt to answer that question was made in his *Scienza Nuova,* published in 1725. In this he acknowledged his debt to Plato, Tacitus and Bacon, of whom the first had described man as he should be, the second man as he is, and the third, by deduction from observed experience, had attempted to systematise the whole range of human knowledge. For his purposes Vico sought out the common elements in the languages and institutions of different nations; indeed, the main purpose of the " new science " was to elucidate these common elements. Ancient Rome and Roman Law provided his starting point, but to both he attached undue prominence, to the neglect of the middle ages and eastern civilisations. The *Scienza Nuova* is thus no more than a fragment, but a fragment which, in later years, has inspired similar and more ambitious attempts.

Vico divided the progress of civilisation into three stages— first, the divine or theocratic, an obscure era, described for the most part in hieroglyphics or language of the priests; second, the heroic or fabulous, the age of great epic poetry, abounding in vivid metaphors as evidenced by Homer who, according to Vico, was not a historical personage, but merely a name given to a succession of minstrels; and, thirdly, the age in which we live, when a literary language has been consolidated. These three ages form the cycle that must be traversed by every nation; to know the evolution of one nation is to know the evolution of the others. Internal decay during the third stage will lead to collapse and return to the first stage. Of political systems which might delay retrogression or promote advance Vico favoured a strong monarchy. About the general progress of humanity, in spite of ups and downs, Vico made no clear pronouncement.

In the generation preceding the publication of the *Scienza Nuova* western Europe had been divided by the controversy between Ancients and Moderns, a controversy which must have seemed immature and even puerile to readers of Vico's book, where new, critical standards were applied to the earliest forms of literature. That book, however incomplete and obscure, opened up new paths of investigation—primitive life was now linked with etymology, early jurisprudence was connected with customs rather than with codes, the modern Homeric theory was anticipated, and mythology was established as a definite stage in human evolution. In these respects Vico was a fore-runner of Mommsen, Niebuhr and Savigny. But this attempt to construct a science of history remained practically unknown in the eighteenth century, nor was notice taken of it until Michelet in the nineteenth century and Croce in the twentieth directed attention to Vico and his book. For most eighteenth-century Italians history meant Muratori and the revival of medieval Italy, or interest in the half-legendary Etruria and Etruscan civilisation;[1] not yet was there any serious approach to the study of the causes accounting for the rise and fall of great empires. Vico had at least shown how important for this investigation are etymology and jurisprud-

[1] above, p. 243.

ence; in this latter subject his lead was to be followed in France by Montesquieu.

Charles de Secondat, Baron de Montesquieu (1689-1755) was born into a family of the *noblesse de robe* and in 1716 succeeded his uncle as President of the *Parlement* of Bordeaux. In 1726 he sold his office in order to devote himself entirely to the cause of learning, and in the following year he was admitted to the French Academy. He travelled widely on the continent and spent two years in England (1729-31). Already in 1721 he had published his *Lettres Persanes,* which both shocked and amused France; in 1748 he produced his *De l'Esprit des Lois,* on which he had been engaged for twenty years. Montesquieu, the most eminent and responsible, though not the most influential of all who contributed to the Enlightenment, was a believer in monarchy but, as a Deist, he was sceptical about many of the religious institutions of his time.

This scepticism was revealed in his *Lettres Persanes* where, by putting his views into the mouths of two young Persians travelling in Europe, he succeeded in evading the censorship. In their letters, ostensibly written to friends and relatives at home, the two travellers, with much innuendo, delineated the anomalies and inconsistencies of western civilisation. The excesses of priestcraft and the mysteries of orthodox theology were not spared. Interspersed with these were aphorisms of a more general character. Thus, on the subject of incredulity, the author notes that opinion depends on bodily constitution; in general, religion does not trouble people when they are in good health, but only when they are ill (letter 75). In punishments there is a large measure of relativity; to a European imprisonment may be a more serious penalty than loss of a limb to an Asiatic (letter 81). Those whose religion is merely tolerated give better service to the state than those of the established church (letter 86). The invention of gunpowder has destroyed the impregnability of fortresses; "I tremble to think of how mankind may discover a speedier method of destroying human life" (letter 106). France generally is governed by women (letter 108). The ultimate effect of colonies is to weaken the mother country. Men should rest where they are. Air acts in such a way that it fixes one's temperament; change to another country may cause illness. The prodigious number of negroes sent to America has not peopled it (letter 122).

It will have been noticed that Montesquieu expressed unusual opinions about air and atmosphere, attributing to these a great influence on illness and health. During his stay in England, he appears to have read a number of books and pamphlets, including those of Dr. Arbuthnot, on the spread of epidemics by air currents, and he adopted the theory, which may be traced back to the ancient Greek philosophers, that atmosphere and climate have a determining influence on temperament and even on character. Some such considerations may have had weight with him when he chose the title *De l'Esprit des Lois* for his magnum opus, because he was concerned with the numerous and intangible things which, taken together, may influence the constitution or polity of a nation. These he enumerated as climate, religion, customs, maxims of government, examples of past history, laws and manners, all resulting in *l'esprit général*.[1] Consequently, a constitution good for one country might be bad for another; in other words he was applying to politics a conception of relativity such as Diderot and others were applying to morals. All this showed a psychological approach—the term is not anachronistic, as it was coming into use among Montesquieu's contemporaries. No longer was political theory reducible to such simple terms as Divine Right or the Social Contract; it was becoming part of a complex which we now term sociology.

Montesquieu adopted a simple classification of states into monarchies, despotisms and republics, the first suited for states of moderate size, the second for large and the third for small areas. He says little of the politics of his own day, though he may have had France in mind when he wrote that

[1] Montesquieu, *De l'Esprit des Lois*, bk. XIX, ch. 4.

there can be no liberty where the executive and legislative powers are joined.[1] So far as one can infer his preference, he favoured monarchy, particularly that of England, with its (alleged) division of powers. So conservative was he that he sometimes appears almost as a reactionary, as in his defence of the ecclesiastical power in Spain and Portugal on the curious ground that it provides a mitigation of royal tyranny. He claimed that the same purpose was served in France by the prerogatives of church, municipalities and seigneurs, these constituting "intermediate powers"—barriers preventing the monarchy from falling into a despotism or a republic.[2] As monarchy is a mean between extremes, its ruler should have regard to honour in his legislation, giving official favour to the hereditary nobility, and ensuring the perpetuation of estates by means of entails.[3] Our author was thus defending some institutions which have since been condemned. He even offered a half-hearted defence of negro slavery on the ground that its abolition would raise the price of sugar.[4]

Throughout the greater part of the book the writer's method is to consider laws in their relation to natural conditions or to various forms of human activity, keeping in view his (over simple) classification of states. The liberty of the citizen he connected with the distribution of executive, judicial and legislative powers; liberty he identified with security, or "the opinion one has of one's security". He advised caution against prosecutions for witchcraft or sorcery,[5] and he condemned penal laws in religion.[6] Commerce, he maintained, leads naturally to peace, and he commended England for three great things—religion, commerce and liberty.[7] In books XIV and XV, where he considered laws in relation to climate, he showed some exaggeration and over-simplification. In cold climates he claimed to find more vigour because the action of

[1] ibid, bk. IX, ch. 6.
[3] ibid, bk. V, ch. 9.
[5] ibid, bk. XII, ch. 5.
[7] ibid, bk. XX.

[2] ibid, bk. III, ch. 4.
[4] ibid, bk. XV, ch. 5.
[6] ibid, bk. XXV, ch. 12.

the heart and the reactions of the nerve fibres are stronger; this, he argues, produces more confidence and courage, whereas in hot climates, he alleged, people tend to be more timid— like old men. Climate also determines reaction to pain—" you will have to scorch a Muscovite if you want to put any sentiment into him ".[1] All this was afterwards to excite the imagination of Rousseau. Of the English climate he said that it caused a certain impatience that is incompatible with tyranny; " servitude always begins with sleepiness ". It is because of climate that slavery is tolerated; it should be limited to those areas where it is a natural institution, and its severity should be mitigated. Climate also influences the relations between the sexes; in hot regions there is a natural inequality between them.

The *De l'Esprit des Lois* is one of the great books of modern literature, abounding in shrewd deductions from observations of institutions as known to the eighteenth-century philosopher. Its author was one of the least subversive and most conservative of men. He book confirmed many of the most debatable assumptions of the *Ancien Régime,* but it raised large question marks about the nature of law and legislation. These had usually been regarded as inhibitions, erratic and inconsequential, as in France; or, as in England, designed mainly to protect private property; in both countries the statute book lagged far behind the level which civilisation had reached. But, in later years France, in consequence of the *Code Napoléon,* and England, in consequence of the reforms of Bentham and Romilly, both created a jurisprudence that might well have satisfied Montesquieu's requirement of conformity with the national genius, and in these achievements may be traced the more remote or indirect influence of the *De l'Esprit des Lois*. Montesquieu taught that law and legislation are organic things which not only vary from nation to nation, but are capable of change and development with the progress or retrogression of the nation itself.

[1] ibid, bk. xiv, ch. 2.

In order to place this in perspective one must compare it with contemporary conceptions of *Jus Naturale*, translated as Natural Law or (more properly) Natural Right. This conception was derived from the Stoic devotion to nature, and was amplified by the eloquence of Cicero; to its fusion with the Roman *Jus Gentium* can be traced the remote genesis of Public International Law. Throughout the middle ages, when it was regarded as a supplement to Revelation, Natural Law was cited for condemnation of such evils as slavery; and, by the seventeenth century, it had acquired so many idealist accretions as to incur the anathema of those two iconoclast thinkers, Hobbes and Spinoza. In the eighteenth century it provided subject matter for professorial chairs and innumerable books. The academic lawyers thrived on it; with its austere and venerable ancestry it was cited in support of many things, including even military aggression.[1] What was this Law of Nature? Vattel said that it consisted of rules of conduct, founded on man's nature, and elucidated by reason; Burlamaqui, more informative, defined a few of its maxims, such as the natural equality of men, the practice of beneficence and fidelity to one's commitments. The Christian form of the law was: " Do unto others as you would that men should do to you ". With some truth Vattel[2] declared that " a good philosophy is necessary for understanding the Law of Nature ". Condorcet stated that the liberty and equality inherent in Natural Law were anterior to human institutions. From all this we may conclude that, by the later years of the eighteenth century, Natural Law was exercising an almost supernatural appeal.

In 1772 there appeared in Paris a curious manifesto—*Les Maximes du Droit Public Français,* which challenged Montesquieu's principle that each nation should have a constitution adapted to its history and institutions; whereas, so it was contended in the *Maximes,* there should be established a rational

[1] By Biefeld, above, p. 43.
[2] Emmerich de Vattel, *Les Loisirs Philosophiques* (1747), p. 74.

organisation of society valid for all countries. Here was the element of danger concealed in the apparently innocent Natural Law. It was now cited in support of an idealist, universal system of government, such as could be realised only by subversion of existing institutions. The teaching of Rousseau and the example set by the American Revolution served to make this doctrine more concrete, and so Natural Law, with its insistence on human liberty and equality, must be numbered among the revolutionary ideas of the century. It was brought into sharper focus by contrast with the conservatism of Montesquieu.

VI VOLTAIRE AND ROUSSEAU

François-Marie Arouet de Voltaire (1694-1778), the son of a Paris notary, was educated at the Jesuit college of Louis le Grand, and was intended by his father for the magistracy. But the boy's strong inclination for a literary career was encouraged by his god-father, the Abbé de Chateauneuf, who introduced him to the Parisian world of fashion and incredulity. In 1715, on the accusation of having written a libel on the memory of Louis XIV, he was imprisoned for a year in the Bastille, where he began the composition of his *Henriade,* an epic commemorating the tolerance of Henri IV. In 1726 he was again in the Bastille (for six months), this time because of an alleged affront to the Duc de Rohan. On his release, he was ordered to leave France, so he went to England, where he spent two years (1726-8), studying English institutions, and consorting with such notables as Bolingbroke and the Deists Tindal and Collins. On his return to France, in addition to writing much verse and many plays, he engaged in financial speculation and, in conjunction with the Pâris brothers, he amassed a fortune, mainly from army contracts. The publication in 1735 of his *Lettres Anglaises* recording his impressions of England, brought on his head a storm of abuse, on the allegation that he had attacked religion; so once more he went into seclusion, this time a voluntary and agreeable seclusion, with Madame du Châtelet at Cirey in Champagne (1736-40). Encouraged by this lady, with whom he had a liaison, Voltaire devoted himself to the study of Newton's *Principia* and began two of his historical works. In 1740 and 1743 he visited Berlin, where he was well received by Frederick, who appreciated the sardonic spirit of his guest. On his return to France, thanks mainly to Madame de Pompadour, he was admitted to the Academy and was appointed a gentleman of the king's bedchamber. This period of royal favour did not last long. After a sojourn with the Duchesse de Maine at Sceaux he was again at Potsdam in 1750, where his sarcasm at the expense of French *émigrés* in Berlin led to estrangement with the king. After travel in Germany he settled down in 1758 at Ferney, in the French province of Gex, within a short distance of the Swiss frontier. There he spent the last twenty years of his life, building up a magnificent establishment, with a model farm, a private theatre and a staff of about 60 persons. Ferney became a place of pilgrimage for his many admirers, and here, with the help of his large library, he devoted himself to literary work. In March 1778, when he was 84, he was induced by his niece to visit Paris, where he was received with such acclamation that his health was affected, with the result that in May he died. His was probably the only notable death hastened by too much handshaking. There were difficulties about according him Christian burial, but in 1791 his remains were deposited in the Pantheon.

Even the severest critics of Voltaire must admit that his career showed agility and versatility. Had he been less circumspect, had he failed to ingratiate himself with the powerful and the police, or had he lived in Paris instead of remote Ferney he might well have experienced longer periods of imprisonment, with a possibility of exile or even death. In character he was astute, malicious and even at times vindictive, with the result that he made many enemies in his own day and is still regarded with abhorrence by a large and influential body of opinion. But it is certain that he was the greatest man of letters in the history of France and the greatest journalist in the history of the world. Poet and dramatist, philosopher and amateur scientist, historian and story teller, he succeeded in perfecting many modes of self expression—short pamphlets, portable dictionaries, amusing " contes " often descriptive of imaginary lands—all of them designed to penetrate to the largest number of readers, if only because they handled *causes célèbres,* or exposed social injustices of which men were conscious, but for which they could find no remedy. He unhorsed his opponent not by rhetoric but by ridicule. As well as this he kept up an enormous correspondence. Even thus, these writings would have failed but for their inimitable style. In his day the French language was becoming standardised, and Voltaire's use of it showed the mastery of the virtuoso, for he could range with ease from sarcasm, innuendo and irony to fierce denunciation and vituperation. Never before and seldom since has the extreme *suppleness* of the French language been demonstrated—its adaptability alike for straightforward narrative or for juggling with whole sets of hypotheses or arguments by skilful use of the subjunctive mood. He himself partly explained the secret of his art in these words : "the most useful books are those of which the readers themselves contribute half; they develop the idea of which the author has presented the seed ".[1]

An example of such a book is the *Lettres Anglaises* (1735) which, by its praise of the comparatively high standard of toleration and prosperity enjoyed by Englishmen, suggested to intelligent French readers a contrast with conditions prevailing in their own country. An ardent disciple of Newton and Locke and a critic of Descartes and Pascal, Voltaire spread a knowledge of English scientific achievement in his *Eléments de la Philosophie de Newton* (1738). In the middle years of

[1] Quoted in G. Lanson, *Voltaire,* p. 148.

the century he was engaged mainly in his historical works—
Le Siècle de Louis XIV (1751 and 1768) and the *Essai sur les Mœurs et l'Esprit des Nations* (1751). In the first of these he presented the reign of Louis XIV not as a series of aggressions, but as a great period of French culture, having its embodiment in the king himself; in the second, beginning with Charlemagne, he outlined the course of European civilisation, reading many eighteenth-century ideas into the past, and censuring unreservedly both the middle ages and the Jews. Nevertheless it was the earliest intelligent approach to the subject, written at the suggestion of Madame du Châtelet who had complained, with good reason, of the low intellectual level of history writing. Other historical works included a biography of Charles XII of Sweden, which exercised his gift of vivid narrative, and an abridgment of universal history showing his wide knowledge of secondary sources. With Voltaire history ceased to be a mere chronicle and became a study of the social and intellectual forces which make up the life of a nation. He had no "philosophy" of history, his belief being that chance is the governing factor in human affairs, and that historical events are brought about by the interaction of great men with fortuitous circumstance.

Voltaire might be described as a Deist or a Pantheist. He found elements of good and bad in all the creeds, and he was a pioneer in the study of comparative religions. Life, in his view, was usually a mean between extremes of happiness and misery; even sustained and exalted virtue would meet with failure and disappointment, as he demonstrated in his *Zadig* (1747). After the Lisbon earthquake of 1755 he became even more critical of excessive optimism, such as had been taught by Leibniz and Pope; this distrust provided the theme of *Candide* (1759), perhaps his best known as it is his wittiest work. Its moral is that all philosophic systems prove unsatisfactory in the end; absolute truth is unattainable, and man's most clear duty is to cultivate his garden.

It was during his stay at Ferney that Voltaire's powers,

now fully matured, were exercised mainly in the cause of humanity. His *Dictionnaire Philosophique* expressed, in convenient abbreviation, his views on a great variety of social and moral questions; but it was his public intervention in several notorious cases of judicial murder that brought him European fame. Two of these—the affairs of Calas and Sirven—had a good deal in common, and served to reveal the tragedies that often accompanied the anomalous position of the Huguenots in France. Calas and Sirven were Protestants; the first had a son who (it was alleged) was on the point of conversion to Catholicism, the second had a daughter of deranged mind, whose conversion was being attempted by a community of nuns. Both son and daughter committed suicide; the unfortunate Calas was tried for murder and was executed. Sirven was sentenced to death by the Procurator of Mazamet, near Castres, but escaped. By his persistent efforts Voltaire succeeded in establishing the innocence of both parents. But he did not succeed in the case of the Chevalier de la Barre who, in 1765, was alleged to have shown disrespect, as a spectator, at a religious procession in Abbeville. For this he was decapitated and burned by order of the municipality. These iniquities were committed not by the clergy but by members of the *noblesse de robe,* whom Voltaire considered more intolerant than the priests.

Like so many of his fellow *philosophes* the sage of Ferney believed in a strong monarchy as a barrier against innumerable tyrannies. He evolved no very original ideas of his own, but he applied his sarcasm and wit to exposure of the inequalities, the inconsistencies and the injustices of his day. The church he attacked only in so far as it supported iniquity. While he wished to see the Catholic establishment preserved in France, he advocated transfer to the secular authorities of such things as marriage, divorce and control of catechisms and religious books. In his view religious communities should be inspected regularly, and no one allowed to take the vows before the age of 25. Although he recommended state education, he did not believe in education for all. Liberty of persons, of conscience, of work and of the Press were among his recommendations; he demanded the abolition of *corvées* and feudal dues, as well as reform of the laws and of the administration of justice. In all this it may be said there was nothing new; Voltaire, it can be argued, was merely continuing, on a larger scale, the propaganda directed by such predecessors as Bayle and D'Argenson; most of his ideas were borrowed from Locke or Newton or the English Deists. But no assailant of intolerance and injustice had ever directed his onslaught over such a wide front, or with such well-balanced masses of light and heavy artillery. If the word Enlightenment means anything, it means the flood of light cast by Voltaire on the obvious injustices of the *Ancien Régime*.

A more penetrating and subversive criticism was that of Jean-Jacques Rousseau (1712-78), who was antagonised not only by the society around him, but by civilisation as it had come to be understood in western Europe. Son of a jeweller of Geneva he received little education and failed to make good in a number of employments. Befriended by Madame de Warens at Anneçy, he abjured his Calvinism for the Catholic faith and, for a time, he taught music in Lausanne. In 1741 he went to Paris with a new method of musical notation, but this had no success; soon he came into prominence by a prize essay. The Academy of Dijon in 1749 offered a prize for the best essay on the question whether advance in science and art had corrupted or purified morals; Rousseau won the prize in spite of his expressed opinion that progress had not elevated morals. Having returned to Calvinism he was befriended by Madame d'Epinay who provided him with a shelter at L'Hermitage in the valley of Montmorency, where he wrote his *Nouvelle Héloise,* the *Contrat Social* and *Emile* in the years after 1756. Universal condemnation of the last-mentioned book caused him for a time to take refuge in Switzerland where he lived a hand-to-mouth existence. By his marriage to a servant maid he had several children whom he left to the care of an orphanage. Offered hospitality by David Hume he lived for a time as his guest in Surrey, but, after a quarrel with his host, he returned to France, where he lived an almost nomadic existence. Apparently suffering from persecution mania, he showed little gratitude to those who befriended him, and it was in a refuge provided for him at Ermenonville that he died. In many respects Rousseau was abnormal. He was a solitary in an eminently sociable age; in the other sex he found not sources of inspiration but protectresses who shielded him from the outside world. Alien in temperament from his contemporaries he proved to be a catalyst, precipitating violent reaction among them, and providing direct inspiration for the French Revolution.

This may be substantiated by reference to two of his most important books—*Du Contrat Social* and *Emile,* both published in 1762 after long meditation in the solitude of L'Hermitage. Like his own life the *Contrat Social* is a disordered book. He does not appear to have started off with any clear idea of his own opinions, but in the course of its composition he managed, to some extent, to clarify his views although, in the absence of revision, the inconsistencies were not removed. The first book opens with a clarion call for emancipation: "man is born free and everywhere he is in chains". Here was the text of a new gospel; the reader did not need to read any farther, and he could repeat this memorable pronouncement in the pulpit or in the fields. But if he did read as far as chapter VIII of book III he would have found that the chains, as they can be accounted for on Montesquieu's climate theory, are both understandable and inevitable, with the result that "liberty is not the fruit of every clime". This was a drastic toning down of the trumpet call which had heralded the book. Had our imaginary reader continued still farther he would have read in the chapter[1] entitled "De la Réligion Civile" that Christianity, which teaches only servitude, should be replaced by a civil religion, having a few

[1] *Du Contrat Social,* bk. IV, ch. 8.

simple moral tenets, together with an avowal of the sanctity of the contract and the laws. All who refuse to accept this state religion should be banished by the sovereign who also may put to death anyone who, having publicly sworn his assent to the contract, acts in a manner inconsistent with the maxims of this civil religion. This *étatisme,* as it has been called, is only one remove from totalitarianism. As Rousseau himself truly remarked : " the *Contrat Social* is a book that ought to be rewritten ".

But this inconsistency does not detract from the main thesis of the book. Rousseau supposed that, in the state of nature, a point was reached when human beings, not yet " civilised ", felt the need for some kind of bond among themselves; such a body of men was " ripe for the contract ". In this contractual association the individual surrenders all his rights to the community, which thereupon becomes " un corps moral et collectif ". This is the sovereign body, indivisible and indestructible, the embodiment of a general will in which each individual will is merged. Once the contract has been entered into a dissentient may be constrained by his fellows—he may be " forced to be free ".[1] The General Will is more than the sum of individual wills, for it is the purified essence of the humanity of the contractants; as such, it cannot err. Here, as in *Emile,* the author is assuming the existence of a latent goodness in mankind. But he safeguards himself by a restriction—his contract is only for those who have not yet been corrupted by civilisation and are still in political adolescence; in his opinion the Corsicans and Poles were in this chrysalis stage. Large, corrupt states such as France lacked the primeval virtue requisite for the General Will; England, with its representative system, was free only during parliamentary elections; Russia, under Peter the Great, had been " policé trop tôt ". The natural tendency of states is to degenerate, but salvation may come from a great legislator, like Moses or Lycurgus or Calvin. The legislator is more than the mere lawgiver, for he

[1] ibid, bk. 1, ch. 7.

has the intuition to perceive the true destiny of the race into which he has intruded himself, as well as the will power to lead it on the proper path. Failing the intervention of such a saviour, the state can resume its upward path only by return to its primitive maxims and simplicity. The *Contrat Social*, with all its ambiguities and inconsistencies, was the text book of the French Revolution.

Emile is a study of childhood and education. "The first cries of infants are prayers", he wrote; with the acquisition of speech they cry less, for one language takes the place of the other. As half the children born into the world will never reach maturity, why make childhood a period of threats, punishments and slavery? This was perhaps the only expression of regret in the eighteenth century that child mortality was so high, and that childhood was so often a period of misery; it was in this deep and exceptional humanity that Rousseau was great. He begins with the assumption that the more a man remains in his natural condition the less he is removed from happiness and virtue; hence the educator should encourage rather than restrain the natural instincts of the child, for these things are essentially good. While so many educators were intent on the forcible expulsion of original sin Rousseau strove to preserve the child's original virtue; here was something new and even revolutionary. Emile, the pupil, is to experience the rigour of things, but not of men; he is to suffer only the punishments inflicted by nature herself. Up to the age of two development of the body is the educator's main concern; until the age of 12 the senses are exercised. The years between 13 and 16 are devoted to *l'esprit*, an untranslatable word; between 17 and 19 the reasoning faculty and "sensibility" are developed; at 20 the moral sense. Judgement rather than knowledge is to be encouraged; natural history is to be taught before human history; Defoe's *Robinson Crusoe* is to be the favourite text book. Emile must learn a craft—he chooses that of carpenter. At the age of 18 God is revealed to him—and here the author digressed into

an account of " la foi du vicaire Savoyard ", describing a
mountain panorama so magnificent that it induces in the
beholder a belief in the existence of God. Religious faith is
therefore derived from sentiment, and the embryonic carpenter becomes a good Deist. After a matrimonial engagement, the young hero has to travel abroad for two years in
order to learn the rudiments of citizenship. On Emile's marriage, the educator's task is done; actually, it was probably
at this point that his real education began, though Rousseau
does not say so.

It is not difficult to see why the book was so generally
condemned. It was the cult of nature run mad. At 20 Emile
must have been a preposterous creature, and certainly no carpenter; but he set a fashion in Europe, as witness the success
of the " Jacobin " type of novel, and the vogue in England
of Thomas Day's *Sandford and Merton* (1783-89), in which
the cultivated, aristocratic young man is contrasted, to his
disadvantage, with the low-born, unsophisticated youth. The
good birth, correct deportment and social accomplishment so
lauded by Chesterfield and his contemporaries had been set
aside in favour of the son of the people, uncouth and unin-
hibited, preserving, for as long as possible, the primitive virtues with which nature had endowed him. " Natural Man "
had invaded the schoolroom, with devastating results, for his
condemnation of civilisation appeared in such sentences as
these : " I hate books; they teach men to talk of what they do
not understand "; " the local accent of the peasants is the soul
of truth, that is why well-born people dislike it "; " there are
more errors in the Academy of Sciences than among all the
Hurons ". These are blasts against organised society itself.
While Voltaire had cheerfully sniped at ugly excrescences on
the eighteenth-century landscape the ever-serious Rousseau
would have erupted the landscape altogether.

Style, nearly as much as content, helps to explain the influence of those books which, for good or ill, have influenced the
progress of humanity. In Rousseau an unbroken chain of

reasoning serves to unite sentences and paragraphs, both of them always varied in length, both characterised by a rhythm and modulation suggestive of the musician. He generally begins with a challenging statement which, after analysis and exposition, leads to a memorable conclusion; as Voltaire compiled " portable " dictionaries, so Rousseau enunciated " portable " phrases and judgements. An element of intellectual integrity, often passionate in its intensity, pervades his writings, giving to them a penetrative quality surpassed only by the language of the Authorised Version of the Bible. His was indeed a new and challenging evangel. Standing solitary and apart, unencumbered by social connection or academic tradition, but endowed with an insight and humanity amounting to genius, Rousseau made a declaration of war on the *Ancien Régime*.

VII CONCLUSION

Though its area had not changed, the Europe of 1783 was larger than that of 1715, for its horizons had been greatly extended. Beyond the Atlantic the republic of the United States offered two things—an object lesson in political theory, and a vast new frontier, inviting penetration by colonist and pioneer. In political theory the Declaration of Independence proved to be the most effective of all charters of human rights; for the infant republic, renouncing power politics and European entanglements, appeared to have answered the question : how could liberty, peace and security be attained? For a time it seemed that the iniquities of the Old World would be redressed in the New; moreover, the opening up of the American frontier served to emphasise the contrast between the servile and semi-servile conditions prevailing in so many parts of Europe with the freedom of enterprise so characteristic of the west. A new commonwealth had been created which appeared to fulfil the highest aspiration of humanity.

Conclusion

This enlargement of enterprise was apparent even in Europe itself, for a wider conception of the functions of the state was coming into existence. There was a decline in the dynastic struggles which had divided the continent for so long. Colonial possessions, trading advantages, maritime supremacy —these were superseding, as objects of policy, the ancient family quarrels, so personal and selfish in their objects, so sterile in their achievements. The nations, gathering strength from their increasing self-consciousness, were now more directly concerned in the wars on which their rulers embarked; the oceans provided vast battlegrounds, and strategy became world-wide in its significance. The long contest for supremacy between England and France, not ended until Trafalgar and Waterloo, has been called the Second Hundred Years War, but how different were these two wars in their objects and results!

In other respects there was less change. By the end of the period described in this volume Europe was still mainly agricultural and pastoral and, before we think in terms of an industrial revolution, we have to recall that transport was still primitive, that many villages lived in an isolation almost inconceivable to-day; coal had not entirely taken the place of wood nor brick of timber; wind and water were still the main sources of energy; clock-work devices served many of the purposes of machinery. But for two revolutions—the Industrial and the French Revolution—this state of things might have continued indefinitely with only gradual changes. These two revolutions precipitated violent consequences throughout Europe and inaugurated the world conditions with which we are familiar to-day. The thesis has here been maintained that the structure of French society was fragile and brittle; lacking resilience, it must break under the strains imposed on it. The strains had long been in action—the *philosophes* had undermined faith in the existing order of things; the privileged minority was becoming more privileged; the disorder in the finances was threatening national bankruptcy. The emotionalism of the French people precipitated the crisis and directed its course.

The eighteenth century has been described by some historians as the Age of Absolutism, by others as the Age of Reason. Neither description is wholly applicable. Monarchs, it is true, were not subject to the restraints which we describe as constitutional, but they were restrained nevertheless—by parliament in England, by the magistracy and the hierarchy of office-holders in France, by a bureaucracy in Austria, by the nobility in Russia. None of the great European states provided the *tabula rasa* on which alone the autocrat can exercise his will. As for the Age of Reason, the period might equally well be called the Age of Sentiment, for the first of these was gradually displaced by the second, and the Romantic Revival was the result. Can we predicate any distinctive characteristic of the period? It was an age when wealth and leisure enabled a small minority to achieve a level in the amenities of life unequalled either before or since, a high standard of civilisation which stimulated the architect, the sculptor, the painter and the musician to creative work which conformed, not to the opinion of the many, but to the taste of an educated few. *Le superflu, chose si nécessaire.* The superfluous establishes the distinction between civilisation and mere subsistence; the eighteenth century was an age of well-directed superfluity. It was sharply contrasted with the misery which afflicted so many of the poor. But the poor we have always with us and, unlike the rich, they leave few memorials.

This well-being of the upper classes engendered a feeling of confidence, even complacency, a sub-conscious assurance that, within the resources at its disposal, a summit of achievement had been reached, unlikely to be surpassed or even equalled by any succeeding age. *Après nous le déluge.* There was some justification for Louis XV's prophecy. Though we cannot reduce this age to simple terms, we can be sure that, in its quantity, if not in its quality, the legacy of the eighteenth century is greater than that of any other, for so much of what has been preserved can be appreciated by everyone. If we except Kant, its philosophy can be understood without any special equipment; its literature is easily available in originals or re-prints; most of its best architecture has been preserved; our galleries are filled with its best paintings and sculptures; its music can be heard on every radio. For us, the eighteenth century is far enough away to be distinctive and self-contained, but not too distant for easy comprehension. Of no other period can such statements be made.

FURTHER READING

The first requisite is a good historical atlas. The best is probably that by W. R. Shepherd, *Historical Atlas*, 8th ed. (London 1956). Reference should also be made to J. S. Bromley and A. Goodwin (eds.). *A Select List of Works on Europe and Europe Overseas 1715-1815* (Oxford, 1956).

I. GENERAL HISTORIES OF EUROPE

Three admirable surveys covering the whole of this period have been published in W. L. Langer's series (London and New York)—P. Roberts, *The Quest for Security 1715-1740*, (1947); W. L. Dorn, *Competition for Empire 1740-1763* (1940); L. Gershoy, *From Despotism to Revolution 1763-1789* (1944).

There are also a number of good surveys in French. Of these one of the best known is: *Clio, Introduction aux Etudes Historiques*. In this series two volumes are devoted to the eighteenth century, the first (Paris 1952) by E. Préclin and V. L. Tapié being a general political survey, while the second (1952), by E. Préclin, includes an account of economic life, art, science and literature. Both volumes are equipped with good bibliographies, but the information is sometimes scrappy. Another French series is: *Peuples et Civilisations*, ed. by L. Halphen and P. Sagnac, of which vol. XI *La Prépondérance Anglaise 1715-1763* is by P. Muret (Paris 1942) and vol. XII *La Fin de l'Ancien Régime 1763-1789* is by P. Sagnac (1941). On a smaller scale is E. Mousnier and L. Labrousse, *Le XVIIIème Siècle: Révolution Intellectuelle, Technique et Politique 1715-1815* (Paris 1953). In English the most recent general account is in The New Cambridge Modern History of which vol. VII, *The Old Regime 1715-1763* was edited by Mrs. J. O. Crawford (Cambridge 1957). This will be followed by vol. VIII, edited by A. Goodwin. The bibliographies are to be published later.

Among the many short surveys of the period may be mentioned M. S. Anderson, *Europe in the Eighteenth Century* (London 1961), valuable for its statistical information, and its accounts of Russia and Eastern Europe.

Further Reading

II. HISTORIES OF THE EUROPEAN STATES

AUSTRIA AND THE EMPIRE: P. Frischauer, *The Imperial Crown: the story of the Rise and Fall of the Holy Roman and Austrian Empires,* (London 1939). H. Hantsch, *Das Geschichte Oesterreichs,* vol. II (Vienna 1950).

BELGIAN NETHERLANDS: H. Pirenne, *Histoire de Belgique,* vol. V (Brussels 1921).

BOHEMIA. H. J. Kerner, *Bohemia in the Eighteenth Century,* (New York 1932). S. H. Thomson, *Czechoslovakia in European History,* (Princeton 1953).

DENMARK. L. Krabbe, *Histoire de Danemark,* (Paris 1950).

DUTCH NETHERLANDS. G. J. Renier, *The Dutch Nation* (London, 1944). B. H. Vlakke, *The Evolution of the Dutch Nation.* (New York 1945). For essays in Dutch and Anglo-Dutch history, see P. Geyl, *Encounters in History* (Cleveland and New York, 1961).

FRANCE. E. Lavisse (ed.) *Histoire de France,* vol. VIII pt. 2 *Le Règne de Louis XV,* (Paris 1911): vol. IX pt. 1 *Le Règne de Louis XVI* (Paris 1911): This is still the best general account. G. Hanotaux (ed.) *Histoire de la Nation Française,* 15 vols. (Paris 1920-7): the volumes are arranged according to subject matter, which includes geography, economic, diplomatic and general history, literature, science and the arts, and are well illustrated. A. Cobban, *A History of Modern France,* vol. I (revised ed. London 1962): the best English account. J. Lough, *An Introduction to Eighteenth-Century France,* (London 1960). Valuable for its account of society and institutions.

GERMANY AND PRUSSIA. A. Waddington, *Histoire de la Prusse,* vol. II, (Paris 1920). G. P. Gooch, *Germany and the French Revolution,* (London 1920): this book contains much valuable information about eighteenth-century Germany. F. L. Carsten, *The Origins of Prussia,* (Oxford 1954) and *Princes and Paliaments in Germany* (Oxford 1959) are both scholarly works. W. H. Bruford, *Germany in the Eighteenth Century* (Cambridge, 1939): although intended mainly for students of literature, this book is of value for students of history. R. Flenley, *Modern German History* (London, 1959) is a good, short survey.

Further Reading

HUNGARY. H. Marczali, *Hungary in the Eighteenth Century* (Cambridge, 1910). D. Sinor, *History of Hungary* (London, 1959).

ITALY. L. Salvatorelli, *A Concise History of Italy* (London, 1940). H. Acton, *The Bourbons in Naples 1734-1825* (London, 1956). P. Valsecchi, *L'Italia nel Settecento* (Milan, 1959). E. P. Noether, *Seeds of Italian Nationalism* (New York, 1951).

NORWAY. T. K. Derry, *A Short History of Norway* (London, 1957).

POLAND. *The Cambridge History of Poland*, ed. W. F. Reddaway and others (Cambridge, 1941). R. Dyboski, *Poland* (London, 1933). O. Halecki, *Borderlands of Western Civilisation* (New York, 1952).

PORTUGAL. H. V. Livermore, *A History of Portugal* (London, 1947).

RUSSIA. P. Milioukov, C. Seignobos and L. Eisenmann, *Histoire de Russie*, vols. I and II (Paris, 1932-3): this is probably the best general history. B. H. Sumner, *A Survey of Russian History* (London, 1944) is a well-informed and suggestive account. R. D. Charques, *A Short History of Russia* (London, 1956). J. D. Clarkson, *A History of Russia from the Ninth Century* (London, 1962).

SPAIN. Altamira y Crevea, *Historia de España y de la Civilizacion Española* (Barcelona, 3rd ed. 1913): there is an English translation by M. Lee (New York, 1949). A. Ballesteros y Beretta, *Historia de España y su Influencia en la Historia Universal* (Barcelona 1918-41): vol. V (1929) deals with the general history of Spain in this period; vol. VI with the institutions and culture; both are profusely illustrated from paintings and prints of the period. H. V. Livermore, *History of Spain* (London, 1958).

SWEDEN. L. Andersson, *History of Sweden*, translated by C. Hannay (London, 1956). B. J. Hovde, *The Scandinavian Countries 1720-1865* (2 vols, Boston, 1948): vol. I contains much information about social and economic conditions.

SWITZERLAND. W. Oechsli, *History of Switzerland 1499-1914* (Cambridge, 1922). E. Bonjour, H. S. Offler and G. R. Potter, *A Short History of Switzerland* (Oxford, 1952).

Further Reading

TURKEY IN EUROPE. H. A. R. Gibb and H. Bowen, *Islamic Society in the West* (Oxford, 1953): vol. 1 deals with the eighteenth century. G. W. Kirk, *Short History of the Middle East* (London, 5th ed., 1961).

III. BIOGRAPHIES AND BIOGRAPHICAL STUDIES

CATHERINE THE GREAT. G. S. Thomson, *Catherine the Great and the Expansion of Russia* (London, 1961).

FREDERICK THE GREAT. G. B. Volz, *Friedrich der Grosse im Spiegel seiner Zeit*, 3 vols. (Berlin, 1934). G. P. Gooch, *Frederick the Great* (London, 1947).

JOSEPH II. F. L. Fejtö, *Un Habsbourg Révolutionnaire: Joseph II*, (Paris, 1953).

LOUIS XV. G. P. Gooch, *Louis XV: the Monarchy in Decline* (London, 1956).

MARIA THERESA. Constance, Lady Morris, *Maria Theresa, the Last Conservative* (New York, 1937). A. Mahan, *Marie Thérèse d'Autriche 1717-1718* (Paris, 1933).

PETER THE GREAT. V. Kliuchevskii, *Peter the Great* (trans. by L. Archibald, London, 1958). I. Grey, *Peter the Great: Emperor of All Russia* (London, 1962).

IV. ECONOMIC HISTORY: SCIENCE: TECHNOLOGY: THE ARTS

T. S. Ashton, *An Economic History of England: the Eighteenth Century* (London, 1955).

C. R. Boxer, *The Golden Age of Brazil 1675-1750* (Berkeley, 1962).

J. S. Bromley and J. H. Kossman (eds.) *Britain and the Netherlands* (London, 1960).

P. W. Buck, *The Politics of Mercantilism* (New York, 1952).

J. Blum, *Lord and Peasant in Russia from the Ninth to the Nineteenth Century* (Princeton, 1961).

R. H. Butterfield, *Origins of Modern Science, 1300 to 1800* (London, 1957).

D. Dakin, *Turgot and the Ancien Régime* (London, 1939).

W. C. Dampier, *History of Science* (Cambridge, 1942).

J. D. Fage, *An Introduction to the History of West Africa* (Cambridge, 1962).

D. J. Grout, *A Short History of Opera* (London, 1961).

A. R. Hall, *The Scientific Revolution* (London, 1954).

Further Reading

A. R. Hall, *From Galileo to Newton, 1630-1720* (London, 1963).

H. Heaton, *Economic History of Europe* (London, 1948).

E. F. Heckscher, *Mercantilism*, 2 vols. (London, 1935).

E. F. Heckscher, *An Economic History of Sweden* (trans. by G. Ohlin, Oxford, 1954).

J. Kulischer, *Allgemeine Wirtschaftsgeschichte*, vol. II (Munich and Berlin, 1929).

G. E. Labrousse, *La Crise de l'Economie Française à la Fin de l'Ancien Régime* (Paris, 1940).

E. Levasseur, *Histoire des Classes Ouvrières et de l'industrie en France avant 1789*, 2 vols. (Paris, 1901).

A. Michel, *Histoire Générale de l'Art*, vol. VII (Paris, 1927).

H. Mousnier, *Progrès Scientifique et Technique au XVIIIème Siècle* (Paris, 1958).

C. S. and O. S. Orwin, *The Open Fields* (Oxford, 1954).

L. B. Packard, *The Commercial Revolution 1400-1776* (New York, 1927).

R. Pares, *Colonial Blockade and Neutral Rights* (London, 1934).

R. Pares, *War and Trade in the West Indies, 1739-1763* (Oxford, 1936).

J. H. Parry and P. M. Sherlock, *A History of the West Indies* (London, 1960).

A. Reichwein, *China and Europe* (London, 1925).

H. Sée, *Esquisse d'une Histoire du Régime Agraire en Europe au XVIIIème et XIXème Siècles* (Paris, 1921).

H. Sée, *La France Economique et Sociale au XVIIIème Siècle* 4th. ed. (Paris 1946). For an English translation see *Economic and Social Conditions in France in the Eighteenth Century* (London, 1927).

C. Singer and others, *A History of Technology*, vols. III and IV (Oxford, 1957-8).

C. Singer, *A Short History of Scientific Ideas to 1950* (Oxford, 1959).

A. P. Usher, *A History of Mechanical Inventions* (Harvard, 1954).

B. A. Voto, *Westward the Course of Empire* (London, 1953).

C. Wilson, *Anglo-Dutch Commerce and Finance in the Eighteenth Century* (Cambridge, 1941).

A. Wolf, *History of Science, Philosophy and Technology in the Eighteenth Century* (New York, 1939).

Further Reading

V. SOCIETY, INSTITUTIONS AND INTELLECTUAL DEVELOPMENT

C. Aubertin, *L'Esprit Public au XVIIIème Siècle* (Paris, 1889). This old book is still useful as it is based on contemporary memoirs and journals.

E. C. Barber, *The Bourgeoisie in Eighteenth-Century France* (Princeton, 1955).

C. L. Becker, *The Heavenly City of the Eighteenth-Century Philosophers* (New Haven, 1932).

R. Bickart, *Les Parlements et la Notion de Souveraineté Nationale* (Paris, 1932).

W. Boyd, *History of Western Education* (3rd ed. London, 1932).

H. C. Burdett, *Hospitals and Asylums of the World,* 4 vols. (London, 1891-3).

J. B. Bury, *The Idea of Progress* (London, 1920).

A. Cobban, *Rousseau and the Modern State* (London, 1934).

K. G. Davies, *The Royal African Company* (London, 1957).

E. Donnan, (ed) *The Slave Trade,* 4 vols. (Washington, 1930-5).

E. M. Earle, *Makers of Modern Strategy* (Princeton, 1944).

R. E. Ergang, *Herder and German Nationalism* (New York, 1931).

H. N. Fairchild, *The Noble Savage* (New York, 1928).

F. L. Ford, *Robe and Swords, the Regrouping of the French Aristocracy after Louis XIV* (Cambridge, 1953).

F. Funck Brentano, *The Old Regime in France* (English trans., London, 1929).

M. Glotz and M. Maire, *Les Salons au XVIIIème Siècle* (Paris, 1944).

A. Goodwin (ed.), *European Nobility in the Eighteenth Century* (London, 1953).

L. Hanson, *Government and the Press, 1695-1763* (Oxford, 1936).

P. Hazard, *European Thought in the Eighteenth Century* (trans. from French, London, 1946).

A. Higgs, *The Physiocrats* (London, 1897).

R. Hubert, *Les Sciences Sociales dans l'Encyclopédie* (Paris, 1923).

G. Lanson, *Voltaire* (2nd ed., Paris, 1910).

G. Lanson, *Montesquieu* (Paris, 1932).

W. T. Maestro, *Voltaire and Beccaria as Reformers in Criminal Law* (New York, 1952).

A. T. Mahan, *Influence of Sea Power on History 1660-1783* (London, 1892).

M. Marion, *Dictionnaire des Institutions de la France au XVIIème et XVIIIème Siècles* (Paris, 1923).

P. Milioukov, *Russian Culture* (Philadelphia, 1934).

Further Reading

D. H. Mohrenschmidt, *Russia in the Intellectual Life of the Eighteenth Century* (New York, 1936).

D. Mornet, *Les Origines Intellectuelles de la Révolution Française 1715-1787* (Paris, 1933).

P. Olivier-Martin, *L'Organisation Corporative de la France d'Ancien Régime* (Paris, 1938).

R. R. Palmer, *Catholics and Unbelievers in Eighteenth-Century France* (Princeton, 1933).

R. R. Palmer, *The Age of Democratic Revolution*, vol. 1 (Princeton, 1959).

F. Pietri, *La Réforme de l'Etat au XVIIIème Siècle* (Paris, 1949).

M. Préclin, *Les Jansenistes au XVIIIème Siècle* (Paris 1939).

H. Richmond, *Statesmen and Sea Power* (Oxford, 1946).

P. Sagnac, *La Formation de la Société Française Moderne* (Paris, 1943).

A. Small, *The Cameralists: Pioneers in German Social Policy* (Chicago University Press, 1909).

A. Sorel, *L'Europe et la Révolution Française* (Paris, 1895-1904). Vol. 1 is still the best general account of the principles and practice of eighteenth-century diplomacy.

A. de Tocqueville, *L'Ancien Régime et la Révolution*. Many editions of this famous classic have appeared since its first publication in 1856. A convenient edition is that of G. W. Headlam (Oxford, 1904). There are several English translations.

C. E. Vaughan, *Studies in the History of Political Philosophy*, 2 vols. (Manchester, 1925).

B. Willey, *The Eighteenth-Century Background* (London, 1940).

H. Wyndham, *The Atlantic and Slavery* (London, 1935).

MAPS

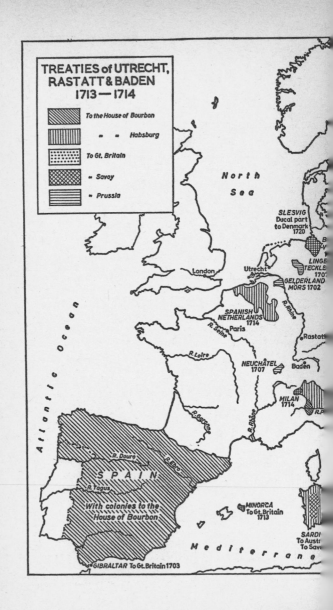

TREATIES of UTRECHT,
RASTATT & BADEN
1713 — 1714

To the House of Bourbon

" " Habsburg

To Gt. Britain

" Savoy

" Prussia

North Sea

Atlantic Ocean

SLESVIG
Ducal part
to Denmark
1720

B
Y

LINGE
TECKLE
170?
GELDERLAND
MÖRS 1702

London

Utrecht

SPANISH
NETHERLANDS
1714

Paris

R. Rhine

R. Seine

Rastatt

R. Loire

NEUCHÂTEL
1707

Baden

R. Rhine

MILAN
1714

R. P

R. Garonne

R. Rhône

R. Douro

R. Ebro

S P A I N

R. Tagus

With colonies to the
House of Bourbon

MINORCA
To Gt. Britain
1713

SARDI
To Austr
To Sav

Mediterrane

GIBRALTAR To Gt. Britain 1703

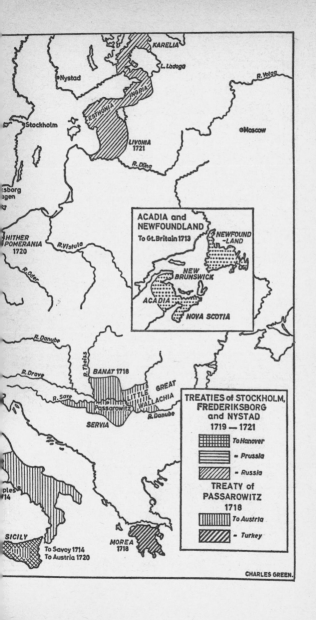

KARELIA

Nystad

L. Ladoga

R. Volga

Stockholm

INGRIA

ESTHONIA

LIVONIA
1721

Moscow

R. Dűna

...sborg
...agen

HITHER
POMERANIA
1720

R. Vistula

R. Oder

ACADIA and
NEWFOUNDLAND
To Gt. Britain 1713

NEWFOUND
-LAND

NEW
BRUNSWICK

ACADIA

NOVA SCOTIA

R. Danube

R. Thelss

BANAT 1718

R. Drave

R. Save

LITTLE

GREAT

WALLACHIA

Passarowitz

R. Danube

SERVIA

TREATIES of STOCKHOLM,
FREDERIKSBORG
and NYSTAD
1719 — 1721

To Hanover

" Prussia

" Russia

TREATY of
PASSAROWITZ
1718

To Austria

" Turkey

...ples
...14

SICILY
To Savoy 1714
To Austria 1720

MOREA
1718

CHARLES GREEN.

TREATIES
1735–1763

Vienna 1735
Belgrade 1739
Breslau 1742
Dresden 1745
Aix-la-Chapelle 1748
Paris 1763
Hubertusburg 1763

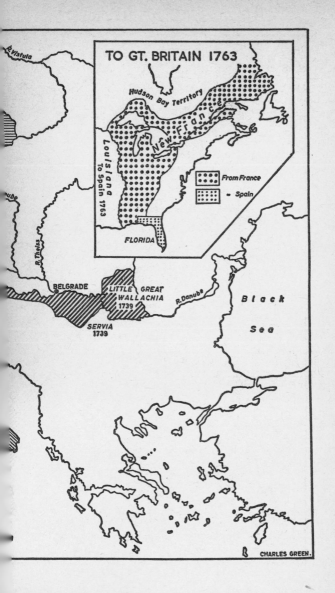

TO GT. BRITAIN 1763

Hudson Bay Territory

New France

Louisiana
To Spain 1763

FLORIDA

····· From France
═══ = Spain

R. Wistula

R. Theiss

R. Danube

BELGRADE

LITTLE
WALLACHIA
1739

GREAT

R. Danube

SERVIA
1739

Black

Sea

CHARLES GREEN.

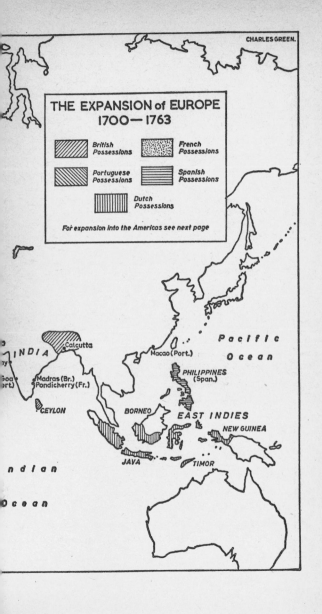

CHARLES GREEN.

THE EXPANSION of EUROPE
1700 — 1763

British Possessions

French Possessions

Portuguese Possessions

Spanish Possessions

Dutch Possessions

For expansion into the Americas see next page

INDIA

Calcutta

Goa (Port.)

Madras (Br.)
Pondicherry (Fr.)

CEYLON

Macao (Port.)

PHILIPPINES
(Span.)

BORNEO

EAST INDIES

NEW GUINEA

JAVA

TIMOR

Pacific Ocean

Indian Ocean

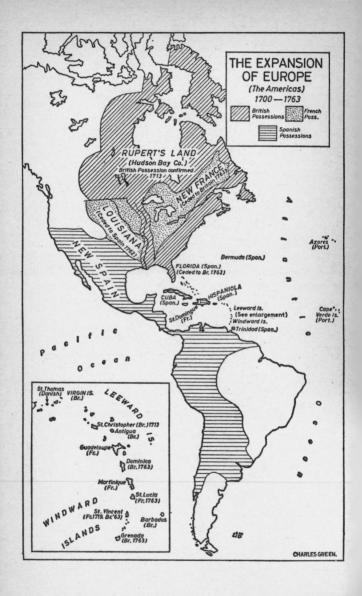

THE EXPANSION
OF EUROPE
(The Americas)
1700 — 1763

British Possessions
French Poss.
Spanish Possessions

RUPERT'S LAND
(Hudson Bay Co.)
British Possession confirmed 1713

NEW FRANCE
(Ceded to Britain 1763)

LOUISIANA
(Ceded to Spain 1762)

NEW SPAIN

Azores (Port.)

Bermuda (Span.)

FLORIDA (Span.)
(Ceded to Br. 1763)

CUBA
(Span.)

HISPANIOLA (Span.)

St.Domingue
(Fr.)

*Leeward Is.
(See enlargement)
Windward Is.*
Trinidad (Span.)

Cape Verde Is. (Port.)

Pacific Ocean

Atlantic Ocean

St.Thomas
(Danish)   VIRGIN IS.
(Br.)   LEEWARD
             St.Christopher (Br.) 1713
             Antigua
             (Br.)
Guadeloupe
(Fr.)
             Dominica
             (Br. 1763)   IS.
Martinique
(Fr.)
             St.Lucia
             (Fr. 1763)
        St.Vincent
        (Fr.1719, Br.'63)   Barbados
WINDWARD   (Br.)
                Grenada
ISLANDS   (Br. 1763)

CHARLES GREEN.

INDEX

INDEX

370

376

379